NEW FORMATIONS

EDITOR:
Judith Squires

CONSULTING EDITORS:
James Donald
Erica Carter

PICTURE EDITOR:
Stephen Johnstone

EDITORIAL BOARD:
Homi Bhabha
Lesley Caldwell
Tony Davies
Simon Frith
Jim Grealy
Stuart Hall
Dick Hebdige
Maria Lauret (Reviews)
Graham Murdock
Ali Rattansi
Denise Riley
Jenny Bourne Taylor
Valerie Walkerdine

OVERSEAS EDITORS:
Ien Ang
Angelika Bammer
Tony Bennett
Jody Berland
Victor Burgin
Hazel Carby
Iain Chambers
Joan Copjec
Lidia Curti
Cora Kaplan
Noel King
Colin Mercer
Kobena Mercer
Edward Said
Renata Salecl
Gayatri Chakravorty Spivak
John Tagg

New Formations is
published three times
a year by
Lawrence & Wishart
144a Old South Lambeth Road
London SW8 1XX
Tel 071–820 9281
Fax 071–587 0469

ADVERTISEMENTS
for enquiries/bookings contact
Ruth Borthwick, Lawrence & Wishart

SUBSCRIPTIONS
For 1994, subscription rates to Lawrence &
Wishart are, for 3 issues
UK: Institutions £50, Individuals £30.
Rest of world: Institutions £52; Individuals £32.
Single copies: £14.99

CONTRIBUTIONS, CORRESPONDENCE
should be sent to
The Editor, *New Formations*,
Dept of Politics, University of Bristol,
12 Priory Road, Bristol BS8 1TU

BOOKS FOR REVIEW
should be sent to Maria Lauret,
Dept of English, University of Southampton,
Highfield, Southampton S09 5NH

Prospective writers are encouraged to contact
the editors to discuss their ideas and to obtain
a copy of our style sheet.
Manuscripts should be sent in triplicate. They
will not be returned unless a stamped,
self-addressed envelope is enclosed.
Contributors should note that the editorial
board cannot take responsibility for any
manuscript submitted to *New Formations*.

The collection as a whole © Lawrence &
Wishart 1994
Individual articles © the authors 1994

No article may be reproduced or transmitted
in any form or by any means, electronic or
mechanical, including photocopying, recording, or any information storage and retrieval
system without the permission in writing of
the publisher, editor or author.

ISSN 0 950-2378
ISBN 0 85315 761 8

Text design by Jan Brown Designs, London
Photoset in North Wales by
Derek Doyle & Associates, Mold, Clwyd
Printed in Great Britain
at the University Press, Cambridge

Notes on Contributors

Benita Parry has written on the literature of imperialism, colonial discourse theory and resistance writing, she is the author of *Conrad and Imperialism* (1983) and is working on a study of imperialist discourses.

Kenneth Parker is Professor of Cultural Studies at the University of East London. His publications include *The South African Novel in English: Essays in Criticism and Society* (London: Macmillan, 1978), *The Letters of Dorothy Osborne* (London: Penguin Classics, 1987) and (with Elleke Boehmer and Laura Chrisman) *Altered State? Writing and South Africa* (Mundelstrup, Denmark: Dangaroo, 1993). He was a founding editor of *The Southern African Review of Books*.

Jon Stratton is a Senior Lecturer in Cultural Studies at Curtin University, Australia. He is author of *Writing Sites* (Hemel Hempstead Harvester-Wheatsheaf, 1990).

McKenzie Wark lectures in the Masters programme in International Communications at Macquarie University, Sydney. His book *Virtual Geography: Living With Global Media Events* will be published by Indiana University Press in 1994.

Kevin Robins works at the Centre for Urban and Regional Development Studies, University of Newcastle. He is co-author of *The Technical Fix* (Macmillan).

John Borneman is Assistant Professor of Anthropology at Cornell University, Ithaca, New York. He is author of *Belonging in the Two Berlins: Kin, State, Nation* (Cambridge University Press, 1992) and *After the Wall: East Meets West in the New Berlin* (Basic Books, 1991).

Anne Beezer lectures in Cultural Studies at the University of the West of England, Bristol and is a member of the *Radical Philosophy* collective.

Marcia Pointon is the Pilkington Professor of History of Art, University of Manchester. Her recent books are *Naked Authority: the Body in Western Art 1830-1908* (Cambridge University Press, 1990), *The Body Imaged: the Human Form and Visual Culture Since the Renaissance* (edited with Kathleen Adler, Cambridge University Press, 1993) and *Hanging the Head: Portraiture and Social Formation in Eighteenth-Century England* (Yale University Press, 1993).

Vassiliki Kolocotroni lectures in English Literature at the University of Edinburgh. She is currently completing her PhD on 'theories of modernism and modernity' for the University of Strathclyde and researching modernism and the work of Julia Kristeva.

Contents
NUMBER 21 WINTER 1994

Post-Colonial Insecurities

ii	*NOTES ON CONTRIBUTORS*	
v	*Judith Squires*	EDITORIAL
1	*Benita Parry*	SPEECH AND SILENCE IN THE FICTIONS OF J.M. COETZEE
21	*Kenneth Parker*	J.M. COETZEE: 'WHITE WRITING'
35	*Jon Stratton*	THE BEAST OF THE APOCALYPSE: THE POST-COLONIAL EXPERIENCE OF THE UNITED STATES
64	*McKenzie Wark*	ENGULFED BY THE VECTOR
80	*Kevin Robins*	THE POLITICS OF SILENCE: THE MEANING OF COMMUNITY AND THE USES OF MEDIA IN THE NEW EUROPE
102	*John Borneman*	TIME-SPACE COMPRESSION AND THE CONTINENTAL DIVIDE IN GERMAN SUBJECTIVITY
119	*Anne Beezer*	WOMEN AND 'ADVENTURE TRAVEL' TOURISM
131	*Marcia Pointon*	'A LATTER-DAY SIEGFRIED': IAN BOTHAM AT THE NATIONAL PORTRAIT GALLERY, 1986
146	*Vassiliki Kolocotroni*	A LITTLE INNER MYTHOLOGY: KRISTEVA AS NOVELIST
	REVIEWS	
158	*Andrew Thacker*	SOVEREIGN SELVES
165	*Eva Bahovec*	TURNING THE SCREW OF SENTIMENTAL EDUCATION

EDITORIAL

> 'Europe, the mighty, the leader of the world, no longer exists; Europe, the source of inspiration for all high cultures, has been exhausted. May it rest in peace.' Agnes Heller and Ferenc Feher

Europe and its nations are no longer what they once were. 'Europeanisation' is now contemplated, not with reference to the rest of the world, but to Europe itself as it struggles to survive the loss of its myths and to come to terms with a world in which its position has been relativised. As the old order gives way, identities (of both colonised and coloniser) are rendered insecure.

These post-colonial insecurities are addressed in this issue from various perspectives. From an assessment of the post-colonial strategies of South African writer J.M. Coetzee, to the changing role of American identities; from the reconstitution of European nations and imaginations to the mobilisation of the national myths of Englishness.

Benita Parry and Kenneth Parker reflect on the work of J.M. Coetzee as an encounter between the legacies of European modernism and the turbulent waters of colonialism. 'Is there a language,' asks Coetzee in *White Writing*, 'in which people of European identity, or ... of a highly problematical South African-colonial identity, can speak to Africa and be spoken to by Africa?' Behind such questions, Coetzee argues, 'lies a historical insecurity regarding the place of the artist of European heritage in the African landscape ... an insecurity not without cause.'

This historical insecurity is now global. For example, the United States is also largely populated by people of European heritage. Thus Jon Stratton argues that despite the fact that the United States gained its independence as long ago as 1782, it is still a post-colonial state in terms of its sense of displacement and its preoccupation with identity. Yet the deployment of a rhetoric of a new world order by President Bush means that the United States loses its claim to having a special quality and is forced to confront its own history as a settler society and to deal with the same problems of displacement, identity and the experience of living in an Other's land which are a part of the histories of other English-speaking settler societies.

McKenzie Wark explores another key manifestation of this shifting world (dis)order: the increasing mobility and flexibility of the media and its now almost saturation coverage of the globe. His claim is that what were once local political crises become the spectacle for a global grandstand of spectators. Kevin Robins takes up the point that national borders no longer seem the appropriate framework for delivering the new types of communications services. For, with reference to European broadcasting policy, we see that national borders are rendered increasingly redundant through institutional and informational integration. One example of such developments is provided by John Borneman in his analysis of the way in which the opening of the Berlin Wall, and the events in the year following it, affected a reordering of temporal and spatial categories in both East and West Berlin.

The insecurities of the post-colonial world are addressed by Anne Beezer through the development of 'adventure travel' – trekking expeditions to the 'remotest areas of the globe'. This form of travel, she argues, indicates a shifting relationship between 'home' and 'away'. It is now loss rather than certainty that impels the journey, a dissolution rather than a vindication of self that is sought.

Finally, turning inwards to look at the insecurities of Englishness as constructed identity, Marcia Pointon addresses that thorny issue of cricket. In April 1993 John Major made a speech invoking county cricket grounds and warm beer as a reassuring image of the survival of essential England. Cricket – struggling for retention of its powerfully symbolic role as an image of national survival – provides a constant reminder of England's colonial conquests. Through its participation in a mythology of nationhood cricket stands not only for the essence of Englishness, it also symbolises orthodox masculinity. Pointon argues that John Bellany's portrait of Ian Botham, commissioned by the National Portrait Gallery, London in 1986, threatened the authority of both.

Judith Squires
October 1993

SPEECH AND SILENCE IN THE FICTIONS OF J.M. COETZEE*

Benita Parry

I

David Attwell maintains that Coetzee's novels are 'directed at understanding the conditions – linguistic, formal, historical and political – governing the writing of fiction in contemporary South Africa'. In turn he offers the volume of interviews and essays he has edited as reflecting 'on an encounter in which the legacies of European modernism and modern linguistics enter the turbulent waters of colonialism and apartheid'.[1] This is an apt and elegant designation of the fictions' moment and space, and I use it as a starting point for considering the ways this fraught confluence is negotiated in self-reflexive novels which stage the impossibility of representation, estrange facticity, and work, in Coetzee's words, to 'demythologize history'.

The Attwell interviews with Coetzee are remarkable in that a reticent writer has been induced to speak about his homeless situation both as an inhabitant and a novelist in but not of Africa. Since one of my concerns is with the variations on the theme of white South African deracination in the fictions, it is notable that such spatial and temporal disconnection is a dilemma on which Coetzee as his own critic has commented. In these conversations he disarmingly confesses that South Africa beyond the Cape 'has always felt like foreign territory to me' (p337); he recalls his apparently failed effort when a graduate student in the United States, to 'find an imaginative (and imaginary) place for myself in the Third World and its narratives of itself' by reading Cesaire, Senghor and Fanon (p338); and he remarks that 'time in South Africa has been extraordinarily static for most of my life' (p209) – a reference to the political order dominated by Afrikaner-Christian nationalism in which he grew up (he was born in 1940) and the culture in which he was educated, 'a culture looking, when it looked anywhere, nostalgically back to Little England'.

In identifying as a predicament the possibility of 'European ideas writing themselves out in Africa' (p339), Coetzee reiterates a problem he had already pursued in a previous book of essays, *White Writing*. Here he had asked: 'Is there a language in which people of European identity, or ... of a highly problematical South African-colonial identity, can speak to Africa and be spoken to by Africa?' This is a matter to which he returned when observing an uncertainty troubling white South African poets about 'whether the African landscape can be articulated in a European language, whether the European can be at home in Africa?' Behind such questions, Coetzee continues, 'lies a historical insecurity regarding the place of the artist of European heritage in

References are to the Penguin editions of Coetzee's novels, excepting *Age of Iron*, Secker and Warburg.

* Although I am aware that they will continue to dissent from the revisions, I am indebted to the stringent criticisms made of an earlier version by Derek Attridge and David Attwell which prompted me to reformulate some of the arguments.

1. David Attwell (ed), *Doubling the Point, Essays and Interviews: J.M. Coetzee*, Harvard, Cambridge, MA 1992, p3.

the African landscape ... an insecurity not without cause.'²

Metropolitan reviewers, as well as those critics whose attention when reading South African novels is focused on detecting condemnations of an egregious political system, are predisposed to proffer Coetzee's fictions as realist representations of, and humanist protests against, colonial rapacity in large, and an intricately institutionalized system of racial oppression in particular.³ Other critics whose concern is with the radicalism of Coetzee's textual practice, and who foreground parody and reflexivity as oppositional linguistic acts, argue that the authority of colonialism's narratives is undermined by subversive rewritings of the genres traditional to colonial fiction, especially those favoured by the traditional white South African novel – the heroic frontier myth, the farm romance, the liberal novel of stricken conscience⁴ – hence opening conventions to scrutiny and confronting the traditional and unproblematized notion of the canon.⁵

Such readings have come from Coetzee's most attentive critics, amongst some of whom there is a tendency to construe the fictions as the calculated transcriptions of the author's known critical stances on the instability of language and the unreliability of narration. The consequence is that paradox and impasse, gaps and silences are accounted for, not as textually generated through the interplay of the referential and the rhetorical, or by the interruptions of incommensurable discourses, but as the planned strategy of a highly self-conscious practice which displays the materials and techniques of its own process of production. More specifically, it has been suggested that by deliberately inscribing ambiguity, indeterminacy and absence, the fiction registers the author's understanding of his own 'positional historicity', thus effecting a formal and aesthetic encoding or fictionalizing of Jameson's premise on the political unconscious, and thereby preempting any effort by critics to theorize elisions and ideological complicities as inaugurated by the texts' spoken and unspoken cultural affiliations. (see Attwell, 1990)

What I will be considering is how novels that weave a network of textual invocations traversing European literary and philosophical traditions, as well as contemporary theory from linguistics and structuralism to deconstruction, circumvent or rather confirm the quandary of white writings' insecurity or dislocation in Africa, which Coetzee as critic has detected. For the principles around which novelistic meaning is organized owe nothing to knowledges which are *not* of European provenance and that *are* amply and variously represented in South Africa; while the disposals of western interpretative paradigms are dispersed in a poised, even hieratic prose uninflected by South Africa's many vernacular Englishes.

That Coetzee's novels do interrogate colonialism's discursive practices is indisputable, through estrangement and irony making known the overdeterminations, fractures and occlusions of such utterances; while the excavations of the uneasy but timid white South African liberal consciousness are amongst the most far-reaching in South African writing. All the same, I want to consider whether the reverberations of intertextual transpositions, as well as the logic

2. *White Writing: On the Culture of Letters in South Africa*, Yale University Press, New Haven 1988, pp7-8, 167, 62.

3. For example Susan Van Zanten Gallagher, *A Story of South Africa: J.M. Coetzee's Fiction in Context*, Harvard University Press, Cambridge MA 1991, and Dick Penner, *Countries of the Mind: The Fiction of J.M. Coetzee*, Greenwood Press, NY 1989.

4. Teresa Dovey, *The Novels of J.M. Coetzee: Lacanian Allegories*, Ad Jonker, Johannesburg 1988; and David Attwell, 'The Problem of History in the Fictions of J.M. Coetzee', in *Rendering Things Visible*, Martin Trump (ed), Ravan Press, Johannesburg 1990.

5. Derek Attridge, 'Oppressive Silence: Coetzee's *Foe* and the Politics of the Canon', in *Decolonizing Tradition: New Views of Twentieth-Century 'British' Literary Canons*, Karen R. Lawrence (ed), University of Illinois Press, Urbana and Chicago 1992.

and trajectory of narrative strategies, do not inadvertently reprise the exclusionary colonialist gestures which the novels also criticize. Let me then put forward the polemical proposition that despite the fiction's disruptions of colonialist modes, the social authority on which its rhetoric relies and which it exerts, is grounded in the cognitive systems of the west. Furthermore, I will suggest that the consequence of writing the silence attributed to the subjugated as the liberation from the constraints of subjectivity – a representation to which I will return – can be read as re-enacting the received distribution of narrative authority.

The paradox, as proposed by this hypothesis, is that in the double movement performed by Coetzee's novels, the subversions of previous texts enunciating discourses of colonial authority are permuted into re-narrativizations where only the European possesses the word and the ability to enunciate, the lateral routes of the virtually plotless novels taking in nothing outside the narrators' world-views, hence sustaining the west as the culture of reference. A failure to project alterities may signify Coetzee's refusal to exercise the authority of his dominant culture to represent other and subjugated cultures, and may be construed as registering his understanding that agency is not something that is his to give or withhold through representation. Yet I am arguing that the fictions do just this, because of which European textual power, reinscribed in the formal syntax required of Literature, survives the attempted subversion of its dominion.

And let me now modulate the terms of the argument. Richard Terdiman maintains that 'no discourse is ever a monologue, nor could it ever be adequately analyzed "intrinsically". Its assertions, its tone, its rhetoric – everything that constitutes it – always presupposes a horizon of competing, contrary utterances against which it asserts its own energies.'[6] Coetzee's preferred modes, the diary, the journal and the letter – where the disingenuous transparency of the earliest forms of novel writing are problematized – make an apparently uncontested arena available to a speaking subject who, in effecting an estrangement of the consciousness she or he articulates, manifests the solipsism of disquisition deprived of dialogue, while intimating another world whose agency is denied, or as in the last novel, *Age of Iron*, deprecated for its modality as a violent political struggle. Perhaps then these narrative solutions stage the process of occluding contending enunciations, of disavowing other knowledges, of constructing and holding in place a hiatus, of construing a 'differend' between a narrator and its other – Lyotard's notion of a speech-act in which the addressee is divested of means to dispute the address.[7]

But whereas the novels do enact the discursive processes whereby 'Bushman' and 'Hottentot' in 'The Narrative of Jacobus Coetzee', the Barbarians in *Waiting for the Barbarians*, the servants in *The Heart of the Country*, the gardener in *Life and Times of Michael K* and the enslaved black Friday of *Foe*, are muted by those who have the power to name and depict them, or as in *Age of Iron*, subjected to acts of ventriloquizing, the dominated are situated as objects of

6. *Discourse/Counter Discourse: The Theory and Practice of Symbolic Resistance in Nineteenth-Century France*, Cornell University Press, Ithaca 1985, p36.

7. *The Differend: Phrases in Dispute*, trans. Georges Van Den Abbeele, Manchester University Press, Manchester 1988 (first published 1983).

representations and meditations which offer them no place from which to resist the modes that have constituted them as at the same time naked to the eye and occult. The question however can be differently phrased to privilege the force of an unspoken presence: do these figures, as Derek Attridge argues, register 'a new apprehension of the claims of *otherness,* of that which cannot be expressed in the discourse ordinarily available to us, not because of an essential ineffability but because it has been simultaneously constituted and excluded by that discourse in the very process of that discourse's self-constitution.'[8]

Consider 'The Narrative of Jacobus Coetzee' (*Dusklands,* 1974), where the mimicry of three chronicles of the colonial enterprise is calculated to display the historical record as ideological fabrication and to undermine the commemoration of a colonialist mission. The narrative route moves from a critique of the colonialist calling that emerges from the anunciations of an acolyte alienating his own rhetoric, to a demythologizing of the hagiographic mode favoured by historians of Afrikaner expansion, to the diagnostic rewriting of a Dutch East India Company report transcribing an expedition made by an illiterate explorer into the hinterland of the Cape in 1760. The style of this last is that of the official chronicle into which the excited and fanciful mode of travel literature has intruded; its substance is an itinerary of the territory Jacobus Coetzee covered, the rivers and mountains he named, the people and physical landscape he encountered. Already through a hermeneutic revision, this supposedly archival testimony is shown to be a construction of how the observing eye of the European and a European nomenclature map a hitherto uninscribed earth; while the parody of Afrikaner scholarship in the 'Afterword' depicts this same 'Coetzee' as one who 'rode like a God through a world only partly made, differentiating and bringing into being' (p116).

The irony that speaks through this naïve pedagogical version of Afrikaner historical recuperation, is exceeded by Jacobus Coetzee's own narrative, where the speaker of a discourse is used by the language he uses in order to enunciate an ontology of white expansion and expose the pathology of the colonialist calling – the speech of an illiterate eighteenth century explorer being invested with the linguistic range and speculative consciousness of an alienated twentieth century intellectual acquainted with the literary canon, the literature of psychoanalysis and contemporary theories of language. In staging a beginning encounter between an explorer and proto-colonizer, and a still undefeated and undomesticated Khoi-Khoi community, Jacobus Coetzee's story rehearses the multiple and conflicting enunciations in a colonial discourse. Hence whereas he details what he had witnessed of the Khoi-Khoi physiques, music, dance, codes, ceremonies, taboos and belief in a creator, his exposition denounces them as a people sexually malformed, without art, ritual, magic, law, government or religion. 'What evidence was there', he rhetorically asks, 'that they had a way of life of any coherence?' Such disavowal is provoked by his perceiving the threat of their having 'a history in which I shall be a term' (p81). Thus it is imperative that they be found 'a place ... in my history' (p97), a

8. 'Literary Form and the Demands of Otherness in J.M. Coetzee's *Age of Iron*' forthcoming in *Aesthetics and Ideology* (ed) George Levine, Rutgers University Press.

move he initiates by depriving them of an immemorial habitation of the land, and incorporating them as inconsequential figures into his chronicle of conquest.

Here the making of a colonial discourse and the process of silencing are dismantled even as they are rehearsed. But what is there in a narrative that is concerned to conceptualize a metaphysics of conquest, to contradict Jacobus Coetzee's doomed discovery that 'in that true wilderness without polity ... everything, I was to find, was possible' (p66), since his victims, the Khoi-Khoi, are relegated as being unable to impinge on and participate in annulling the discourse of mastery disclosed by an auto-critique? Is the silence of these strange and defeated people deployed here as a textual strategy which counters the colonizing impulse and impudence in simulating another's voice? Alternatively can it be construed as a mute interrogation and disablement of discursive power? – a possibility offered by Derek Attridge who reads Coetzee's fictions as a continued and strenuous effort in figuring alterity as 'a force out there disrupting European discourse', a force which is both resistant to the dominant culture and makes demands on it, not by entering into dialogue, but by 'the very intensity of an unignorable "being there" '. ('Literary Form and the Demands of Otherness') On the other hand, does this muteness intimate a narrative disinclination to orchestrate a polyphonic score, because of which the silenced remain incommensurable, unknowable and unable to make themselves heard in the sealed linguistic code exercised by the narrating self, and hence incapable of disturbing the dominant discourse?

Tzvetan Todorov, whose discussion of the other constituted by colonialism enlists the work of Levinas, has written: 'one does not let the other live merely by leaving him intact, anymore than by obliterating his voice entirely ... Heterology, which makes the difference of voices heard, is necessary.'[9] This suggests a notion of commerce with alterity as a contact taking place in an intersubjective space which leaves both 'I' and 'you' separate and intact but enhanced, and where the non-identity of the interlocutors is respected and retained. A text written from within this interval or 'in-between' would register the opening of one's own discourse to strange accents and unfamiliar testimonies, but without suppressing or erasing difference, without pretending to simulate another's authentic voice or speaking on another's behalf, and without imprinting an ontological dissimilarity which simultaneously offers an explanation and an excuse for oppression. Such a procedure would engender a recombinant, 'neologistic' idiom, which because it inscribes alterity not as a dumb presence but as an interlocutor, would counter what Levinas names as 'the eclipse, the occultation, the silencing of the other.'[10]

II

Within the discussion of colonial and postcolonial discourse, silence has been read as a many-accented signifier of disempowerment and resistance, of the

9. Tzvetan Todorov, *The Conquest of America: The Question of the Other*, trans Richard Howard, Harper and Row, NY 1982, pp250, 251.

10. *Totality and Infinity*, trans A. Lingus, Dequesne University Press, Pittsburgh 1969. On Levinas, see *The Provocation of Levinas*, Robert Bernasconi and David Wood, (eds) Routledge, London 1988. For the deployment of Levinas's theories in discussions of the other constructed by colonialism, see Todorov, *op.cit.*, and Peter Mason, *Deconstructing America: Representations of the Other*, Routledge, London 1990.

denial of a subject position and its appropriation. Emphasizing its ambiguity, Christopher Miller has written that because 'the voice remains our central metaphor for political agency and power ... silence is the most powerful metaphor for exclusion from the literary mode of production', adding that while some insist on its oppressivity, others 'find in silence itself a different kind of word to be listened to, perhaps a strategy of resistance.'[11] In keeping with this recognition of the multiple resonances silence, some critics have construed Coetzee's deployment of the topos as if this is notated by the text to be intelligible as an emblem of oppression, or to be audible as that unuttered but inviolable voice on which discourses of mastery cannot impinge, and hence as an enunciation of defiance.

Gayatri Spivak in her discussion of *Foe* designates Friday as 'the unemphatic agent of withholding in the text'; and Graham Huggan maintains that Coetzee's figuration of silence is an exemplary instance of a postcolonial writing where it is not an absence or an incapacity of speech, but rather 'a different kind of speech, a muteness to be perceived either as a form of self-protection or a gesture of resistance'. Paola Splendore reads Michael K, the Barbarian Girl and Friday as 'characters who cannot speak or who refuse to speak the language of the foe, but whose silence shouts as if they were a thousand people screaming together'; and for Derek Attridge 'a mode of fiction that exposes the ideological basis of canonization ... that thematizes the role of race, class and gender in the process of cultural acceptance and exclusion, and that, while speaking from a marginal location, addresses the question of marginality ... would have to be seen as engaged in an attempt to break the silence in which so many are caught.' Debra Castillo, on the other hand, who observes that 'neither of the two narrative voices of *Dusklands* proposes itself as the voice of the other, a shadowy presence at best and one that retains an unreadable silence in all of Coetzee's novels', refrains from attributing intelligibility to the representations of aphonia.[12]

However I will suggest that the various registers in which silence is scored in Coetzee's novels, speak of things other than the structural relationship of oppressor/oppressed, or the power of an unuttered alterity to undermine a dominant discourse, and that these other things are signs of the fiction's urge to cast off worldly attachments, even as the world is signified and estranged. I have already tried to show how in 'The Narrative of Jacobus Coetzee', the process of muting is staged as an act of conquest. My hypothesis about Coetzee's figures of silence in the subsequent novels is that although they are the disentitled, and therefore are available to be read as manifesting subordination to and retreat from a subjugated condition, the critique of political oppression is diverted by the conjuring and valorizing of a non-verbal signifying system.

By observing the texts' correspondence to the templates of psychoanalytic theories, and in particular to Kristeva's propositions on the transactions within the signifying process between the modalities of the 'semiotic' and the 'symbolic' or the 'thetic'[13], it is possible to gloss the textual connections between

---

11. *Theories of Africans: Francophone Literature and Anthropology in Africa*, Chicago University Press, Chicago 1990, pp248, 250. On silence as a privileged signifier of postcolonial writing, see Bill Ashcroft, Gareth Griffiths and Helen Tiffin, *The Empire Writes Back: Theory and Practice in Post-colonial Literatures*, Routledge, London 1989. In Paulo Freire's writings, silence signifies a culture of defeat and resignation.

12. 'Theory in the Margin: Coetzee's *Foe*' 'Reading Defoe's *Crusoe/Roxana*', in *Consequences of Theory*, Jonathan Arac and Barbara Johnson, (eds) Johns Hopkins, Baltimore and London 1991, p172; 'Philomela's Retold Story: Silence, Music and the Post-colonial Text', *Journal of Commonwealth Literature* 25, 1 (1990), pp12-23; 'J.M. Coetzee's *Foe*: Intertextual and Metafictional Resonances', *Commonwealth* 11, 1

the trope of silence and the simulacra of woman's writing as two different discourses of the body performed by those who are outsiders to a patriarchal linguistic/cultural order. Shared by Coetzee's male protagonists of silence is an absence or extreme economy of speech which is in all cases associated with sexual passivity or impotence: the hare-lipped Michael K, a gardener and progenitor of fruits and vegetables, lacks a father, a patronymic and sexual desire, and remains bonded to the mother (*Life and times of Michael K*, 1983); it is intimated that the dumb Friday is possibly without either tongue or phallus (*Foe*, 1986); while the taciturn Vercueil of *Age of Iron* (1990) is perceived by the narrator as unable to beget children, his semen imagined as 'dry and brown, like pollen or the dust of this country' (p180). These deficits have been read as signalling their location on the fringes of the phallocentric social order, whose dominance through their speechlessness and asexuality they evade.[14]

Yet although the silence of each has a distinctive tenor, what all signify is not a negative condition of lack and affliction or of sullen withdrawal, but a plenitude of perception and gifts: Michael K's aphasia facilitates a mystic consciousness; the verbal abstinence of the drunken and incontinent Vercueil, who means more than he says, is appropriate to his metaphysical status as the unlikely incarnation of an annunciation – 'verskuil' in Afrikaans means to obscure, conceal or mask; while the outflow of sounds from the mouth of Friday gives tongue to meanings? desires? preceding or surpassing that which can be communicated and interpreted in formal language. It could then be argued that speechlessness in the fiction exceeds or departs from the psychoanalytic paradigm it also deploys, to become a metaphor for that portentous silence signifying what cannot be spoken – the undifferentiated echo of a Marabar Cave, a presence too sacred, revered and adored to be rendered in profane speech, or an event too terrible to be told and that is told of in *Beloved*: 'the holes – the things the fugitives did not say ... the unnamed, the unmentioned'.

Coetzee's figures of silence are not without a quotidian dimension, and an inequality in social power is marked by the disparity between the obsessional will to utterance in Coetzee's female and European narrators – who literally perform the constitution of the subject in language and author a discourse of the body – and the inaudibility of those who are narrated: Michael K who is cryptically identified as Coloured (p96), is a propertyless labourer; Friday is a black slave and Vercueil is a tramp of unspecified race. However this incipient critique of how deprivation inflicts silence on those who are homeless in an hierarchical social world is deflected by the ascription of value to the disarticulated body, since the reader is simultaneously offered intimations of a non-linguistic intuitive consciousness, and is invited to witness the fruits of speechlessness when there is a failure of the dialectic between the 'Imaginary' and the 'Symbolic' or in Kristeva's vocabulary, the 'semiotic' and the 'thetic'.

Both surmises can be referred to Michael K who is written as a being without an identity, outside the writ where the Law of the Father runs, and as the exemplar of a mind turned inward. Spoken for in the narrative – his

(1988), pp55-60; Derek Attridge 'Oppressive Silence', pp4-5; 'Coetzee's *Dusklands*: The Mythic Punctum', *PMLA*, 105, 5 (1990), 1108-1122.

13. Julia Kristeva, *Desire in Language: A Semiotic Approach to Literature and Art*, Leon S. Roudiez (ed) trans Thomas Gore, Alice Jardine and Leon S Roudiez, Blackwell, Oxford 1981; Toril Moi, *Sexual/Textual Politics*, Methuen, London 1985; *The Kristeva Reader*, Toril Moi (ed), Blackwell, Oxford 1986; Ann Rosalind Jones, 'Writing the Body: Toward an Understanding of l'Ecriture feminine', in *The New Feminist Criticism*, Elaine Showalter (ed), Virago, London 1986; John Fletcher and Andrew Benjamin (eds), *Abjection, Melancholia and Love: The work of Julia Kristeva*, Routledge, London 1990.

14. See Dovey, *op.cit.*

representation depends on 'he thought', 'he found', 'he said' – he is interpreted as being too busy with fantasy 'to listen to the wheels of history' (p217), 'a soul blessedly untouched by doctrine, untouched by history' (p207), who lives in 'a pocket outside time' (p82), has access to a numinous condition when he 'emptied his mind, wanting nothing, looking forward to nothing' (p74); he attains an ineffable state of bliss on eating a pumpkin he had reared in a parodic act of parental nurturing.

Although the narrative gloss has him likening himself, a gardener, to 'a mole, also a gardener, that does not tell stories because it lives in silence' (p248), Michael K is attributed with an ambition to interpret his own solitary, eidetic consciousness; 'Always when he tried to explain himself to himself, there remained a gap, a hole, a darkness before which his understanding baulked, into which it was useless to pour words. The words were eaten up, the gap remained. His was always a story with a hole in it' (p150-1). Here failure to attain and articulate self-consciousness is not rendered as disappointment, since silence is privileged as enabling the euphoria of desire unmediated by words; and if Michael K is perceived as dramatizing the inability to achieve a voice in the Symbolic order, then we can note that his 'loss of thetic function' is not represented as a lapse into psychosis but as a path to the visionary.

Because Friday's inner consciousness is not narrated, his silence is more secret and less available to the attention of conjectural readings, a sign of which is that he is offered alternative futures by the fiction, one within and the other outside the formal structures of language. In the discussion on how to bring Friday into the realm of representation, Susan Barton protests at Foe's proposal that he be shown writing, believing that since 'Letters are the mirror of words', Friday who has no speech, can have no grasp of language. For Foe, on the other hand, writing is not a secondary representation of the spoken word but rather its prerequisite: 'Writing is not doomed to be the shadow of speech ... God's writing stands as an instance of a writing without speech' (pp142, 143). It is Foe's view which would seem to prevail in the first narrative turn where the prospect of Friday as a scribe is prefigured. Once the pupil of an Adamic language taught by Cruso, and a pictographic script offered by Barton, Friday who previously had uttered himself only in the 'semiotic' modes of music and dance, now seated at Foe's desk with his quill, ink and paper, and wearing his wig, appropriates the authorial role.

His mouth likened by Barton to an empty buttonhole, Friday begins by forming Os, of which Coetzee has written 'The O, the circle, the hole are symbols of that which male authoritarian language cannot appropriate' (cited Dovey, p411). All the same it is intimated that he will go on to learn *a*, a portent of his acquiring linguistic competence. There is however yet another narrative turn, when the dreamlike quest of a contemporary narrator for Friday's story, takes him into the hold of a wrecked ship, and this time Friday does not cross the threshold into logical and referential discourse, remaining in that paradisal condition where sign and object are unified, and the body, spared the traumatic insertion into language, can give utterance to things lost or never yet heard, whose meanings, we are given to understand, will water the globe:

> But this is not a place of words ... This is a place where bodies are their own signs. It is the home of Friday ... His mouth opens. From inside him comes a slow stream, without breath, without interruption ... it passes through the cabin, through the wreck; washing the cliffs and shores of the island, it runs northward and southward to the ends of the earth. (p157)

It would seem then that although the figures of silence are the subordinated, and hence intimate disarticulation as an act of discursive power, they are not only 'victims' but also 'victors', since they are credited with possessing extraordinary and transgressive psychic energies. Furthermore since it is explicitly posited in the fiction that writing does not copy speech and is not its symbol or image, can we consider whether for Friday and the other disempowered figures who cannot or will not make themselves heard in the recognized linguistic system, their bodies are to be read as encoding a protowriting?[15] Friday's home is designated as 'a place where bodies are their own signs'; and to the Magistrate in *Waiting for the Barbarians*, who cannot understand the gestures of the Barbarian Girl, and who can communicate with her only in makeshift language without nuance, her body is a script to be decoded in the same way as the characters on the wooden slips he has excavated.

It is therefore notable that when Coetzee's novels stage another discourse of the body, it is not in the scripted silence of the lowly and the outcaste, whose oppression is also the condition for their access to intuitive cognition and transcendental states, but as the progeny of women who speak, albeit uneasily, from a position of entrenched cultural authority, while also articulating their homelessness in and opposition to the patriarchal order. Three of Coetzee's narrators so far have been women, and while it would seem that he is enlisting the notion of the body as progenitor of woman's language which has been posited by some feminist theorists (for a critique see Moi, 1985 and Jones, 1986), it is less certain that the writing does transgress standard usage to register the irruptions of repressed libidinal elements into the performative text.

What is evident is that the female narrators explicitly represent the body as the agent of language: Mrs Curren of *Age of Iron* declares in her letters to an absent daughter, that her words 'come from my heart, from my womb' (p133), assigning to writing the properties of the genetically communicated code – the phylogenetic inheritance made flesh in print: 'These words, as you read them ... enter you and draw breath again ... Once upon a time you lived in me as once upon a time I lived in my mother; as she still lives in me, as I grow towards her, may I live in you' (p120). In another register, Susan Barton of *Foe*, who asks 'Without desire, how is it possible to make a story?' (p88), asserts 'The Muse is a woman, a goddess, who visits poets in the night and begets stories upon them' (p126); while Magda of *In the Heart of the Country* rejects her

---

15. Are there echoes here, as in the representation of a silent consciousness, of Derrida's critique of Husserl? See *Speech and Phenomena and Other Essays on Husserl's Theory of Signs*, trans with and introduction by David B Allison and Newton Garver, Northwestern University Press, Evanston 1973: 'The autonomy of meaning with regard to intuitive cognition ... has its norm in writing ... The use of language or the employment of any code which implies a play of forms ... also presupposes a retention and protension of differences, a spacing and temporalizing, a play of traces. This play must be a sort of inscription prior to writing, a protowriting without a present origin, without an *arche.*' pp97, 146.

'father-tongue' as a language of hierarchy which is not 'the language my heart wants to speak', and longs for 'the resonance of the full human voice ... the fullness of human speech' (pp97, 47).

In Coetzee's imitations of woman's writing there is a tension between the striving after a discourse of the pre-symbolic and the language of the symbolic in which this is articulated: Magda's search for a condition before the body's insertion into the homelessness of language alights on the speech of the Coloured servants as the repository of a prelapsarian condition (in this reiterating a colonialist conceit); while her utterance of the aspiration to that euphoric consciousness discernible in the figures of silence – 'a life unmediated by words, these stones, these bushes, this sky experienced and known without question' (p135) – succeeds where they failed in authoring a story from which, as in the rejected discourse, the testimony of the 'brown folk' is erased. Similarly Mrs Curren's praise of motherhood, far from being saturated with joy and ecstasy, is delivered in a vocabulary and syntax appropriate to her status as an educated white South African, while her representations of Africans issues in pastiches of naturalist reportage and morally outraged protest writing, modes which Coetzee is known to despise and which are directed at displaying the banality of white South Africa undertaking to write the voice of the oppressed. (Yet against the grain of a novel which parodies the liberal mode of making known the inner world of Africans by mediating their speech, *Age of Iron* does register an African woman's eloquent contempt for the white world in her laconic responses to the narrator's expressions of sympathy for her servant's grief at the death of a son killed by the police.)

All Coetzee's female narrators resolutely position themselves as authors of their own narratives:

> I have uttered my life in my own voice ... I have chosen at every moment my own destiny. (Magda, p139)
> I am a free woman who asserts her freedom by telling her story according to her own desire ... the story I desire to be known by is the story of the island. (Susan Barton, pp131, 121)
> How I live, how I lived: my story ... my truth, how I lived in these times, in this place. (Mrs Curren, pp140, 119)

However in terms of dis/identification with masculine narrative traditions, each produces a differently accented script, and whereas the recitations of Magda and Mrs Curren do ostentatiously enunciate maternal desire, Susan Barton in *Foe*, while insisting on her freedom as a woman to choose her speech and her silence, affirms her wish to be 'father to my story' (p123), holding out against Foe in suppressing 'the history of a woman in search of a lost daughter' (p121), and thus refusing to write a discourse of motherhood.

Furthermore, alone amongst Coetzee's narrators, Barton articulates a reluctance to exert the narrative power which she as an Englishwoman, however disreputable, holds over those who are muted, when she resists Foe's urgings to invent Friday's story 'which is properly not a story but a puzzle or hole in the narrative' (p121). It is in *Foe*, which amplifies its status as a book about writing a book, that the disparate stratagems of novelistic authority are conspicuously and self-reflexively dramatized. The dialogue of Foe and Barton condenses a contest between gendered protagonists holding different positions on language and representation. With her commitment to the priority of speech, Susan Barton formulates the task as descending into Friday's mouth, that is of finding a means to use Friday as an informant in order to fill the gap, in her narrative: 'It is for us to open the mouth and hear what it holds' (p142). But to the exponent of Writing's primacy and the father of linear realist narrative – 'It is thus that we make up a book ... beginning, then middle, then end' (p117) – it is the author's brief to fabricate another's consciousness and circumstances: 'we must make Friday's silence speak, as well as the silence surrounding Friday ... as long as he is dumb we can tell ourselves his desires are dark to us, and continue to use him as we wish (pp142, 148).

Is Coetzee's fiction free from the exercise of that discursive aggression it so ironically displays, since it repeatedly and in different registers feigns woman's writing? The artifice of the rhetoric perhaps serves to foreground that these texts are artefacts contrived by a masculine writer pursuing the possibilities of a non-phallocentric language. But why does a male novelist take the risk of simulating woman's speech, indeed her self-constitution in language (Magda declares 'I create myself in the words that create me', and Mrs Curren writes 'I render myself into words'), while this same white novelist refrains from dissemblinig the voices of those excluded from the dominant discourses (where such voices are audible, their status as written by a white narrator is made apparent), instead elevating their silence as the sign of a transcendent state? If, as I have suggested, both the topos of silence and the imitations of a woman's writing act to transcribe and valorize the body as agent of cognition, then the claim that the fiction manifests an identification with feminism, and the charge that it consigns the dispossessed to a space outside discourse, could be dismissed as irrelevant to the novels' interests. Such an argument overlooks that the effects of bestowing authority on the woman's text while withholding discursive skills from the dispossessed, is to reinscribe, indeed re-enact the received disposal of narrative power where voice is correlated with cultural supremacy, and aphonia with subjugation; just as the homages to the mystical properties and prestige of muteness disperses the critique of that condition where oppression inflicts and provokes silence.

It is tempting to associate Coetzee's deployment of silence with the mute Africa of *Heart of Darkness* which in its 'unknowability' and its own 'overwhelming reality' is resistant to incorporation into European discourse, its unrepresentable presence rendered in Marlow's obscure, ornate and obfuscatory language and engendering a crisis in his adherence to a stern ethic of work and duty. Thus were Coetzee's figures of alterity to be read as dramatizing the texts' destabilization by a wholly different discursive realm, then its modality as an other-worldly state beyond subjectivity and the secular sets the same limits on its power to oppose the dominant discourse as does Conrad's metaphysical 'Africa', the space of both novels remaining sealed from that heterology in which the narrative discourses are inflected by the tones, accents and testimony of other voices.

Coetzee as critic surveying the South African pastoral novel has written with regret about the ways we now read silence:

> Our ears today are finely attuned to modes of silence. We have been brought up on the music of Webern: substantial silence structured by tracings of sound. Our craft is all in reading *the other*: gaps, inverses, undersides; the veiled; the dark, the buried, the feminine; alterities. To a pastoral novel like *The Beadle* we give an antipastoral reading ... alert to the spaces in the text ... Only part of the truth, such a reading asserts, resides in what writing says of the hitherto unsaid; for the rest, its truth lies in what it dare not say for the sake of its own safety, or in what it does not know about itself: in its silences. It is a mode of reading which, subverting the dominant, is in peril, like all triumphant subversion, of becoming the dominant in turn. Is it a version of utopianism (or pastoralism) to look forward (or backward) to the day when the truth will be (or was) what is said, not what is not said, when we will hear (or heard) music as sound upon silence, not silence between sounds? (*White Writing*, p81)

Without reiterating the implications of turning his discriminating gaze on his own fiction, I would suggest that Coetzee's writing, rather than exploring the dialectic between sound and silence, or teaching us to hear sound as trespassing on silence, situates the inarticulate protagonists, who intimate the mystery of enigmatic, non-verbal modes of cognition which they are unable or unwilling to narrate, as the objects of another's narratives. This secretion of contradictory meanings suggests that 'what [his] writing says of the hitherto unsaid' may be other than what the critics are saying about Coetzee's silences.

III

I have attempted to argue that Coetzee's narrative strategies both enact a critique of dominant discourses, and pre-empt dialogue with non-canonical knowledges through representing these as ineffable. I now want to consider whether the noticeable absence of inflections from South Africa's non-western cultures in the narrative structure, language and ethos of the fictions, registers and repeats the exclusions of colonialist writing, omissions on which Coetzee has remarked when noting 'the baffling and silencing of any counter-voice to the voice of the farmer/father' in the South African farm romance (*White Writing*, p135). The eclipse, the occultation, the silencing of the other, is what South Africa's settler colonialism, as the self-appointed representative of western civilization in Africa, was intent on effecting. Hence the cognitive traditions and customs of the indigenous peoples were derogated and ignored, as were those of the practitioners of two world religions whose communities in South Africa were initially formed by the importation of slaves from the Dutch East Indies in the seventeenth century and of indentured labourers from the Indian sub-continent in the nineteenth century.

The paradox is that whereas South Africa's institutional structure internally duplicated the divide between the hemispheres, and its state apparatus has exercised an imperialist ascendency over neighbouring and *de jure* autonomous territories, within the orbit of imperialism's global system it was and remains an outpost complicit with but on the boundaries of the west's power centres, its mining, heavy and high-tech industries dominated by multi-national capital, and its white comprador classes deferential to the cultures of the metropolitan worlds. This inessential status in relationship to Europe was registered in the beginning novel of white South African writing in English, Olive Schreiner's *The Story of an African Farm*. Here the books in the loft belonging to Em's English father, the shelf of books cherished by the German overseer and the books given to Waldo by his French-looking Stranger, are signs of a secular explanatory system imported from Europe into a land which is deemed as having no native resources in which to validate itself – the Dutch too had brought a book with them, but only The Book.

Such subservience was perpetuated, as Coetzee has shown in his essays, in the adoption/adaptation of established European fictional genre by both English and Afrikaans literatures. These until the 1950s were overwhelmingly aligned with and served to naturalize the ideology of white supremacy and segregation coterminous with Afrikaner, British and subsequent, diverse European settlement. Such writing is now virtually extinct, while a literature predominantly in English, but also increasingly in Afrikaans, has positioned itself as opposed to the status quo.

The identification of white literature with the traditions of the first world has been a given for writers: a remark of the expatriate novelist Dan Jacobson that settler colonial societies cannot sustain a culture, suggests how resolutely he turns his back on the possibilities of this settler society participating in generating new formations through interactions with the cultures of South Africa's volatile non-European communities who have been instrumental in effecting transculturation; while the flight of the Sestigers, a group of young Afrikaner writers, from the constraints of a militant nationalism took them during the 1960s, not towards those ethnically diverse groupings resisting the regime and ethos of white South Africa, but to Paris, perhaps in search of their seventeenth-century Huguenot ancestors who had disappeared into the Afrikaner nation. To the culturally insecure and dislocated white South African writers, Europe is the imaginary and imagined homeland from which they have been exiled, and whether it is to classical and modernist realism, or to postmodernism that they turn for inspiration and sustenance, they have remained dependent on metropolitan modes – although critics are now claiming that the later Nadine Gordimer and those younger white writers who have transgressed cultural insulation and assimilated knowledges and accents from which previous generations were, through circumstance and choice isolated, are on the brink of inventing other forms in their plurally-located and multiply-voiced 'post-apartheid' novels.[16]

Meanwhile, the predominant mode of the South African novel, white and black, remains social realism, and from this Coetzee in his critical writings has intimated his distance. Reviewing a study of Gordimer in 1980, Coetzee disputed the author's contention that her writing is 'engaged in undermining the structures of time that the realist novel as a genre embodies', arguing that 'whatever she is, Gordimer is not an innovator in narrative method. *The Conservationist*, technically her most complex novel, does not use any technique that had not been used by 1930.' When in a subsequent review Coetzee noted her interest 'in herself as the site of a struggle between a towering European tradition and the whirlwind of the new Africa', and commended 'an oeuvre that constitutes a major piece of historical witness', his appreciation in no way reverses his earlier judgment of her modes as conventional.[17]

If Coetzee's own writing defamiliarizes the practices of white South African fiction, then the subversions of the representational paradigm also set his novels apart from black writing, which for complex historical reasons is similarly indebted to established western modes. Shared by the black novel and short story, often autobiographical in inspiration, and historically concrete in location and moment, fictionalized journalism/journalistic-fiction was first devised in the 1950s by the *Drum* generation, and populist realism of prose, performance poetry and drama was generated by the Black Consciousness Movement of the 1970s and 1980s, and which found a home in the magazine *Staffrider*, is an impulse to register the heterogeneous black experience in its own oppositional terms and its own resistant voice. Although spokesmen for the project of a 'new black aesthetic' mooted during the 1970s and 1980s had declared 'we are going to kick and pull and push and drag literature into the form we prefer', recommending a violently innovative diction, dislocated syntax and explosive narrative structures that would produce a literal enactment of social disjunctions and political conflicts, this radical programme was largely implemented in further experiments within an urgent social realism which often issued as an extreme 'naturalism'.

The persistence of an overwhelmingly testamentary writing led a critic working in the United States to consider 'why black South African literature remains outside the problematic of a modernist or postmodern culture', to ask if a pre-modern literature is not a 'necessity ... for a dominated and struggling people', and to question whether to reflect on modernity and modernism, postmodernity and postmodernism is not 'always already ethnocentric because it excludes one important dimension of the current global system of capitalism by concentrating on an issue that belongs solely to the "first world"?'[18] The congruence and incongruence of forces in South Africa's combined and uneven development — a mineral capitalism dependent on a pre-capitalist labour-force is a striking instance; the coexistence and overlap of

16. On Nadine Gordimer, see Stephen Clingman, *The Novels of Nadine Gordimer*, Allen and Unwin, London 1986, and Brenda Cooper, 'New Criteria for an "Abnormal Mutation"? An Evaluation of Gordimer's *A Sport of Nature*', in *Rendering Things Visible*. The notion of the white 'post-apartheid novel' has been mooted by Graham Pechey in numerous reviews that have appeared in the *Southern African Review of Books*.

17. *Researches in African Literature*, 11, 2, (Summer 1980) pp253-6; and *Doubling the Point*, pp386, 387. The question of which mode exercises the most subversive power under contemporary South African conditions has been raised by Neil Lazarus who argues for the subversive power of modernism; 'Modernism and Modernity: Adorno and Contemporary White South African Literature', *Cultural Critique*, 5 (1986/7) pp131-155.

18. Jochem Schulte-Sasse, *Introduction* to issue *Modernity and Modernism, Postmodernity and Postmodinism: Cultural Critique*, 5, (1986/7) pp5-22.

different modes of production, distinctive heritages and multiple vernaculars, as well as the recombined cultural forms and innovative Englishes engendered by the black majority, indicates rather the relevance of these issues to the critical discussion, and also suggests that the very disjunctions and contradictions, as well as transactions and flows between pre-modern and modern forms, would have stimulated innovatory literary modes.

However the designation of black writing as 'pre-modern' could be disputed and dismissed, for while white South Africa denied itself the pleasures of cross-cultural inventions, the black communities because of urbanization, albeit in situations of planned deprivation, of participation in high-tech industries, albeit as a massively exploited work-force, and of an educational system designed to keep them in their subordinate place, but which gave restricted access to literacy, have been the agents of transculturation processes in South Africa. If English, the language of the cities, remains the predominant medium of print culture, it has enabled transnational perspectives, since not only English sources but the writings of European, Asian, African and Latin American novelists, intellectuals and revolutionaries, are accessible in translation, making possible the recitations of Cesaire's poetry, Fanon's addresses and the prose of Baldwin and Baraka as public events. Nor does a literature of attestation preclude the enlargement of realist form, or the infiltration of pre- and post-realist discourses, procedures which have been effected by the transgression of generic frontiers between documentation and fabrication, autobiography and fiction, as well as the incorporation of older, oral ways of story-telling within narrative styles adapted from those developed on other continents and in other times.

In these departures, critics argue, the writing of black women, delayed by their more effective separation from the technologies of the text, which occupies what one critic describes as 'the ravaged ground where class, race and gender oppression intersect', has been prominent. Such writing, it is maintained, has challenged the masculine accents of the black literary tradition and the newer fighting literature, both of which while protesting class and race oppression, continued to thematize woman's subordination and project male agency. Furthermore, a writing which negotiates the tensions between the female self, still largely conceived as wife and mother, and the affiliation to being black within narratives which foreground the immediate conditions and social forces making for woman's multiple oppressions, both criticizes patriarchal relations extant within traditional structures, and transgresses the preoccupation with the black urban experience by calling on the epistemological and linguistic resources of now disrupted peasant societies. In this it has forged a link between urban and rural women, and broken the silence about the ancestors imposed by the regime's invention of distinct and incompatible ethnic traditions in the interests of maintaining segregation through the fiction of separate African 'nations'.[19]

While the material conditions of oppression generated a literature bearing witness to black experiences and aspirations, the question of why writers

19. For information and analysis I am indebted to the work of contributors to a special issue of *Current Writing: Text and Reception in Southern Africa*, vol.2, (October 1990) on *Feminism and Writing*; to the essays of Brenda Cooper,

turned to existing fictional forms must be asked. Perhaps the restricted privilege of a liberal education shaped by a British-influenced academic practice, delivered the ready-made example of the European novel as the unsurpassable medium of social and ethical critique. Certainly such a training brought with it the constraints of a literary aesthetic privileging the organicism, coherence and moral seriousness of the classic realist text. Noticably, two prominent black critics of older generations, both of whom censure the limitations of protest writing, appear inhospitable to formal experimentation, recommending in the one case a literature documenting 'the vicissitudes of African society at major points of crisis', reconstructing the African past and chronicling the struggle against colonialism; and in the other positing the necessity of producing 'compelling imaginative recreations of hitherto ignored themes and settings'.[20]

The preference for a responsible realism reclaiming black history and registering black agency was reinforced on different grounds by 'cultural agendas' devised by the most visible organizations of the liberation movements. These decreed that writers commit themselves to developing a purposeful, expressive and accessible literature depicting oppression, illuminating the struggle, and serving to raise consciousness. Such demands in turn generated a 'solidarity criticism' which by arguing that evaluation should be based on cultural function, encouraged the praise of unmodulated and declamatory prose, poetry and drama and inhibited the debate on what might constitute a revolutionary art.[21] A climate in which established Anglo-American critical paradigms vied with political programmes for the arts is now changing. This is evident in the founding of at least two journals participating in the transnational debates on critical theory and postcolonial criticism, and in the self-interrogations of critics and writers who as members of one or another community are aligned with the struggle, and as scholars or artists are aware that the discussion on autonomy and commitment in cultural production, as this has been conducted in South Africa, is in urgent need of redefinition.[22]

IV

It is from within this specific literary landscape that I want finally to look at Coetzee's implementation of what he has referred to as 'a politics of writing for postcolonial literatures.' Detached from the predominant modes of South African writing, obliquely situated to the prevailing intellectual formations of his native land, whether white nationalist or liberal, socialist-liberationist or black consciousness, and little touched by the autochthonous, transplanted and recombinant cultures of South Africa's African, Asian and Coloured populations, Coetzee in his fictions negotiates 'South Africa' as referent through defamiliarizing strategies which efface its spatial and temporal specificity, denying it the identity of a social space and the site of cultural meanings. In one of the Attwell interviews, Coetzee, while speaking with

---

op.cit, Dorothy Driver, 'M'a-Ngoana O Tsoare Thipa ka Bohaleng – The Child's Mother Grasps the Sharp End of the Knife: Women as Mothers, Women as Writers', and Karen Press, 'Building a National Culture in South Africa', all in *Rendering Things Visible*; and to Rob Nixon, 'Border Country: Bessie Head's Frontline States', forthcoming *Social Text*, Spring 1993, to be reprinted in Liz Gunner and Susheila Nasta (eds) *Commonwealth Literatures*, 1993.

20 Lewis Nkosi, 'The New African Novel: A Search for Modernism', in *Tasks and Masks: Themes and Styles of African Literature*, Longman, Harlow 1981, p55; and Njubulo Ndebele, 'Redefining Relevance', *Pretexts*, vol.1, no.1, Winter 1989, pp45-50. See also Kenneth Parker, ' "Traditionalism" versus "Modernism": Culture, Identity, Writing', to appear; and Tony Morphet, 'Cultural imagination and cultural settlement, in *Pretexts*, 2: 1 (Winter 1990), pp94-103. For an assessment of the radicalism of Ndebele's criticism, see Anthony O'Brien, 'Literature in Another South Africa: Njabulo Ndebele's Theory of Emergent Culture', *Diacritics* 22:1 (Spring 1991), pp67-85.

21. See Ingrid de kok and Karen Press (eds), *Spring is Rebellious: Arguments about Cultural Freedom*, ed. Buchu

admiration about the 'passionate intimacy with the South African landscape' of fellow writer Breyten Breytenbach (p377), and the ostensible pleasure which playwright Athol Fugard takes in the beauty of South Africa (p369), explains his own refusal to contrive 'nature description' of the Cape on the grounds that this represented no challenge to his 'power of envisioning', threatening 'only the tedium of reproduction'. (p142)

Such abstinence, I would argue, has further implications. In his critical writing, Coetzee has detected an impulse in the South African pastoral mode 'to find evidence of a "natural" bond between *volk* and *land*, that is to say, to naturalize the *volk's* possession of the land', observing too that 'the politics of expansion has uses for a rhetoric of the sublime' (*White Writing*, p61). It is these connections between landscape and the legitimizing narrative of the white nation which the novels sever by ostentatiously failing to register any signs of splendour in scenery that has inspired rhapsody.

Hence the terrain mapped by 'The Narrative of Jacobus Coetzee' constitutes an ideological cartography, the naming by an eighteenth century explorer and proto-colonialist of rivers and mountains, and the designation of flora and fauna as yet uncatalogued in European taxonomies, establishing the authority of the invader's nomenclature and marking the act of territorial acquisition. Magda of *In the Heart of the Country*, atones for her confession 'I am corrupted to the bone with the beauty of this forsaken world' (p138), by spurning the tropes and topoi of the South African pastoral tradition and rendering the scene as existentially sterile, her lapses into humanizing the spectacle swiftly followed by recantation. The pastiche of naturalist conventions in the litany of place names tracking Michael K's journey through the Cape Province registers the past occupation of the territory by Afrikaner and British settlement, but screens the meticulously inventoried locations from the infiltration of affect. In *Age of Iron* the romance and promise with which European voyagers infused their accounts of the fairest Cape in all the world, The Cape of Good Hope, are demystified when the majestically serene and smiling peninsula of legend is configured in a rain-soaked suburb built with bricks made by convict labour, and the drably named 'False Bay' is redesignated a 'bay of false hope'.

In thus estranging and decathecting a landscape named as the Cape, Coetzee's narrators effect a distancing from that historic claim to the land celebrated by white settler writing. But does not rendering a locale as null and void repeat that 'literature of empty landscape' which Coetzee has designated as a literature of failure because it speaks a homelessness in Africa? Further does not restricting the site of the colonial drama to the Cape act to produce a truncated version of the narrative of conquest which the fiction invents in 'The Narrative of Jacobus Coetzee'? Because here the beginning colonial confrontation is played out between Afrikaner and Khoi-San, the so-called Hottentots and Bushmen, whose resistance was effectively crushed, whose populations were decimated and whose cultures were dispersed, the boundedness of the staging excludes the violent and prolonged struggles between the white settlers, as they moved across the southern sub-continent, and

Books, Cape Town 1990. My review of the above appeared in *Transition* 55 (1991), pp125-134. For a thoughtful piece on the culture of opposition in Central America, see Timothy Brennan. 'Forward into the Past', *Transition* 57 (1992) pp110-121.

22. *Current Writing: Text and Reception in Southern Africa* published by the English Department, Univ of Natal at Durban, Durban 4001; and *Pretexts: Studies in Literature and Culture*, published by the Arts Faculty, Univ of Cape Town, Private Bag, Rondebosch 7700. See also *Rendering Things Visible* and *Spring is Rebellious*, and Nadine Gordimer, 'Turning the Page: African Writers on the Threshold of the Twenty-First Century', and 'The Future is Another Country: A Conversation with Stephen Clingman', *Transition* 56 (1992), pp4-10 and 132-50.

the Nguni and Sotho speaking peoples, where military defeat and dispossession did not entail genocide. And indeed since the fiction only leaves the Cape and its immediate hinterland for the unnamed and unspecified imperial frontier of *Waiting for the Barbarians,* and the textually received locations of *Foe,* it can perhaps even be seen as turning its face from Africa.

When Africans do enter the South African present of the most recent novel, *Age of Iron,* the passing of so pitiless an era is contemplated by the narrator as a return to kinder times, to the age of clay, the age of earth. A novel which speaks an intimacy with death has been welcomed in reviews as an allegory where the narrator's affliction with cancer is a figure of a diseased body politic – and certainly this is a connection which her rhetoric does insistently make. But since the narrative of Mrs Curren's dying occupies a different discursive space from the story of South Africa's bloody interregnum, her terminal illness is detached from the demise of a malignant social order; while her salvation, effected by Vercueil, the tramp-as-figure-of-deliverance who ensures that in the disgraceful state of South Africa she will die in a state of grace, draws attention to the absence of any prospect on another, transfigured South Africa. The withholding of a gesture to a politics of fulfilment, in a novel which does intimate a personal redemption, is made all the more conspicuous because the aspiration of the oppressed for emancipation unhinges the narrator from an attachment to a liberal-humanist ethic, and the text's refusal to countenance the hope for a tomorrow – 'the future comes disguised, if it came naked we would be petrified by what we saw' (p149) – is perhaps the strongest signification yet of the fiction's urge to mark its disengagement from the contingencies of a quotidian world in transition from colonialism.

All the same, another ending narrated by *Age of Iron* has very different resonances, for in taking to its limits the only political discourse to which she has access, the narrator recites a requiem for South African liberalism. Because her wrath and loathing are directed against the Afrikaners, whom she blames as the architects of the 'crime' committed in her name, Mrs Curren could appear to be acquitting her own English-speaking community of any culpability – as she explicitly does when speaking the customary protest of South African liberalism against an illegitimate and irrational domination which stops short of unequivocal support for radical change. Yet when she discerns the exclusions in an old photograph taken long ago in her grandfather's burgeoning garden, self-exculpation is suspended and nostalgia for the golden days of her childhood, 'when the world was young and all things were possible' (p51), is annulled:

> Who, outside the picture, leaning on their rakes, leaning on their spades, waiting to get back to work, lean also against the edge of the rectangle, bending it, bursting it in? ... No longer does the picture show who were in the garden frame that day, but who were not there. Lying all these years in places of safekeeping across the country, in albums, in desk drawers, this picture and thousands like it have subtly matured, metamorphosed. The

fixing did not hold or the developing went further than one would ever have dreamed ... but they have become negatives again, a new kind of negative in which we begin to see what used to lie outside the frame, occulted (pp102-3).

That this act of erasure in white self-representation cannot be restored by her story is the burden of a narrative whose efforts to bring the blacks into the realm of representation issues in bathos when pastiches of the benign naturalism and moral outrage all too familiar in the South African protest novel are offered; and the exhaustion of the liberal tradition of white fiction which this signals is confirmed by the death of its author. But does not this extended metaphor of the eclipse, the silencing, the occultation of the other in the chronicle of white South Africa have yet further reverberations which hark back to the exclusions, the holes in the narratives, 'the baffling of counter-voices' in Coetzee's own novels?

V

Within the current South African discussion, there are critics who argue for the oppositional energies of Coetzee's novels, defending his project against those who castigate his fictions as out of touch with the sensibilities of the times, and indifferent to the existential conditions of contemporary South Africa.[23] The question of 'who speaks' in Coetzee's writing, which has been the concern of this essay, cannot be disconnected from 'who listens' and how the novels are received. Translated into Western and Eastern European languages, as well as Turkish and Hebrew, and widely read in the Anglophone world, which of course includes many once-colonized territories, Coetzee's fiction has won important South African, British and European literary awards, as well as the Jerusalem Prize, and has been widely embraced as a powerful moral critique of apartheid. It is also at home in the global if restricted discussion on the radicalism of postmodernism and the revolutionary innovations of postcolonial writing. Towards these last cognitive circles Coetzee has been hospitable, having spoken of the cultural affinities between communities in what are known as the peripheries of the metropolitan world, their title to an international language, and their shared engagement in developing a politics of writing for postcolonial literature.[24] But who in South Africa does Coetzee's fiction address and whose attention has been procured? That the recent comprehensive *Bibliography* on Coetzee lists few contributions from black critics and writers,[25] is a sign of how the system has until now inhibited the numbers of black literary scholars; it may also suggest continuing cultural schisms between the communities and their different interests, perceptions and concerns.

Although Coetzee, who is publicly cool about embattled South African writing, has participated in the activities of the Congress of South African Writers, he is notable amongst contemporary white writers for his refusal to be

23. For example, Michael Chapman, a white Professor of English, who in a review of *Foe* charged Coetzee with elitism; *Southern African Review of Books*, 2: 2 (Dec 1988/Jan 1989), p14. See also the 'Round Table' discussion in *Commonwealth* 9,1 (1986), issue devoted to Coetzee. For a critique of Coetzee's critics, see Attwell (1990).

24. Cited in *Southern African Review Books*, 2: 3 (Feb/March, 1989) p13.

25. *J.M. Coetzee: A Bibliography*, compiled by Kevin Goddard and John Read, intro. Teresa Dovey, National English Literary Museum, Grahamstown, South Africa 1990. The

drafted into the struggle against the South African state or to offer himself as the conscience of his community. Whereas Nadine Gordimer has spoken of the white writer's forbidding responsibility to change the consciousness of white people, and André Brink has written of 'the need for literature to take arms within and against the socio-political relations of South Africa'[26], Coetzee has been concerned to safeguard his fiction from incorporation into a critique of the South African condition. In an interview during the early 1980s with students from the University of Cape Town, where he is a Professor of Literature, Coetzee insisted: 'what I am now resisting is the attempt to swallow my novels into a political discourse ... because, frankly, my allegiances lie with the discourse of the novels and not with the discourse of politics' (cited in Dovey, p55). He has since strongly endorsed the notion of a novel as a text 'that operates in terms of its own procedures and issues in its own conclusions ... that evolves its own paradigms and myths, in the process ... perhaps going so far as to show up the mythic status of history – in other words, demythologizing history' (cited in Attwell (1990), p101).

Perhaps the constraints of a critical environment commending functionality and demanding overt commitment, prompted Coetzee to protest the autonomy of literature, while the coarse vocabulary of cultural agendas and the impassioned rhetoric of the liberation movements may have nourished his Olympian distaste for 'all political language'. Pondering on this proclivity in the third person, Coetzee has said: 'As far back as he can see he has been ill at ease with language that lays down the law, that is not provisional, that does not as one of its habitual motions glance back skeptically at its own premises. Masses of people wake in him something close to panic. He cannot or will not, cannot and will not, join, shout, sing: his throat tenses up, he revolts' (Interview: *Doubling the Point*, p394).

In protesting against the predication of writing's compliant instrumentality, Coetzee as his own critic appears determined to detach his novels from their worldly connections. While it does not follow that the novels are so dissociated, I have considered whether a body of fiction which is at such pains to avoid playing 'the flat historic scale', does not position barriers against readings that would privilege its secular particularity. In his Introduction to the Field Day *Anthology of Irish Writing* (1991), Seamus Deane, who rejects the truism that all writing is profoundly political, has written: 'We are concerned rather to show how this is sometimes openly acknowledged and at other times urgently concealed'. The apparent referents have encouraged literal interpretations of Coetzee's fiction as protests against colonial conquest, political torture and social exploitation, while critics have argued that by subverting colonialism's oppressive discourses, his work performs 'a politics of writing'. What I have attempted to suggest is how a fiction which in its multivalence, formal inventions and virtuoso self-interrogations of narrative production and authority, remains unmatched in South African literature, is marked by the further singularity of a writing practice that diverts and disperses the engagement with political conditions it also inscribes, while remaining, as a critic has said of his work, 'ethically saturated'.[27]

---

exception to the silence of black critics on Coetzee's work, is a review of *Foe* by Neville Alexander, political activist, writer and educationalist, who reads the novel as politically radical; 'A plea for a new world', in *Die Suid-Afrikan* (1987), p38.

26. Nadine Gordimer, *The Essential Gesture: Writing, Politics and Places*, (Stephen Clingman, ed and intro) Cape, London 1988; André Brink, *Mapmakers: Writing in a State of Siege*, Faber, London 1983.

27. Neil Lazarus, 'Modernism and Modernity: Adorno and Contemporary White South African Writing', *Cultural Critique*, 5, 1986/7, pp131-155.

J.M. COETZEE: 'WHITE WRITING'

Kenneth Parker

As critic, J.M. Coetzee is probably best-known for his collection of essays, *White Writing: On the Culture of Letters in South Africa*.[1] That critical reputation is noteworthy for two features: first, that it depends most on the appraisals of European and North American, rather than South African, critics; and second, that the Euro-American response tends to obscure affinities, both with his fiction and with the rest of his critical output, much of which has less to do with the natal space of South Africa than with that imagined space of a Europe of the past that has never ceased to be the imagined literary homeland for white writers. One objective of this paper, therefore, will be to seek to establish some of the connections not only between the different critical and cultural modes of his writing, but also between the different historical and geographical locations that mark his interests.

At the outset, then, a number of general observations might be in order. The first is that several of the essays in *White Writing* date back to the beginning of the 1980s; they are the outcome of the critic's return from Britain and the United States to South Africa in the early 1970s and of subsequent critical and pedagogical concerns in English studies in white South African universities at that time.[2] Coetzee's critical interventions in the early 1970s have (with one exception) nothing to do with South Africa; his concerns deal, instead, with preoccupations which stem from his doctoral thesis on Samuel Beckett, and consist, for the most part, of articles published in critical journals outside the country of his birth.[3]

Important to note is that these articles on Beckett predate the publication of his fiction: while his first novel, *Dusklands*, was published in South Africa in 1974, two years after his return to that country, it was only with *In the Heart of the Country* (1977) that his fiction was first published abroad. Indeed, *Dusklands* was not published in the UK till 1982, and 1985 in the USA. His is therefore a critical recognition not only achieved in a very short space of time, but one that is overwhelmingly the creation of the 'cross-border' reader, who exists '… at the point where the South African subject of discourse attempts to interpellate the reader across these borders, from the confines of his or her own community, with its own specific values and cultural interests, in order to define his or her own unique identity. This 'cross-border' reader seems … to be of great importance as one of the constitutive principles in the shaping of South African literature'.[4]

What should be noted, therefore, is that a substantial proportion of Coetzee's critical output has been devoted to themes and topics that loom as large as, and precede, his interest in, white South African culture: those of linguistics[5] and of

---

I should like to express my appreciation to Ms Jean Albert, formerly of the South African Public Library and the Cape Town City Library, for locating and making available to me copies of newspaper articles and reviews on, or by, J.M. Coetzee.

1. J.M. Coetzee, *White Writing. On the Culture of Letters in South Africa*, New York and London, Yale University Press, 1988.

2. Of the seven chapters that constitute *White Writing*, 'Blood, Taint, Flaw, Degeneration: The Novels of Sarah Gertrude Millin' first appeared in *English Studies in Africa* vol.23, no.1, 1980, pp41-58; 'Idleness in South Africa' first appeared in *Social Dynamics* vol.8 no.1, 1982, pp1-13 and, in a revised version, under the title 'Anthropology and the Hottentots' in *Semiotica* vol.54, no.1-2, 1985, pp87-95.

3. Coetzee's doctoral thesis, conferred by the University of Texas at Austin in 1969, is entitled 'The English Fiction of Samuel Beckett: An Essay in Stylistic Analysis'. Relevant

the broad sweep of European culture, especially as manifested in the tradition of the classic realist text.[6] Succinctly stated, one aspect of my case is that Coetzee is, himself, the paradigm for a genre which he depicts, in a central argument of *White Writing*, as writing that '... is white only insofar as it is generated by the concerns of people no longer European, nor yet African' (*White Writing*, p.11).

I *WHITE WRITING*: CONTEXT AND CON-TEXTS

The most striking feature of *White Writing* is that Coetzee nowhere attempts to state his position concerning what it is to be, or to become, African. Like virtually all other critics in, and about, South Africa, Coetzee is entrapped by the (invariably) uncritical acceptance of a rhetoric of an overarching binarism between 'European' and 'African', which totalising discourse thereby marginalises what is specific about the South African experience, namely its hybridity. It is noteworthy that what today connects the old discourses of racism on the part of the dominant, and the new ones of liberation on the part of the oppressed, is the rhetoric of 'authenticity' that is anti-intellectual, anti-academic, often deeply philistine. However, unlike (for instance) Njabulo Ndebele, about whose work he, as we shall see, writes approvingly, Coetzee shows scant recognition of the historical and ideological reasons for that privileging of the doctrine of the 'authentic'. What distinguishes the criticism of Ndebele is, precisely, his rootedness within a shared history of being oppressed, even when he is sceptical of some of the more extravagant pronouncements on the part of the arbiters of the culture being transformed. What characterises Coetzee's position is, equally precisely, his detachment from such a rootedness.

It is important to be clear. My argument here is not in support of any populist belief in the myth of roots, especially when such attachments are of relatively recent manufacture. My argument is that, notwithstanding its many excellences of insight and revision, this failure to define what it is to be, or to become African, is the most intrusive silence that marks (and, indeed distorts) the text. Instead, the feature that most marks the text is how 'white South African' the text is, despite disclaimers to the contrary by author, as well as influential critics. For instance, although Coetzee informs us that his is a '... mode of reading which, subverting the dominant, is in peril, like all triumphant subversion, of becoming the dominant in turn' (*White Writing*, p81), Martin Trump is surely right in his assertion that Coetzee's practice, with its '... resistance to the accepting, without skepticism, of any dominant order ... is drawing deeply from the sweetest waters of the wells of liberalism.'[7]

The case for what might appear to be a somewhat maverick interpretation might be made in another way: if the question of identity for white South Africans is an unresolved tension between 'Europe' and 'Africa' (no matter how these are defined), there is increasingly an awareness of an equally unresolved tension between the claims of a dominant liberal tradition and an emergent and countervailing postmodernism as political culture. Coetzee, the writer of fiction, is at ease with the latter; Coetzee the cultural critic, continues to be, resistingly, attached to the former. The point can be made succinctly: as writer of postmodernist fiction, Coetzee deserves the international acclaim he has acquired; but participant in the current concerns of postcolonial criticism he is not!

It is the ideological and critical consequences of that distinction that is the burden of this paper: note that it is precisely in the history of one of the most powerful myths of the liberal tradition of the 'civilising' rôle of Europe that *White Writing* has its origins.

The epigraph to *White Writing* is that section from Ovid's *Metamorphoses* 3, where it is narrated that 'Pressing his lips to foreign soil, greeting the unfamiliar mountains and plains, Cadmus gave thanks ... Descending from above, Pallas told him to plow and sow the earth with the serpent's teeth, which would grow into the future nation.' What that epigraph omits is the context: Cadmus, son of Agenor, finds himself on foreign soil as a consequence of his wanderings in search of his sister Europa, who had previously been kidnapped by Jupiter. In Boeotia, the teeth of the sacred serpent he had slain grow into an army of sewn men (Sparti), who warn him against meddling in their civil war. From that war, five survivors join Cadmus to found the city of Thebes. Later, Cadmus marries Harmonia, to whom he presents a sacred robe and necklace, which will bring misfortune to whoever possesses it.

One central theme of the fable is therefore that of transformation: broadly, that of the creation of harmony and order out of chaos, more specifically, that of the founding of a future nation under the leadership of the male settler who will be assisted by some members of the dispossessed. The central assumption here is that the land to which Cadmus comes was unsettled (in the sense of uninhabited, as well as marked by conflict), as well as unsown; hence the argument in support of transformation from culture as 'agriculture' to culture as 'civilization', later developed into that well-known thesis by John Locke, which asserts that: '....subduing or cultivating the earth, and having dominion over it, we are joined together. The one gave title to the other, so that God, by commanding to subdue, gave authority so far to appropriate.'[8]

The Cape of Good Hope, as landscape as well as landed property, has featured, historically, as an object of colonial discourse that constructs it as different again from those of the New World as well as of the Orient. If by colonial discourse is understood '... an ensemble of linguistically-based practices unified by their common deployment in the management of colonial relationships ...',[9] the question arises: who narrates? This issue of narration is especially pertinent when considered in the context of one key theme of *White Writing*, that of the supposed uncertainty about the nature of white identity – therefore about the conventional justifications for the rôle of dispossessor.

In the recent past, in the con-text(s) of the rhetoric of a 'new South Africa' (or is it a 'new' South Africa, or even a new 'South Africa'?), this has become a somewhat fashionable assertion. The history has been somewhat different:

Pale Fire and the Primacy of Art', *UCT Studies in English* 5, 1974, pp1-7; 'Confession and Double Thoughts: Tolstoy, Rousseau, Dostoevsky', *Comparative Literature* vol.37, no.3, 1985, pp193-232; 'Censorship and Polemic: The Solzhenitsyn Affair', *Pretexts*, vol.2, no.2, Summer 1990, pp1-36.

7. Martin Trump, review of 'White Writing', *Unisa English Studies*, vol.27, No.1, 1988, pp62-63.

8. John Locke, *Of Property*, p35.

9. Peter Hulme, *Colonial Encounters: Europe and the Native Caribbean 1492-1797*, London, Methuen, 1986, p2.

until now, the dispossessor has had no doubts about the rightness of the role, only about its mechanisms and practises, one dominant feature of which has been the exclusion of blacks from virtually all aspects of participation in the, nevertheless common, society. It is only in the aftermath of changed material circumstances for whites, brought about by the combination of popular resistance at home, political change in adjacent African states, and pressures from abroad that the white state has sought to articulate alternatives to the policy of apartheid.

While those articulations, on the part of the white state, have resulted in evident material transformations (the release of political prisoners; the return of 'exiles'; the talks with the African National Congress and other liberation organisations; the removal of signs demarcating space reserved for white-skinned people from those of others), the dominant objective of these initiatives has been the attempt to maintain white hegemony by the incorporation of selected sections from within the ranks of the black communities.[10] Indeed, *White Writing* often unwittingly makes this clear: blacks are either obliterated from the common landscape, or explained as being present only as interlopers to what is presented as white space. At the heart of these discourses of transformation, in the state, as well as in the contemporary fiction, there is a paradox: that if the hitherto existing history of South Africa is that of racism as crucial to the needs of capitalism, the present would appear to argue its abrogation – in the interests of the transformed needs of capitalism.

One of the weaknesses of *White Writing* then is that it does not really foreground the historical specificity of these moments of transformations in black/white, as well as white/white, relations from the moment of white conquest and settlement in 1652. History cannot be separated from narrativity; if the former is context, the latter might be said to be con-text, not only for what it states, but especially for what it conceals. First, what is to be deduced from a largely linear progression that starts with the implantation of white settlement, but would appear to end in the mid-1950s of the present century? To read that termination as the moment of the demise of 'white writing' would be misleading, especially with reference to the second con-text: that of the moment of the constitution of Coetzee's own text – in the aftermath of radical resistance in the black townships, and in the parallel development of new departures in black writing.[11]

One of the consequences of the breakdown of the certainties of a civil society characterised by white racist hegemony has been the problem it has posed for white intellectuals, the institutions in which they work, and the interests they represent. Not only are these intellectuals enlisted to ensure the retention of Europe's implantations and to re-educate all sections of public opinion, but so too must the very concept of the law be enlisted to ensure that new customs, new habits can be brought into being: uncannily reminiscent of Antonio Gramsci's notion of 'spontaneous consent'.[12] Many white academics, especially those openly committed to the national liberation organisations in the halcyon 1960s, have a distinguished record in this regard. Coetzee was never part of

10. One of the most noteworthy features of the 'new South Africa', to which I was allowed to return at the beginning of 1991, for the first time since leaving at the end of 1964, was precisely how this double process of incorporation of factions from within the ranks of the oppressed, while simultaneously marginalising even further its most vulnerable elements, was part of deliberate state policy. It is appropriate, here, to acknowledge my indebtedness to John Coetzee – it was as a consequence of his support that I spent a most congenial and intellectually profitable three months in the University of Cape Town. For that kindness I shall be forever in his debt.

that commitment. To draw attention to this non-participation is not to criticise; in the 1960s, Coetzee's position was the norm in white South African academia. What was singular about his position then, a position that continues to mark his responses to this day, is a self-effacing fastidiousness.

It is partly a matter of style – Coetzee has tended to eschew the rhetorical flourish, to avoid being censorious. Above all, it is a matter of ideology: in the negotiations between the descendants of the Cadmus who came to the Cape, and the descendants of the peoples these settlers encountered there, where does he fit in? One conclusion is that, following on the recognition that the founding myths cannot be sustained, these myths have to be reconfigured not only for those (white South African, as well as 'cross-borders') readers, but also for those who are to be incorporated – those survivors who will join the Cadmus-figure in the building of the new Thebes at the Cape!

Of these reconfigurations by Coetzee, the one that has arguably been hardest to digest by white South African critics is the one which asserts that 'the fairest Cape' was neither part of the terrestrial paradise of the New World, nor the City on the Hill serving Europe as an example of true spiritual reformation, but rather a 'Lapland of the south'. While Coetzee has been taken to task by white South African critics[13] for his 'distorted representation' of (especially Afrikaans) writing, his selective appropriation of the white literary record is perhaps (unintentionally) the most paradoxical con-text of the book: even if his critics are right about his selectivity, what stands out is the poverty of the culture of white writing in South Africa; inclusion of additional texts would not have significantly altered the conclusion that white implantation is not only random and spotty, but tenuous, precarious. Coetzee's contribution to the dismantling of the myths of white South African attachments to a claimed European heritage overwhelmingly outweighs the critique to be offered hereafter.

II DE-MYTHIFICATION AS DE-TACHMENT

Just as Ovid did before him, Coetzee tackles particular and specific myths, and then proceeds to make connections between these in a broadly linear historical framework: from (not quite first) encounters at the Cape in the seventeenth century, via dispossessions in the hinterland in the eighteenth century, to temporary victory of Boer over Black and Brit in the more recent past. Unlike Ovid, however, Coetzee's critical practice is to read silence in the texts – especially about people who are not white – as signs of meanings that are not only withheld from, but not open to, white interrogation:

> Our ears today are finely attuned to modes of silence ... Our craft is all in reading *the other*: gaps, inverses, undersides; the veiled, the dark, the buried, the feminine; alterities ... Only part of the truth, such a reading asserts, resides in what writing says of the hitherto unsaid; for the rest, its truth lies in what it dare not say for the sake of its own safety, or in that which it does

11. A selective listing might include the following: Piniel Shava, *A People's Voice: Black South African Writing in the Twentieth Century*, London, Zed Books, 1989; Jane Watts, *Black Writers from South Africa: Towards a Discourse of Liberation*, London, Macmillan, 1989; Michael Vaughn, 'Literature and Populism in South Africa: Reflections on the Ideology of Staffrider' in *Marxism and African Literature*, George M. Gugelberger ed., London, James Currey, 1985; *Research in African Literatures* vol.19, no.1 Spring 1988 – special issue on Black South African Literature since 1976; *Current Writing: Text and Reception in South Africa*, vol.1, no.1, 1989 for articles by David Maughan-Brown, Njabulo Ndebele, Mbulelo Vizikhungo Mzamane and Boitumelo Mofokeng.

12. Antonio Gramsci, *Selections from the Prison Notebooks*, edited and translated by Quintin Hoare and Geoffrey Nowell Smith, London: Lawrence & Wishart, 1971, pp12-13.

13. Helize van Vuuren, 'Verwronge beeld van Afrikaanse letterkunde in *White Writing*' (Distorted portrayal of Afrikaans literature in *White Writing*), *Die Suid-Afrikaan*, December 1988, pp46-49; Hennie Aucamp, 'Skerpsinnig – maar altyd wáár?' (Trenchant – but

<small>always true?), *Die Burger*, 15.9.1988, p12; M. van Wyk Smith, review of *White Writing* in *English in Africa*, vol.17, no.2, October 1990, pp91-103; Christopher Hope, 'Language as Home: Colonisation by Words', *Weekly Mail*, July 22 to July 28, 1988, p15.</small>

<small>14. Benita Parry, review of *White Writing* in *Research in African Literatures*, vol.22, no.4, Winter 1991, p199.</small>

not know about itself: in its silences. (*White Writing*, p81).

Perhaps so. But who constitute the 'our'? Furthermore, while the critical stance is congruent with the position adopted in the fiction (the dumb Friday, the nearly-mute Michael K, the woman in *Waiting for the Barbarians* who is speechless, Verceuil in *Age of Iron* with his associations with 'verskuil'/(concealment; deception)), what remains unclear is why. Are these, Benita Parry asks, '... figures of witholding speech as an act of resistance? Or are they the victims of textual strategies that disempower them by situating them outside the linguistic order? Does not Coetzee's own principled refusal to exercise the power of the dominant culture by speaking for the other itself paradoxically perform the discursive process of silencing?'[14]

This seems particularly to be the case when contrasted with the self-awareness that is conferred on even the most marginalised whites: Magda, immured in festering loneliness asserts that her '... stories are stories, they do not frighten me, they only postpone the moment when I must ask: Is this my own snarl I hear in the undergrowth?' Yet it is Magda who can go on to ponder whether or not a speculative history is possible. (*In the Heart of the Country*, p36; p40). Much later she will go on to observe that 'This is no way to live'. (p190)

The crucial example, though, is that of 'The Narrative of Jacobus Coetzee'. Compared with Foe, who is bereft of a speaking voice, and the real Jacobus Coetzee, who was illiterate and had to have his narrative transcribed, the fictional Jacobus is afforded all kinds of assistance to fashion (fabricate?) the realisation of his 'positive act of the imagination' (*Dusklands*, p109): he becomes not only editor, but author, one who not only acts out the 'civilizing mission', but who consciously differentiates between what he writes in his diary, and what he tells the 'Hottentots' and 'Bushmen' amongst whom he finds himself: 'From the fertile but on the whole effete topos of dreaming oneself and the world I progressed to an exposition of my career as tamer of the wild', by which process he begins to lose a sense of his boundaries, which, in turn, leads to his 'casting off attachments'.

'Casting off attachments', the loss of a sense of boundaries, has to do not only with how the history of these encounters is presented, but especially with the self who presents that history. For a story that has as its epigraph Flaubert's observation that 'What is important is the philosophy of history', what is to be made of the three accounts of the same journey: the 'original' first person narrative; the third person edition and commentary by S.J. Coetzee, with its editorial intrusions; the 'translation' by J.M. Coetzee? If one assessment of colonial discourse is that it silences alternative versions of historic encounters, to what extent is Coetzee's project itself a colonialist act in its imposition of elaborate layers of silencing? It is here that the question of the constitution of the self is central:

All versions of the *I* are fictions of the *I*. The primal *I* is not recoverable.

Neither of the Words *I* and *You* exist pure in the medium of language. Indeed, after the experience of the Word in relation to one's own existence, life cannot go on as before. 'Self-annihilation' (i.e., annihilation of the self) is the essential form of the God-relationship', writes Kierkegaard (*Concluding Unscientific Postscript*, p412).[15]

This intertextual digression has been necessary in order to emphasise what *White Writing* is fundamentally about: the casting off of 'attachments' to white South African myths: of origin and first encounters ('Idleness in South Africa'); of European aesthetics ('The picturesque, the sublime, and the South African Landscape'); of pastoral as an appropriate literary form ('Farm Novel and Plaasroman'; 'The Farm Novels of C.M. van den Heever'); with which is associated an appropriate language ('Simple Language, Simple People'), especially that of the overarching myth of race 'purity' ('Blood, Taint, Flaw, Degeneration'); finally that of coming to terms with the recognition of being 'strangers to Europe' ('Reading the South African Landscape').

For Coetzee, this is the moment of the inscription of new myths about white settlement, as well as white writing about that settlement, in South Africa: 'As apartheid began to be implemented', he writes, 'moral ties were severed too; and from being the dubious colonial children of far-off motherland, white South Africans graduated to uneasy possession of their own, less and less transigent internal colony' (*White Writing*, p11). This rhetorical circumlocution reveals, as I have tried to show elsewhere,[16] a somewhat tendentious reading not only of the historical record of conquest and dispossession, but also of historical method. Myth-breaking though it is in many ways, *White Writing*, nevertheless, ultimately suffers from one central silence that Coetzee (quite justifiably) criticised the late Michael Wade for in a review of the latter's monograph on Nadine Gordimer: 'What is missing here is a sense of Gordimer's own existential relation to history and to fictional historiography and, in particular, a sense of the darkly prophetic stance she has now taken up.'[17] Whether he would agree with it or not cannot be established in any incontrovertible sense, but Coetzee would seem here to be in with Frederic Jameson's notion of 'cognitive mapping': the schema whereby it might be determined how subjects are positioned in history, by analysing their discursive practices.[18]

III 'DARKLY PROPHETIC': HIS-STORY AS PARADOX

Alternatively stated, one theme that has exercised Coetzee, as critic, has been that of the conditions that might enable the emergence of a 'national' literature. Even more striking is how the cognitive map that Coetzee draws has surprisingly sharp symmetries with white South African formulations of racial identities: of so-called 'Coloureds', of black Africans, of Afrikaans- and English-speaking whites. In seeking to establish the presence of that symmetry, it is essential to enter in an important caveat: not only are the reviews on

15. John M. Coetzee, Achterberg's ' "Ballade van de gasfitter": The Mystery of I and You,' *PMLA* 92, 1977, pp285-296.

16. Kenneth Parker, 'Coetzee on Culture', *Southern African Review of Books*, vol.1, no.4, Summer 1988, pp3-6.

17. J.M. Coetzee, review of Michael Wade: Nadine Gordimer, in *Research in African Literatures*, vol.11, no.2, Summer 1980, p255.

18. Fredric Jameson, 'Postmodernism, or The Cultural Logic of Late Capitalism', *New Left Review*, 146, July-August 1984, pp53-92.

which my assertions are based few in number, they are also located in specific historical conjunctures that materially affect their production. Nevertheless, that the reviews are concerned with authors who are described as exemplary of racial identities and of political culture (Alex La Guma; Njabulo Ndebele; Breyten Breytenbach and André Brink; Nadine Gordimer and Christopher Hope) vastly mediates the qualms I have about the case I now wish to make.

It seems to me significant that Coetzee's first major critical intervention, an interrogation of Alex La Guma's *A Walk in the Night and Other Stories* (1967), provides him with an opportunity to range La Guma against Lewis Nkosi.[19] Nkosi had asserted that, with the exception of La Guma, whose writing he admired for its 'enthusiasm for life as it is lived', it was 'impossible to detect in the fiction of black South Africans any significant and complex talent which responds with both the vigour of their imagination and sufficient technical resources to the problems posed by conditions in South Africa'.[20]

Bearing in mind Fredric Jameson's observation about the positioning of the subject in history, it is important to look at Coetzee's observations in some detail, with reference not only to the moment of the review, but also to the moment of La Guma's text. It should be remembered that *A Walk in the Night* was first published by Mbari in Nigeria in 1962, the same year in which its author was banned under the Suppression of Communism Act, and that it appeared in its Heinemann edition only in 1967, a year after the author (who had not only been detained in prison without charge on numerous occasions, but who had also been placed under house arrest that specifically forbade him to communicate with friends or family, or to leave his house), had finally left for England on a one-way exit permit with his family. Equally importantly, it should be recalled that La Guma was one of the leaders of the liberation movement against whom the 1956 arrest for 'treason' had ended in ignominious defeat for the state when all were acquitted in 1960. The three years between acquital and banning were therefore crucial not only for his writing, but also for his political activity as one of the leaders of the South African Coloured Peoples Congress, a constituent part of the alliance led by the ANC. It was also the period when the white state first announced its intention to remove the inhabitants of District Six, the setting for the first novel, from the centre of Cape Town and to relocate them in the sandy waste known as the Cape Flats.

Coetzee, like most other critics at the time, appears to be unaware of this history – either of the author, or of the community whose humanity is measured by acts of resilience to acts of vicarious brutality by the agents of the white state, as well as from inside its ranks. He makes three related criticisms in the novella from which the title derives: first, about the 'considerable weight of political statement'; second, about the ancestral and formal aspects of La Guma's fiction; third, socio-cultural glosses on the nature of the community depicted. Taken together, these criticisms serve to vindicate Martin Trump's detection of a liberal strain in the critic. The assertion, on my part, is not that Coetzee was part of the influential consensus of liberal-humanist criticism that

19. J.M. Coetzee, 'Alex La Guma and the Responsibilities of the South African Writer', *Journal of the New African Literatures and the Arts*, September 1971, pp5-11. Coetzee will write about la Guma again in *English in Africa*, edited by Alan Lennox-Short, Cape Town: Nasou, 1973, pp111-112 and in *Studies in Black Literature*, vol.4, no.4 [misnumbered: should have been vol.5, no.1], 1974, pp16-23. It is tantalising to speculate on the reasons why Coetzee should have chosen to publish in *Jonala*, which had originally appeared in 1966 as *Journal of the New African Literature*. Its editor, Joe Okpaku, was to argue later on that the aim 'was to encourage writers to give expression to their own inclinations, no matter the straightness or waywardness of their works'. This 'New Generation' of 'young men' [sic] 'refused any patronage, denounced the Negritude-Tigritude debate as irrelevant, and declared that there was no such animal as 'universality' in the jungle of genuine criticism. This term *universality* was just another euphemism for *European* or *Western*'. There was, of

dominated South African English culture (and arguably still does!), but that his critical position is an index of the difficulty of breaking with it.

When influential white South African liberal critics in those years displayed an antipathy toward 'political statements' in literature, that should be read, not as antipathy to politics *per se*, but toward particular formations: usually the two which liberal ideologies saw themselves pitted against – either a Marxist politics expressed formally as 'socialist realism' (La Guma), or an emergent Africanist discourse developed initially by people like Ezekiel (later Es'kia) Mphahlele and culminating in the Black Consciousness movement of the 1970s.[21] That there was a ferocious – but hardly admitted – battle for control, might be judged from an analysis of the 'little magazines' of the period.[22] It is in some of these contexts that Coetzee assesses La Guma.

The critique stemming out of antipathy towards politics is, at best, confused. The 'main line of the plot', Coetzee asserts, shows 'men overwhelmed by forces they do not understand'. Not only is this a misreading of the text – it is not that they do not 'understand'; what they lack is often the language and the logic to give expression to their material situation. To therefore proceed to declaim that 'we are entitled to ask what purpose a literature serves which only chronicles the lives and deaths of little people, the victims of fates too dark for them to comprehend ...', and from there to conclude that '*A Walk in the Night*, despite its naturalist assumptions and its doom-laden atmosphere, contains embedded in it an analysis of the political weakness of the Coloured society in South Africa, and hence implies an explanation of the negativeness of a fiction that realistically portrays that society' is (at its simplest) perverse. By which criteria, and on what basis, is the charge of 'weakness' sustainable? From 1947, when the white regime's very first act was to institute apartheid on the Cape Town suburban train network, through a whole range of legal measures to do with education, work, place of abode, the abrogation of the last vestiges of a franchise, the community had been especially singled out for attack. What is remarkable, and a matter of public record, is their resistance – a resistance in which Alex la Guma was a leading figure. How La Guma's text can be read as implying the 'negativeness' of a fiction that seeks to portray that society, warts and all, is unclear.

What is clear, however, is his ascription of literary relations: for Coetzee, the 'godparents' for *A Walk in the Night* are *An American Tragedy* and *Native Son*. Not only does this ascription deny a role for the classic nineteenth century realist novelists whom La Guma asserts were crucial to this formation (writers whom Coetzee himself continues to value), but in locating La Guma's precursors in the USA, rather than in Europe, Coetzee would seem to be denying to black writers from South Africa a share in the literary ancestry located in Europe that white South African writers claim for themselves.

It is important to press this point. Coetzee's argument is not that La Guma's novel is flawed because of the failure to manage the formal features of the European text; instead, for him the key flaw in the novella is that it is 'a novel without a hero: this fact is of itself the most comprehensive political statement

course, at the same time the material reality of the South African situation: not only was La Guma a banned person, but that banning prohibited the quotation of his words inside the country.

20. Lewis Nkosi, 'Fiction by Black South Africans, in *Introduction to African Literature*, Ulli Beier ed., Evanston: Northwestern University Press, 1967.

21. For liberal-humanist debates on the rôle of the writer, see especially the 'Foreword' by Jack Cope to the inaugural number of *Contrast* (Summer 1960, vol.1, no.1). The recalcitrance of that position may be measured by subsequent modified reiterations by Geoffery Haresnape – see especially *Contrast*, 60, December 1985, *Contrast* 63 (July 1987), *Contrast* 65 (July 1988). For the later period, see especially *Current Writing*, vol.1, no.1, 1989, for articles by David Maughan-Brown, Njabulo Ndebele, Mbulelo Vizikhungo Mzamane, and Boitemulo Mofokeng.

22. Stephen Finn, 'The South African Short Story 1960-1990; the writers, the editors, the agendas', in *Altered State? Writing and South Africa*, edited by Elleke Boehmer, Laura Chrisman & Kenneth Parker, Mundestrup, Denmark: Dangaroo Press, 1993.

La Guma makes'. Now, this is quite wrong-headed: like other South African Marxists of the time, La Guma believed passionately in the notion of 'the people' as hero. From amongst these, went the argument, there arose individuals who may, from time to time, assume certain short-term leadership roles. And, indeed, the history of the struggles of that moment did precisely that: Gramsci's 'organic intellectuals' like La Guma himself, as well as his father before him; trade union leaders like Johnny Gomas and Reggie September; civil rights activists like Zainunissa (Cissie) Gool and George Peake.

Ultimately, Coetzee's misreading is the outcome of a lack of historical and socio-cultural understanding that often also mars his otherwise scintillating insights into white writing. In the La Guma text it is there in small details, as well as broader theory. One example of the former is to categorise the thug Willieboy's fury at the visit of American sailors to the 'Coloured' brothel as 'unreasonable', and as 'represent[ing] a cultural introvertedness'. It is an observation that fails to recognise an important distinction: while those 'Coloured' males will doubtless claim their male 'right' to oppress 'their' women, their protest is political recognition of not only how the women are victims, but also of their powerlessness because of who they are.

The broader general theoretical assertions are equally debatable: to say that the community 'has become a social class in a capitalist society', that 'uncertainty before the promise of bourgeois security creates a lack of cohesiveness in it', and that it 'lacks political awareness' points not only to Coetzee's unfamiliarity with the social theories he adduces, but especially with what these assertions suppress.

The history of the community La Guma portrays will show that, whatever the tangled relations between class and colour at any one moment in history, in South Africa's capitalist phase the so-called 'Coloured' community has been a proletariat – whether urban, or rural, that has been its material reality. And even though a fraction of the community (teachers, medical doctors, skilled craftspeople) lived ostensibly bourgeois lives, even that was severely circumscribed by the overriding facts of apartheid. There never was a 'promise' by the white state – neither of bourgeois security, nor anything else except even more rigorous apartheid! Indeed, historians of the moment of Afrikaner hegemony over others in the common society might do well to look into the especial virulence with which that new ruling faction set about dismantling the last vestiges of 'privilege' which members of that community had by which it was differentiated from other blacks who had no rights of any kind whatsoever. To charge the community with a 'lack of political awareness' is therefore perverse.

That there were, at that time, considerable differences about the nature and form of the liberation struggle is a matter of record – notably between the policies advocated by the Non-European Unity Movement, and those of the South African Coloured People's Organisation. What is also a matter of record that is suppressed in Coetzee's discourse is the manner in which the white state sought to prevent resistance by legislation. Perhaps it is for these reasons that the community lacked 'political awareness'. Their struggles against (for instance) the imposition of apartheid in the transportation network (1947), against the Group Areas Act that designated racially specified ghettoes (1951), against the abrogation of a limited franchise in white elections (1951) and (in common with all other groups) in the Defiance Campaign against Unjust Laws (1952), are all matters of record. So, too, is their resistance to the draft of racist laws that mark the period of the early Sixties which inspire La Guma's writing and Coetzee's later commentary.[23] Unwittingly, perhaps, we are back to where we started: the white liberal refrain of those times, to the effect that these people were being offered the 'wrong' kinds of political leadership.

The case might also be made from the opposite position, that of the understanding of apartheid itself, and how to abolish it. Not only does he assert that 'As an episode in historical time, apartheid is overdetermined', but he then goes on to say that, writing not as a historian but as a literary scholar, 'it is ultimately in the lair of the heart that apartheid must be approached. If we wish to understand apartheid, therefore, we cannot ignore its testament as it comes down to us in the heartspeech of autobiography or confession.'[24] While recognition should be accorded to the spirit that motivates such an approach to the unrepentant 'ignorance and madness' (Coetzee's words) of one of the formative figures of Afrikaner nationalism, it is important to insist that such magnanimity suppresses a crucial aspect about power relations: the capacity that a white skin has to enable and confer autonomy over self and others that a black skin disbars. To adapt an injunction, 'Look into thy heart, and destroy apartheid', will not do, if only because it is not an option that is open to the mass of the oppressed: it is only those who have power who can afford to be that magnanimous!

Fifteen years will have passed, and a deservedly international reputation gained, before Coetzee will review the work of another black writer, Njabulo Ndebele.[25] In view of the critique he will offer soon after about the failure of 'white writing' to become 'African', it is important to see why he values Ndebele. Ndebele 'writes the clear, polished English of someone who is clearly not only at home in the language but has passed through an orthodox literary apprenticeship', an apprenticeship which Coetzee tells us is in striking contrast with what he calls a 'Soweto school' which is marked by being unliterary to the point of being anti-literary, or even sub-literary.

While there is much to commend the distinction, as well as the recognition that the formal characteristics of the 'Soweto school' owes its existence as much to an affirmation of proletarian origins as to a 'segregated' (sic) society, the valuing of Ndebele would appear to depend upon a paradox: if white writing is in peril because it has not yet become 'African', and the 'Soweto school' is not an alternative because of the deficiencies Coetzee asserts, how then to account for Ndebele? For Coetzee, Ndebele (unlike La Guma) has succeeded precisely because he has made the transition from African to being 'at home' in 'English' – in other words, by acquiring, through apprenticeship, that which is the best that Europe can offer: to become, if you wish, 'white', by marginalising that which is 'African', most notably the oral and the popular. Furthermore, for

23. It is perhaps necessary to interpolate a personal note. Much of the factual knowledge upon which I draw comes from participation in these struggles, of the late 1950s and early 1960s, as a member of the South African Coloured People's Congress, during which period (as a part-time student in the University of Cape Town at the same time as earning a living) I was also actively engaged in student politics. The interpolation is not to seek to privilege personal experience; it is merely to place on record that my friendship with Coetzee, as well as with La Guma, dates from that time.

24. 'The Mind of Apartheid: Geoffrey Cronjé (1907-)', *Social Dynamics: A Journal of the Centre for African Studies, University of Cape Town*, vol.17, no.1, 1991, pp1-35. For a further insight into Coetzee's current views on the nature of the relationship between the writer and the state, particularly with reference to censorship, see his 'André Brink and the Censor', *Research in African Literatures*, vol.21, no.3, Fall 1990, pp59-74. See also the article by Chris Louw, 'Satan and

Coetzee, Ndebele's value lies in the fact that he can, like Ayi Kwei Armah, be a teacher and healer of his people. And why? Because of the reverberations in Ndebele of Dostoevski – the figure Zamani in *Fools* 'in particular is a Dostoevskian holy fool, a man with a dark past – a "lovable evil" '.

The problem is that, whether he will concede my reading of the paradox at the heart of his assessment or not, Coetzee is fundamentally correct about the broader context; he uses his review of *Fools* to observe that it seems to him that 'a feature of the South African novel for some while has been that its writers have not known how to end what they had begun, or what the times they are representing have begun for them. It is as though the end, the true and just end, has assumed the aspect of that which cannot be imagined, that which can be represented only as fantasy ...'.

Stripped of the encrustations of metaphysics, what Coetzee quite correctly highlights in his reading of *Fools* is that old chestnut about the 'South African National Novel'. The problem is that the posing of the issue forces not only a discursive practice circumscribed by metaphysics, but also a European literary pantheon as metrestick. Writing for one of the most influential journals of state and big business opinion in the country, Coetzee remarks:

> The question is, can we find anyone who *knows* South African society well enough to present it in the depth and fullness that we (and our descendants, and the outside world) would – legitimately – demand from a Great National Novel? Or, to put the question in quite a different way: Has South African society that degree of organic unity that it can actually be known and represented from the inside out, as let us say, Tolstoy does for mid-nineteenth century society at all levels?[26]

The formulation takes us back to the central paradox that marks Coetzee's criticism (and perhaps his fiction as well): if the future for white writing is to become 'African', it will have to break with the traditions of the liberal bourgeois classic realist text tradition; yet, recourse to that tradition is imperative in order to write the Great South African Novel. It is important to recognise that Coetzee's best work is marked by his endeavour to tease out that paradox; it is equally important to recognise that Ndebele's best work is produced precisely because of his explicit recognition of hybridity, notably with reference not in this case to the formal elements acquired from Europe, but especially the forms and practices of collectivity that are the characteristics of black experience in its resistance to oppression that is not simply to do with race and colour: the stories are also about class (*The Music of the Violin*) and gender (*The Prophetess*).

There is a further paradox: because of the skills present in Ndebele's work, it must be inferred that he, rather than the white, English-speaking liberal writer, is best placed to effect such a resolution. Is it being excessively cynical to suggest that it was ever thus: for blacks to create for white South Africa what it is unable to do for itself? Indeed, the only moments of passion in Coetzee's writing is when he offers a critique of a white liberal tradition from which he

---

Censorship', *Southern African Review of Books* vol.2, no.3, February/March 1989, p13, translated and extracted from *Die Suid-Afrikaan*, December 1988/January 1989, which reports Coetzee's principled attack on the 'dis-inviting' by the Congress of South African Writers of their invitation to Salman Rushdie, under pressure from Islamic fundamentalists. Coetzee's criticism of Nadine Gordimer's role in that event, and her response, is especially relevant in the con-texts of this paper.

25. Review of 'Fools', *New Republic*, December 1986, pp36-38.

26. 'The Great South African Novel', *Leadership South Africa*, vol.2, no.4, 1983, pp74, 77, 79. See also 'Into the Dark Chamber: The Novelist and South Africa', *New York Times Book Review*, 12 January 1986, pp13, 35.

cannot wholly free himself. Thus, reviewing Christopher Hope's *White Boy Running*, he asks, explicitly: 'Why should liberal whites have proved so fickle, so spineless? And why should so natural a liberal as Hope – middle class, individualist, pacific – have lost all faith in the relevance of liberal ideals?' Coetzee's answer is that we need look no further than the history of South Africa since 1960, which provides '… eloquent proof that reasonable suasion, legal argument, and peaceful protests are ineffectual against an adversary to whom *raisons d'etat* are the only reason …'[27]

Now, not only is this a perception of a power struggle between the two dominant white groups, it again points to a deformation of the historical record. The history of South Africa is marked by one overriding fact: that of white hegemony over black; indeed, one of its most distinguishing features is how the rhetoric and practises of European (especially English) liberalism have been used to maintain blacks in positions of inferiority. The history of white liberalism in South Africa is not allied to a tradition of freedom, but rather to one of oppression, even though that oppression differs in form, as well as in justification, from that of its Afrikaner antagonist. Battles between Boer and Briton have historically been about technologies for the oppression of blacks.

It is in writing about the Afrikaner that Coetzee most obviously excels, especially when he deals with the complex dialectics that marks the work of Breyten Breytenbach. Two observations, in particular, merit citation, in that they not only point to a different trajectory from that of the past English liberal tradition, but might also have some bearing on a future literary practice. For the makers of Afrikaner cultural policy, Coetzee observes, 'There is an interest in not acknowledging that there can coexist in a single breast both a belief in a unitary democratic South Africa and a profound Afrikaans *digterskap*, poetness. Hence the notion that the 'terrorist' in Breytenbach can be incarcerated and punished while the poet in him can be let free.' By contrast, as far as the poet is concerned, Coetzee draws attention to the fact that a feature of Breytenbach's poetry is that 'it stops at nothing: there is no limit that cannot be exceeded, no obstacle that cannot be leaped, no commandment that cannot be questioned. His writing characteristically goes beyond, in more senses than one, what one had thought could be said in Afrikaans.'[28]

IV PARADOX RETAINED

The primary objective of this paper has been to show that, notwithstanding his location within a postmodernist tradition of fiction-making, when it comes to criticism, J.M. Coetzee continues to inhabit the unresolved landscape of the deformations brought about by a continuing hold of an aesthetics of liberalism in South Africa.[29] If such a position can be characterised, commonsensically, as 'ambivalence', Stephen Watson has sought to account for what he calls such 'ambivalences' in Coetzee, by skilful use of Albert Memmi's notion of the 'dissenting coloniser.'[30] Although I continue to live in the hope that, one day, a white South African will write a novel which delineates what it is like to do the

27. Review of 'White Boy Running', *The New Republic* 13 June 1988, pp37, 39.

28. 'A Poet in Prison'. Review of 'The True Confessions of an Albino Terrorist' and 'Mouroir', *Social Dynamics: A Journal of the Centre for African Studies*, University of Cape Town, vol.11, no.2, 1985, pp72-75.

29. See, for instance, Michael Vaughn, 'Literature and Politics: Currents in South African Writing in the Seventies', *Journal of Southern*

[margin notes:]

African Studies, vol.9, no.1, October 1982, pp118-138.

30. Stephen Watson, 'Colonialism and the Novels of J.M. Coetzee', *Research in African Literatures*, vol.17, no.3, Fall 1986, pp370-392.

31. J.M. Coetzee. 'Surreal Metaphors and Random Processes', *Journal of Literary Semantics*, vol.VIII, No.1, April 1979, pp22-30.

[main text:]

oppressing, there is much to be said for Watson's case with specific reference to Coetzee's situations, one feature of which has always been precisely that which he values in Breytenbach: the willingness to go beyond, in more senses than one, what one had thought could be said in white South African writing. Yet the characterisation 'dissenting coloniser' reinforces the paradox at the heart of the project: to the extent that he decentres the ruling myths, Coetzee is clearly a dissenter; yet it is precisely the privilege of being one of the descendants of Cadmus that empowers him to dissent. Put another way, colonisers have power to withdraw from their historic roles in a way that the colonised have not because of their lack of power. That Coetzee is arguably, with Breytenbach, and a new generation of white Afrikaans women writers (Jeannette Ferreira, Emma Huismans, Rachelle Greef), a highly principled example of the category of 'dissenting coloniser', is worthy of celebration and recognition as contributions to the struggle for liberation; but that still does not qualify him (or the other white writers mentioned) as attached to the 'postcolonial' project: the 'post' in post-apartheid South Africa will still have to wrestle with the 'post' in postcolonialism, as well as in postmodernism – context with con-text.

Perhaps the last word about the intellectual project should go to the critic himself. Having analysed and compared the first two lines of a translation of a poem by André Breton with one written by a computer, Coetzee observes that:

> we are left with a paradoxical phenomenon: two texts ... which, if subjected to formal analysis, are describable in much the same terms, but whose background histories (to speak metaphorically) are utterly divergent ... In the beginning the two texts are very similar. We read one of them in terms of the intentionality of its creator, the other in terms of grammatical theory. In the course of the readings, the texts grow apart. Where we first saw likeness, we now see difference. But the truth is that neither the likeness nor the difference was inherent in the texts. Likeness and difference were meanings we did not find but created.[31]

THE BEAST OF THE APOCALYPSE: THE POSTCOLONIAL EXPERIENCE OF THE UNITED STATES

Jon Stratton

> But the funniest thing was
> When I was leavin' the bay,
> I saw three ships a-sailin'
> They were all heading my way
> I asked the captain what his name was
> And how come he didn't drive a truck
> He said his name was Columbus
> I just said, 'Good Luck'.
>
> (Bob Dylan, 'Bob Dylan's 115th Dream')

This paper is about the American structure of culture in the post-Second World War period. I use the term 'structure of culture' to refer back to Raymond Williams's analytical term structure of feeling,[1] whilst emphasising the importance of cultural specificity.[2] In this article I want to take the United States of America as a specific cultural entity. I want to examine briefly a number of inter-related American myths as they have been articulated in literature, music and film, and discuss the relation of the myths to the specific experience of the United States of America as the first postcolonial state. I am using the term postcolonial here to refer to the complex of concerns surrounding the problem of identity which characterise the experience of states, and in particular settler states, which have their origins in the European practice of colonisation. Over the last half a century or so it has become clear that independence from the colonising state does not solve the problem of identity for such new states. It is equally clear that a sense of place is a fundamental constituent in the formation of the identity of the modern state. Despite the fact that the United States gained its independence as long ago as 1782, it is still a postcolonial state in terms of its sense of displacement and its preoccupation with identity.[3] Perhaps the most important way in which a settler state expresses this experience of displacement is in its construction of the indigenous inhabitants of the land.[4] The myths with which I will be concerned are characteristically utilised by the American white, Anglo-Irish, male middle class. This is because this group has dominated the power structure of the United States. Nevertheless, other groups within the United States can and do make use of the same myths for their own purposes.

1. On the idea of a structure of feeling see Raymond Williams *Marxism and Literature*, Oxford University Press: Oxford 1977. On the idea of culture as a whole way of life see Raymond Williams *Culture and Society 1780–1950*, Penguin: Harmondsworth 1961.

2. I developed the term structure of culture as a way of designating cultural specificity in Jon Stratton, 'Australia – this sporting life' in Geoffrey Lawrence and David Rowe (eds) *Power Play*, Hale and Iremonger: Sydney 1986.

3. Postcolonialism is a term increasingly fraught with difficulty. One good introduction, and one

to which I am indebted, is Bill Ashcroft, Gareth Griffiths and Helen Tiffin, *The Empire Writes Back*, Routledge: London 1989.

4. I have discussed this construction further in relation to the Australian experience in 'A Question of Origins', *Arena* 89, 1989, pp133-151.

The myths with which I am concerned can be grouped together in the context of the dominant mythology of the apocalypse. I will argue that the idea of the apocalypse has been a fundamental myth in the American experience. There are three other significant myths which operate in relation to the myth of apocalypse. These are the frontier, the promised land and the road. In general terms these myths relate to the myth of apocalypse in the following way. The American myth of apocalypse is ultimately based in the Christian story of apocalypse described in the New Testament book of the Revelation of St. John the Divine. As it has become a part of the American structure of culture, the myth of apocalypse refers to the period during which the United States, or the world, undergoes a series of extraordinary upheavals and cataclysms. It is during this time that the beast of the apocalypse rules. The chaos and decimation performs a cleansing on the people out of which only the chosen survive. The chosen are then able to live in the promised land. The temporal moment between the time of the last days and the time of the promised land is materialised as the geographic moment of the frontier. The road takes on significance as the time which is travelled towards the salvation of the promised land. I have been deliberately vague in this outline because one of my main points is that since the myth of apocalypse is articulated differently at different times in American experience, what the terms refer to has varied considerably. This article is taken up with precisely this issue.

Those people familiar with the Christian story of apocalypse will note that I have left out what is usually considered to be the most important topos in this story, the day of judgement. This is because in the secular American myth of apocalypse the day of judgement is always already present in the American experience. The United States stands judgement on itself. Through the transformations in the American myth of apocalypse this condition has remained stable. It provides what I shall go on to describe, following Baudrillard, as the moral perspective which binds the United States together. Whether or not the United States has found itself wanting has depended on the particular myth of apocalypse in place at the time the judgement was being made.

As I have already noted, the American experience of the myth of apocalypse does not remain the same over time. As a consequence the American experience of the frontier, the promised land and the road also changes over time. This article will concentrate mainly on one period. This is the period from the development of the atomic bomb to the end of the Cold War. However, in order to understand what was so special about this period I will refer back to the earlier period. I will also begin an examination of the transformation in the American experience of apocalypse, and some of the implications of this transformation, in the wake of the Cold War. It is becoming common to describe the period of intensified hostility which was roughly coincident with Ronald Reagan's presidency as the Second Cold War. I am taking the period around 1989/90, which includes Gorbachev's reforms and the beginning of the break up of the Eastern Bloc, as the main historical marker for the end of the period with which I am concerned. The final end of the Cold War around 1989/90 marks a critical moment in the American experience of the apocalypse and its associated myths.

The myths of the frontier, the promised land and the road all operate within the general myth of the apocalypse. Nevertheless, these myths began to be transformed rather earlier. One marker of this shift can be found in the assassination of President Kennedy in 1963, another is the moral crisis over the waging of the Vietnam War. A third is the final loss of that war in 1975. These events provoked a reconstruction of the three subordinate myths. Nevertheless, these myths did not receive the final blow to their post-Second World War significance until the end of the Second Cold War forced a more general reconstruction in the articulation of the myth of apocalypse itself.

President Bush's deployment of the rhetoric of a New World Order, a global promised land, marked one attempt to reconstitute the apocalypse myth. It depended on a conviction that the apocalypse has already happened and that the whole world has been led to a post-apocalyptic new world by the United States. President Clinton's much more inward-looking and isolationist rhetoric draws on post-Second World War images of the United States as the promised land. However his preoccupation is fundamentally nostalgic. It is common knowledge that Clinton has modelled himself on John F. Kennedy. Clinton's speeches look backwards to the promised land of 1960s American prosperity. Neither Bush nor Clinton have a way of understanding the internal problems of the United States through the apocalypse myth. Where Bush looked outwards to the world, Clinton looks backwards to the past. The problem is this. If the United States thinks of itself as living in a post-apocalyptic world, can it sustain an identity for itself, and a meaning, when it can no longer view itself as the specially constituted promised land? Clinton's rhetoric of nostalgia can not be strong enough to sustain American identity given that Americans now experience themselves as living in a post-apocalyptic world. In this claimed post-apocalyptic global promised land the United States loses its ability to judge itself from a special moral perspective. As a consequence the United States is increasingly unsure of the grounds which might justify its attempt to impose that same moral perspective on the world. Simultaneously, the generalisation of the American moral perspective in terms of an achieved global promised land means that the United States can no longer, as in the post-Second World War period, present itself to itself, and to the world, as an exemplary promised land. The moral crisis which began in the mid-1960s has begun to take on a new dimension.

The United States is a unique ex-colony. It is the only settler state to have developed an industrial and financial capitalism powerful enough to dominate the global order. The end of World War II, when an intact American economy was able to expand into the decimated countries of Europe and Europe's old markets, inaugurated this period. It ended around 1974 when, in the wake of the oil crisis, it became increasingly apparent that the global economic order could no longer be controlled by one country no matter how much military control it could exercise. In the United States this crisis was reinforced by the loss of the Vietnam War. The reconstruction of Eastern Europe and the breakup of the USSR. in the late 1980s and early 1990s marks the high point of the transitional period which began around 1974. During this period the position of the United States in the global order changed considerably. At the same time that it became impossible for the United States to dominate the world economically, the Cold War was ending. The effect of this has been to problematise the position of the United States as the defender of the Free World. After all, it is now more problematic as to who constitutes the Free World and more problematic as to what it might be being defended from. Meanwhile, in the aftermath of the Vietnam War and the failed attempt to rescue the Iranian hostages, absolute confidence in the combination of military power and moral right which characterised the post-Second World War American martial experience was put into question both in the United States and in the countries which viewed themselves as a part of the Free World. For the USA these changes signal a crisis in the way it has come to terms with the postcolonial experience.

I EUROPEAN FANTASY AND THE AMERICAN DREAM

It has become a theoretical commonplace to describe the USA as part of the core of the world-system.[5] This assumes a community of interest and capitalist power between the USA and the old colonialist states of Europe. In broad rhetorical terms it is the USA and Europe along with the rest of the settler states which go to make up 'the West.' In the post-Second World War period this construct was legitimated by the opposition of the United States to the USSR. 'The Free World of the West' was opposed to the Other of the communist world, with the rest of the world's countries bit players classified since the mid-1950s as the Third World. This classification was itself one constructed by the Western First World which sought to incorporate the diversity of the non-Western world in terms of an evolutionary development/ underdevelopment model.

From a European perspective at the end of the modern period, that is the era of state-based production capitalism, the world was dominated by two peripheral powers, two non-European states. Russia and the United States acted out modernist European myths of utopia. The Russian Revolution provided a temporally mythic moment for the Leninist attempt to materialise the Hegelian and Marxist narrative of an End to History. Russia was colonised by European ideas just as surely as Europe physically colonised the American continent (which, of course, it also named). Both states emulated the European states by becoming colonisers in their own right. The similarities between the two unions of states are remarkable but I do not want to extend the comparison here. My purpose is to suggest that from a European perspective the Cold War was fought out between two versions of the utopian myth which underlay the experience of European modernity. If the communist version 'lost' it did so

5. On the idea of the world-system and the core/periphery distinction see I. Wallerstein *The Modern World-System*, Academic Press: New York 1974.

because it was fundamentally contradictory. On the one hand it wanted to live out the European bourgeois fantasy of the connection of reason to unlimited industrial power. On the other hand it attempted to do this from within a theoretical critique of the capitalist free market and in terms of an attempt to create a 'workers' paradise', a communist utopia that had its ideological origins in the same nineteenth century bourgeois thought that dominated European constructions of the United States. My point in relation to this paper, which I will develop below, is that the construction of the Cold War enabled the United States to transpose the experience of its identity crisis as a settler colony of displaced people from a relation with the indigenous people of the country – the aggressively mis-named Indians – to a state beyond the United States.

With the collapse of the Soviet Union the United States will have to find a different way to deal with the problem of displacement and identity. The development of the Western film genre in the post-Second World War period is worth examining in this context. As the Western developed through the 1950s, native Americans – the Indians – were less and less represented as people who occupied land and more and more as existing as 'part-civilised' people in urban settings associated with white American 'civilisation'. Gradually Westerns became primarily concerned with 'good' and 'bad' cowboys. Finally, at the height of the Cold War in the late 1960s Westerns themselves declined as a genre. The increasing invisibility of native Americans corresponded to the American certainty of its mission to defend the Free World. In this light it is possible that *Dances With Wolves* signals the return of the native American to the settler consciousness as the end of the Cold War returns the United States to the experience of its own insecurity as a settler state.

Where colonialist Europe has constituted itself in terms of self-identity, troped by the idea of home, the settler colonies have always experienced themselves in terms of displacement. The point of contact between the American colonial experience and the European experience of the United States has been the myth of apocalypse and particularly the subordinate myth of the promised land. The American construction of the United States as the promised land is a reworking in terms of the apocalypse myth, of the European fantasy of a forthcoming utopia (as exemplified in Marx's work) which itself has a heritage in Judaeo-Christian myths of apocalypse. The promised land/utopia myth forms the basis for both the European construction of the United States and the United States' experience of itself. The connection between the two aspects of the myth is explicit in the idea of America as a New World. The appropriation of the colonising continental name for itself by the United States signals its simultaneous appropriation of the myth of the promised land/utopia. The United States as the New World is a rhetorical turn which has informed the American image throughout this century. It colludes with the European preoccupation with the United States. In American rhetoric there is a complex relation between the terms 'America' and 'United States'. The use of the term United States began before independence but was established at independence. It has become marker of the 'real', literally postcolonial, state of the United States. America, on the other hand, collapses the United States into the mythic order of the New World. The adjective American, used for both terms, conflates both sets of connotations.

From de Toqueville to Eco and Baudrillard the United States has been constructed as a mythic Other which has, either successfully or unsuccessfully, for better or for worse, realised the fantastic hopes and fears of bourgeois Europe. Baudrillard's book on the United States is called *America*. The name signifies the mythic heterotopian experience of the European visitor. From a European perspective life in the United States is experienced as a European fantasy. At the same time the idea of the American experience as the realisation of European bourgeois fantasy pervades the American structure of culture and forces the question of the status of American reality. This is why the myth of apocalypse is fundamental to the American structure of culture. Robinson has argued that 'The American Dream as European Dream was fundamentally a Protestant dream of historical apocalypse – a dream of a transformation *of* history *in* history that would consummate and so give meaning *to* history.'[6] I will go on to describe how this dream of an historical apocalypse informs the American postcolonial experience.

In his discussion of Hegel's *Phenomenology of Mind*, assembled by Raymond Queneau from Alexandre Kojève's lectures, we find Kojève saying:

> One can even say that, from a certain point of view, the United States has attained the final stage of Marxist 'communism.' ... I was led to conclude that the 'American way of life' was the type of life specific to the post-historical period, the actual presence of the United States in the world prefiguring the 'eternal present' future of all humanity.[7]

Baudrillard's *America* echoes this position, albeit with a likely touch of Baudrillardian irony. There is a section entitled 'Utopia Achieved'. Kojève ignores the colonial background to the American experience. As a consequence the United States becomes the culminating moment in the Hegelian and Marxist grand narrative of History. The United States realises the world about which bourgeois Europe dreams. Baudrillard presents a commentary on this idea. He writes: 'For the Old World [colonization] represents the unique experience of an idealised substitution of values, almost as you find in science fiction novels (the tone of which it often reflects as in the US), a substitution which at a stroke short-circuited the destiny of these values in their countries of origin'.[8]

One of Baudrillard's points is that the process of colonization allows the colonizer to impose his (sic) fantasy on a land unencumbered by his own country's historical tradition.[9] It has become traditional to take the bourgeois French Revolution of 1789 as one marker of the beginning of modernity. The French Revolution is the clearest case in which a European bourgeoisie attempted to construct a European bourgeois state. American independence from its colonial power was achieved seven years before that Revolution. In its

6. Douglas Robinson, *American Apocalypses: The Image of the End of the World in American Literature*, Johns Hopkins: Baltimore 1985, p2.

7. Alexandre Kojève, *Introduction to the Reading of Hegel's Phenomenology of Mind*, p161 quoted in Julian Pefanis, *Heterology and the Postmodern: Bataille, Baudrillard and Lyotard*, Allen and Unwin: Sydney 1991, p2.

8. Jean Baudrillard, *America*, Verso: London 1988, p78.

9. The characteristic gendering of the colonising situation marks the European colonising power as male and the colonised as female.

aftermath de Toqueville travelled the United States to see what democracy held in store for France. Already for secular Europe the United States was thought to be prefiguring the bourgeois modern experience. In this sense the United States was already thought by Europe to be 'ahead' of European history.

The experience of America was the prototypical colonizing experience. The distinction between the Old World and the New articulates the apocalyptic representation of European fantasy in the realisation of the United States. In this sense the United States acts out the European bourgeois fantasy. There are two main aspects to this fantasy. One is best described in terms of the French sociological tradition. In this tradition, in which the major thinkers are Comte and Durkheim, we have the bourgeois myth of the social as the governing interpretive term. The social is the theorisation of the lived experience described as 'society'. Society is claimed to be founded on the nuclear family and hegemonically articulated through a shared moral order. The other aspect of the fantasy is psychoanalysis. Perhaps when Freud remarked to Jung as they travelled to the United States that they were bringing the plague, Freud had an inkling of the importance Americans would find in psychoanalysis. In reference to this pairing of functionalism and psychoanalysis it is suggestive to think that the success of the ideology of the nuclear family as a privatised entity in the United States has led, in turn, to the conservative success of Freudian psychoanalysis as a way of dealing with the problems of the nuclear family.

In commenting on the importance of morality to the American experience Baudrillard notes that, 'If America were to lose this moral perspective on itself, it would collapse.'[10] If American reality is constructed in terms of bourgeois European fantasy, then sociological functionalism and psychoanalysis are the theoretical gifts of Europe which discursively articulate the American experience. The sociological development of American functionalism (epitomised in the work of Talcott Parsons) and the spread of psychoanalysis both occur in the post-war period. Together they provided a bourgeois theoretical structure which incorporated, legitimated and expressed the American moral perspective during the Cold War when the United States viewed itself as the promised land.

There is one more context for the American post-Second World War articulation of the myths of apocalypse and the promised land. It was during this period that the United States expanded into the world economy as the major purveyor of consumption goods. This occurred in the context of a shift in capitalism generally from an emphasis on production to an emphasis on consumption. With the spread of a fetishistic concern with commodities the utopian European experience of the United States was transformed. The United States was reconstructed as the site of apparently limitless consumer goods at a time when Europe was suffering a scarcity even of staples. This reworking of the myth of utopia enabled the United States to be constructed as the place of the materialisation of the nexus of concerns which articulated the commodity fetishism of consumption capitalism: youth, sexual desire, female beauty, leisure being the main ones.

The United States, for its part, attempted to transform itself into the

10. Baudrillard, *America*, p91.

bourgeois fantasy it had inherited from Europe. Ewen and Ewen[11] have described how the United States forged itself into a homogeneous society through the early part of this century by means of Hollywood films and commodities. In 'The Meaning of Memory'[12] Lipsitz has demonstrated how this homogenising strategy of the early part of the century was continued using television. The image offered for realisation was again that put forward in functionalism and psychoanalysis: a society with a unified moral order based on the nuclear family. This image was both the way Americans experienced themselves (European fantasy as American reality) and the way Americans and Europeans aspired to be (the American Dream as European fantasy) inflected through the desire articulated in the American originated consumption capitalism first deployed in the United States. Ethnic differences, languages, moral precepts, extended families and working class experience and culture were all subjugated to a bourgeois American experience of a society in which identification through consumption formed the basis for social order.

II AMERICAN APOCALYPSES

In post-war American capitalism consumption articulated the moral order. At the same time apocalypse became the medium of commentary. In order to understand this we must take a closer look at the place of apocalypse in the American structure of culture. Robinson argues that 'the whole question of the apocalyptic ideology, of the transformation of space and time from old to new, from corruption to new innocence, from death to rebirth, is fundamental to American literature.'[13] Robinson goes on to argue that, whilst this is the case, American literary criticism has consistently devalued authors who work in the apocalyptic mode. This is understandable when we remember that American literary criticism developed in the colonial shadow of a British literary criticism which privileged a bourgeois patrolled realism. As writers who have attempted to come to grips with 'the problems raised by the apocalyptic thrust of the American Dream'[14] Robinson lists Emerson, Poe, Hawthorne, Melville, Twain, Henry James, Faulkner, West, Ellison and Barth. In addition he adds Coover, Pynchon and Vonnegut.[15]

From a European perspective the apocalypse marks the transition from Old World to New. In the American experience it suggests the problem of the status of American reality. In the pre-Second World War period the American apocalypse was always imagined as taking place within the United States itself. Robinson argues that:

> One of the most obsessive concerns for American apocalypses in the centuries since Wigglesworth [*The Day of Doom* 1662] has been the task of infusing the biblical revelation with the visionary force of locality, the *American* power of dream. American apocalypses, to the extent that they are American, *are* American dreams – and dream becomes the characteristic American revision of the apocalypse.[16]

11. Stuart Ewen and Elizabeth Ewen, *Channels of Desire: Mass Images and the Shaping of American Consciousness*, 1982.

12. George Lipsitz, *Time Passages: Collective Memory and American Popular Culture*, University of Minnesota Press: Minnesota 1990.

13. Robinson, *American Apocalypses* pp2-3.

14. *Ibid*, p3.

15. There is another minor but significant American myth, that of the Great American Novel. There is, however, no myth of the Great British Novel, or French Novel. There is a myth of the Great Australian Novel. The idea of the great novel, the one which will encapsulate and articulate the American – or Australian – experience is an idea

Whilst from a European perspective the United States, located in the New World, has always had a post-apocalyptic hyper-real quality to it, this is not the case in the American experience of itself. Here the image of apocalypse traces the insecurity of displacement. It is the coming apocalypse which will invest the American experience with a sense of presence which it requires to be reality. This is the importance of the dream in American apocalyptic rhetoric. The burden of the oneiric prophesy is that, like the psychoanalytic experience of the dream, it expresses a reality of greater substance than that of everyday life. In American rhetoric, then, the dream foretells the post-apocalyptic reality. This is the reason for the signifying power of the myth of the Great American Dream. The post-apocalyptic dream-world will be the world of American fulfillment, and identity. Dylan's songs of the 1960s such as 'The Gates of Eden' and 'The Times They Are A-Changin',' are suffused with apocalyptic imagery. 'Bob Dylan's 115th Dream' can be read as a commentary on the American experience of displacement. In it the narrator visits the United States before Columbus has discovered America. He leaves just as Columbus is arriving. Perhaps the most well-known use of the dream metaphor during this period was that of Martin Luther King. King's 'I have a dream' speech, made in 1963, shows well how dominant cultural myths can be reworked by non-dominant groups within the culture for their own purposes.

born of the experience of settler colonies. The myth of the Great Novel is a part of the colonial baggage of the settler colony.

16. Robinson, *American Apocalypses* p62.

As the United States became the world's leading capitalist country and was forced into a leading international political role through its need to develop export markets, the American experience of apocalypse was transformed. Where previously the apocalypse had signalled the settler state's insecurity with its own identity and sense of place, it now began to be used to assert that identity and sense of place. We can best understand this by going back to Robinson's insight that the Protestant apocalypse was a transformation in history which gave meaning to history. The logic of this is that the United States will have achieved its identity once the apocalypse has happened, or possibly has begun to happen. To put this more simply, the moment of the apocalypse is the key marker in the American construction of identity. If the apocalypse is still in the future, then so is the achievement of American identity. However, after the apocalypse the United States will have achieved its identity. It would then be able to take a secure place as a part of the core, those European nation-states certain of their identities from which capitalist modernity, including colonialism, emanated. The cultural moment in this transition was the American production of the atomic bomb.

In American military and political rhetoric the explosion of the atomic bomb marked the beginning of a new era. From this moment on American rhetoric divided the world into those who had 'The Bomb' and those who did not. After the first test of the atomic bomb in July 1945 Robert Oppenheimer, the scientist in charge of work on the bomb, made the religious connection explicit. He said that after the explosion he thought of a line from the *Bhagavad-Gita*, 'I am become death, the shatterer of worlds.' The previous lines of the *Bhagavad-Gita* compare the radiance of a thousand suns bursting in the sky to the splendour of God. The simile could easily have come from the Christian book of the Revelation. The atomic bomb was constructed as the beginning of a secular apocalypse, an apocalypse produced by the United States. The exploding of the atomic bomb marked the rhetorical beginning of the last days. World events could now be constructed and interpreted apocalyptically. The end of the eschatological period would be the moment of Armageddon, the final battle. Armageddon was rhetorically constructed in terms of global nuclear destruction.

Many of Dylan's songs are, in the first place, American apocalypses looking towards a better, more realised post-apocalyptic United States. However in a lot of his songs, as in many other places where the image of apocalypse was used in the post-Second World War period, the United States is not specified and is merged rhetorically with the rest of the world. In Dylan's 1963 song 'A Hard Rain's Gonna Fall' the traditional local American apocalypse was connected with the new global apocalypse. In Dylan's *oeuvre* there is a marked decline in the usage of the apocalypse myth after the late 1960s. Dylan stopped using the apocalypse myth as a medium to describe and critique the United States around the time the United States lost its post-war certainty of itself as the promised land. The concomitant shift to a concern with personal salvation, which, as we shall see, is a theme of the road movie genre, is reflected in Dylan's biography in his own religious conversion.

As late as 1989 in their song 'Wake Up' from their *Yellow Moon* album the Neville Brothers sing:

> We're living in the times
> the Bible calls Revelation
> It seems keeping peace on Earth
> is man's greatest tribulation
> But you know the greatest crime of all
> the greatest sin
> The next war will be the final conflict
> and no one's gonna win

By transforming the American experience of apocalypse into a global eschatology the Americans were able to change the quality of their reality. In doing this they were able to give themselves an identity and a sense of place in the global order. In other words, by externalising the themes through which it articulated its insecurity and displacement as a settler society the United States was able to claim security and identity for itself.

From within this eschatology came the rhetoric of the Cold War. The Cold War was the period of the last days. Inglis has described the Cold War as 'the supreme fiction of our epoch.'[17] He argues that the narrative began with George Kennan's article 'The Sources of Soviet Conduct' published in *Foreign Affairs* in 1947. Inglis describes this article as announcing 'the advent of the Cold War as America's historic and unrefusable opportunity to assume

17. Fred Inglis, *Popular Culture and Political Power*, Harvester-Wheatsheaf: Hemel Hempstead 1988, p35.

leadership of the free world.'[18] Previously the United States had been concerned with an American apocalypse, now the apocalypse was constructed as global and the United States identified itself as the saviour of the world or, in more pedestrian rhetoric, as the global policeman.

It was in this eschatological context that the construction of the myth of the Cold War enabled the United States to act out the Manichean battle between God and the Devil, good and evil, as the battle between the Free World epitomised in, and defended by, the United States, and communism materialised in the demonised Soviet Union. In 1959 Albert Wohlstetter published 'The Delicate Balance of Terror' in *Foreign Affairs*. This article articulated the theory of nuclear deterrence. In a capitalist order newly dominated by spectacular consumption we have a theory of the Cold War in terms of display. The nuclear warheads must be produced and must be displayed so that the other side can see their spectacular existence, but they must not be used.

Throughout the 1950s and into the 1970s the final battle between good and evil was represented allegorically in countless films until, near the end of the narrative, Reagan was able to draw on *Star Wars* for his Manichean description of the USSR as the 'Evil Empire'. Around the same time Reagan's military Strategic Defence Initiative became popularly known in the United States as Star Wars, suggesting the extent to which the *Star Wars* trilogy of films enacted on an apocalyptic scale, a galaxy, the American eschatological experience of the Cold War. *Star Wars* was released in 1977 shortly before the easing of tensions that led to the 'end' of the First Cold War. As the ideological narrative of the Cold War weakened, the experience of the Cold War became more obviously fictionalised and spectacular. *Star Wars* was perhaps the most successful representation of Cold War mythology. Where earlier Cold War films had tended to construct a metaphorical or literal communist threat to a real United States, *Star Wars* constructed an eschatology of galactic dimensions. It provided an interpretation of the Cold War narrative which was itself eschatological. The Second Cold War can be understood as a spectacular attempt to recapitulate the narrative of the First Cold War using *Star Wars* as a mythic touchstone.

Star Wars forms a pair with the made-for-television-film *The Day After* (1983). Where other post-Second World War apocalypse films used the nuclear apocalypse strategically to construct an Other world, *The Day After* was an attempt to realise the nuclear apocalypse itself. It was only at the moment around 1980, when the myth of the Cold War was becoming unsustainable as a consequence of changes in the USSR, that a film concentrating on the nuclear Armageddon itself became a possibility.[19] This was because the construction of the post-Second World War period in terms of the last days left no space for thinking about an actual post-apocalyptic world. Indeed, the idea of an actual world of revelation was a contradiction in terms. Real nuclear Armageddon was constructed as the End of the World rather than as the cleansing moment of transition to a revealed hyper-real world. The idea of nuclear war as being unthinkable, not only morally but literally also, reinforced

18. *Ibid.*, p36.

19. In Britain Peter Watkins had made a film entitled *The War Game* about the nuclear apocalypse for broadcast by the BBC in August 1965. It was banned and was only finally shown on

television in August 1985. Around the time of The Day After *the British made* Threads. *Where* The Day After, *as its name suggests, concentrated on the immediate effects of the nuclear apocalypse,* Threads *emphasised the continuities and differences in people's lives before and after a nuclear war.*

the idea of the last days as being in themselves endless. It was in this context that nuclear war could become a fictional trope for the construction of Other Americas in which aspects of life in the United States could be discussed. This is the mythic basis for the use of apocalypse as a means of social commentary on post-Second World War American life.

I have explained that the American transformation of the myth of apocalypse allowed a new experience of American life as complete, as real. The apocalypse movies use the topos of apocalypse to comment on that experience by presenting a secular post-apocalyptic future in history which is defined by lack. The post-apocalyptic future is constructed as not having everything from consumer goods to security. All these things can be generalised as a lack of society. (We can note here how remarkably similar these post-apocalyptic worlds are to Thomas Hobbes's image of the state of nature, as outlined in his *Leviathan* (1651). C.B. McPherson, in *The Political Theory of Possessive Individualism* (1962) has argued that this image is a representation of the ideology of possessive individualism when there are no imposed constraints, when there is no state.) To make use of a trope to which I will return, as the present is reconstructed as the promised land of plenitude so the post-apocalyptic future becomes a site for commentary on the present.

The Day the Earth Stood Still was released in 1951. In this apocalyptic scenario an alien arrives in Washington in a flying saucer. Klaatu explains his mission. The other civilised planets are concerned about the combination of aggression and atomic capability that they see on Earth. Whilst they do not mind Earth destroying itself they do not want to have Earth disrupting their peaceful coexistence. To this end Klaatu leaves behind a robotic policeman who will enforce the wishes of the other planets. This policeman seems to have much the same sort of role as the United States imagined for itself in the post-war period. Klaatu is a messianic figure. He heralds the last days which are the days of atomic capacity. In terms of the American narrative of apocalypse it is inevitable that Klaatu's flying saucer should land in Washington. Whilst Klaatu wishes to speak to all the world leaders his speaking position is, literally, from Washington. Klaatu connects Washington with a Higher Authority, the civilised planets/God, but he also articulates the role of the post-war United States as the global policeman. This was one of the first of a genre of films which I shall call apocalypse movies.

The common theme in this genre is the end of civilisation – for which we should read American middle class society – usually by nuclear destruction. This apocalyptic scenario surrounding the atom bomb is signalled in the title of a 1947 dramatised documentary about the development of the bomb, *The Beginning or the End*. Early films of the genre tended to concentrate on the threat and the destruction. A good example is *The Beast from Twenty Thousand Fathoms* (1953) in which a prehistoric animal is thawed out of the Arctic ice by the heat generated by nuclear tests and attacks New York. In this film, as in many of the 1950s films using nuclear capacity as a motif, the destruction is not caused directly by nuclear explosions but rather is an indirect effect. By the late

1950s there began to be made films dealing with nuclear destruction and life afterwards. *Beyond The Time Barrier* is mostly set in 2024 when people live underground to avoid nuclear contamination. The 1962 film *Panic in Year Zero* described the effects of a nuclear attack on Los Angeles. Later films which show life after the apocalypse include *The Omega Man* (1971), *The Ultimate Warrior* (1975) and *Damnation Alley* (1977).[20] *The Terminator* (1984) described a future in which the defence computers of both the United States and the USSR have united to set off a nuclear war intended not only to destroy civilisation but to wipe out humanity. There is also the more recent *Cyborg* (1987).

20. Leslie Halliwell, see *Halliwell's Film Guide*, 2nd Ed Granada: London 1979.

All these films imagined a dystopian post-apocalyptic future which provides a contrast with an American present which, by virtue of the contrast, is idealised. In this way they reinforced the experience of living in the last days which was the fundamental experience of the Cold War. The gradual ending of the Cold War, despite the best efforts of the political and military-industrial complex in the United States, led, on the one hand, to an ability to conceptualise the American experience of global apocalypse in *Star Wars* and, on the other hand, an ability to think and to realise – that is to remythologise as a conceivable experience – nuclear war. The very title of *The Day After* shows a new ability to conceptualise nuclear war as an event in history rather than as an inconceivable end to history. *Terminator 2* was released in 1990. Its subtitle was *Day of Judgement*. Interestingly, given what I have been suggesting about the transformation in the myth of apocalypse around 1990, the narrative is dominated by the attempt to eradicate from history the nuclear war precipitated in the future by the machines which was outlined in *The Terminator*. At the end of the film we are led to believe that the attempt to change the future has been successful. There will now no longer be the war which led to the terminators being sent back in time. The apocalypse will now not occur. In this development the film erases its own narratival reason for existence. This erasure occurs at the same time that the American post-Second World War construction of apocalypse was being transformed, with the apocalypse itself being eliminated.

III POSTCOLONIAL INSECURITIES

The problem with the post-Second World War transformation of the apocalypse myth is that it meant that the United States could never be thought of as being the losing side. The certainty of the United States as the chosen country in a global order living through the last days had to come from its success in defending the Free World. By the early 1960s this reconstruction of the United States as the post-apocalyptic promised land led to the messianic overtones associated with John F. Kennedy and the idea of the United States as Camelot. Jacqueline Bouvier Kennedy remembered, after Kennedy's assassination, that Kennedy loved listening to the record of the musical *Camelot*. The lines he loved most were 'Don't let it be forgot, that once there was a spot, for one brief shining moment that was known as Camelot.' It was Jacqueline

Bouvier Kennedy who went on to describe the period of Kennedy's presidency as a Camelot lost at his assassination. In his speech on his adoption as the Democratic candidate in 1960 Kennedy said, 'We stand today on the edge of a new frontier.' Martin Luther King's 1963 'promised land' speech echoed this idea although, as I noted earlier, he used it in relation to the position of black Americans. In 1964 Lyndon Johnson described his policy for a 'great society'. During a speech at the University of Maryland he said that: 'The challenge of the next half-century is whether we have the wisdom to use wealth to enrich and elevate our national life – and to advance the quality of American civilisation – for in your time we have the opportunity to move not only towards the rich society and the powerful society, but upward to the Great Society.' Any major political, economic or military loss would throw this reconstruction of the apocalypse myth into question, and with it the United States' sense of identity and purpose.

There is no need here to document the traumatic effects of the American loss of the Vietnam War or the strenuous attempts in films like *Rambo* to reconstruct history to fit American eschatological reality. However I want to look briefly at *Apocalypse Now* as an American postcolonial film. *Apocalypse Now* can be categorised within that genre of postcolonial fiction which can be briefly described as a supplementary writing back. Typical of such works are J.M. Coetzee's *Foe* (1986) which reworks Defoe's *Robinson Crusoe* and Jean Rhys's *Wide Sargasso Sea* (1966) which traces the life of Bertha Mason, Rochester's 'mad' wife whom he keeps locked in the attic in Charlotte Brontë's *Jane Eyre*. In these works the colonialist assumptions of the earlier English novels are challenged and unsettled by the new point of view.[21]

Apocalypse Now is a reworking of Conrad's *Heart of Darkness*. Although it is not a self-conscious writing back, it nevertheless operates as a postcolonial reworking of a novel from the core, inflecting it with distinctively American concerns. By virtue of reworking a core text concerned with colonialism it becomes itself a commentary. The change of concern is apparent in the film's title. Where Conrad's book located its narrative in the movement from English civilisation to African savagery, *Apocalypse Now* locates its concern in the American post-war experience of apocalypse. It belongs in the genre of apocalypse movies, but features no nuclear holocaust. Because of the connection between nuclear warfare and the apocalypse the Vietnam War in the American experience could not be the final battle between good and evil, the mythical nuclear war ending to the eschatological Cold War. The Vietnam War was thought of as only one battle within the Cold War.

Still, the loss of the Vietnam War called the post-war mythic structuring of the global apocalypse with the United States as the saviour into serious question. The title of *Apocalypse Now* can be understood as a commentary on this crisis. The film examines the post-war American experience of apocalypse from an awareness that the crisis in the experience of the myth is itself apocalyptic. *Heart of Darkness* offers a reading guaranteed by the certainty of the colonial order. Its narrative traces the voyage out from an English certainty

21. This genre of novels is discussed by Helen Tiffin in 'Comparative literature and post-colonial counter-discourse', *Kunapipi*, 1987, 9, 3.

of place. *Apocalypse Now* describes a doubled colonial experience. In literal terms the film shows an independent settler society fighting a colonial war. In *Heart of Darkness* Marlow returns to Europe unable to articulate what he has experienced. In spite of this his new knowledge is made safe by the certainty of place in England. In *Apocalypse Now* there is no certainty to make safe the horror of the lost colonial adventure for a country for which the loss itself unsettles the myth on which it has, as an ex-settler colony, attempted to construct its own identity, its presence in and to the world.

Apocalypse Now was made in the mid-1970s and released in 1979. Released two years after *Star Wars, Apocalypse Now* connected the American crisis of identity, which was a consequence of the loss of the Vietnam War, with the deeper crisis associated with the ending of the narrative of the Cold War itself. In *Apocalypse Now* we have a clear expression of the renewed uncertainty of the United States about its own identity, epitomised in its uncertainty over place. In *Heart of Darkness* the story is told from England. Marlow's story is narrated from the core. Within the narrative Marlow tells his story of leaving England for Africa and of his eventual return to Europe culminating in his visit to Kurtz's fiancée. In *Apocalypse Now* we never see the United States. The film's entire narrative is set in Vietnam and Cambodia. Early in the narrative Willard, the rewritten figure of Marlow, muses on his inability to live in the United States. At one point he comments 'I'd been back and it just didn't exist anymore.' The United States was no longer the promised land of America.

There are three different versions of the end of the film. In none of them does Willard return to the United States. In *Heart of Darkness* Marlow returns to Belgium and lies to Kurtz's fiancée about his final words. In *Apocalypse Now* it seems unlikely that Willard will return to the United States to tell Colonel Kurtz's story to his son as Kurtz has asked him to do. Unlike *Heart of Darkness* the narrative of *Apocalypse Now* does not supplant Kurtz's final expression of his feelings, 'The horror, the horror.' Marlow was able to reconstruct Kurtz's experience for his fiancé, from within the certainty of place and identity of the core. For Willard, however, there is no place from which to understand and reinterpret his experience. He will have grown up in the post-Second World War United States. His ideal is to kill without judgement. Ironically this apocalyptic loss of vision is precisely the loss of moral perspective which Baudrillard argues would be so disastrous for the United States. The loss of the promised land implies this loss of vision. Willard, a member of the next generation, does not have to struggle to be like Kurtz. Coming from a settler society which now has no certain identity or moral perspective, Willard is already like Kurtz.

Heart of Darkness is narrated from the certainty of place and of morality of the colonising core. *Apocalypse Now* is narrated in colonial uncertainty. The established reading of the relation between the two texts understands *Apocalypse Now* as radicalising *Heart of Darkness* as a strategy for clarifying and critiquing the American involvement in Vietnam as a colonial enterprise. Whilst accepting this reading I am suggesting something further. Made after the Vietnam War, after the oil crisis and towards the end of the narrative of the Cold War, *Apocalypse Now* articulates the renewed uncertainty of the United States as a settler society.

Apocalypse Now constructs the Vietnam War itself as an apocalyptic moment in post-Second World War American experience. The film opens with an American helicopter airstrike. On the soundtrack The Doors sing 'The End'. In light of my earlier discussion of the 'Great American Dream' the Vietnam War marked the apocalyptic end to the living of that dream as real. Within the film Willard's journey up the river to Kurtz is a movement towards the apocalyptic moment. In this sense Willard's journey is a transformation of the journey in American road movies which I will discuss further below. When Willard reaches Kurtz's camp there is a white-washed sign on a wall which reads 'Apocalypse Now'. The code for the airstrike which Willard is supposed to call up is 'Almighty'. In one ending Willard calls up the airstrike and the film closes in an apocalyptic conflagration. In another ending Willard kills Kurtz and returns to his boat. On looking through Kurtz's typescript Willard, and the viewer, sees that Kurtz has scrawled across one page, 'Drop the Bomb, Exterminate them all.' In *Heart of Darkness* Marlow's visit to Kurtz is crucial but it is not apocalyptic. In *Apocalypse Now* the failed American colonial adventure marks the loss of moral certainty. In this apocalyptic moment the United States loses its eschatological claim to being the chosen country and returns to being a settler society searching for its own identity.

I have argued that Dylan's use of the apocalypse topos was always within its traditional American formulation, using the apocalypse to condemn aspects of American life. In 1983 he recorded a song which went unreleased until 1991 entitled 'Blind Willie McTell.' This was perhaps the only Dylan song since 'All Along the Watchtower' recorded in 1968 to make significant reference to the apocalypse mythology. In 'Blind Willie McTell' Dylan describes a corrupt 'world' – he means in the first place the United States – which is condemned 'all the way from New Orleans to Jerusalem.' However, the purpose of the song is not to describe this condemned world as such. The song is a blues which laments the lack of any present-day singer, such as the dead Blind Willie McTell, who can adequately describe the present state of affairs. In this song, then, Dylan's apocalypse is not related to the state of the United States but to the loss of an apocalyptic vision appropriate to the subject matter. In this way 'Blind Willie McTell' takes up and develops the same concerns as *Apocalypse Now*.

Both these texts suggest that the real American apocalypse is the one suggested by Baudrillard, that if the United States – the mythic America – were to lose its moral perspective on itself, it would collapse. There is, however, a more profound possibility. Whilst both *Apocalypse Now* and 'Blind Willie McTell' articulate the experience of apocalypse in the post-Vietnam War United States, the late 1980s saw the collapse of the 'evil empire', not in a global nuclear Armageddon but in a loss of totalitarian communist political control. This end to the myth of the Cold War entails also an end to the secular eschatology which has secured the identity of the United States since the end of the Second World War. It is in this context that the United States has been forced back into a postcolonial search for its own sense of presence, its place in the world. The American post-war transformation of the myth of apocalypse can no longer be sustained. If Bush's New World Order is, indeed, post-apocalyptic the question is, how can the United States sustain its sense of identity in a world without apocalypse? One answer is to be found in the American rhetoric of the promised land, a reworking of the modern European idea of utopia.

IV THE PROMISED LAND, WON AND LOST

The post-apocalyptic New World Order is being constructed in terms of a utopian myth of a world concert of democratic states all operating within an endlessly dynamic global capitalism. The phrase itself is intriguingly ambiguous. Is it a New (pause) World Order or a New World (pause) Order? From an American point of view it is both.[22] In the idea of a New World Order we have another externalisation of an American myth internalised from the colonial period. This myth is most succinctly summed up in the title of a late 1950s Chuck Berry song, 'The Promised Land'. The myth developed as an inflection of the colonial Christian understanding of apocalypse. For the Puritans who settled New England, the New World was the promised land. When the group under the leadership of John Winthrop founded Boston, Winthrop was not only looking for a new site for Zion; he was extending the frontier. In this millenarian view the frontier literalises the moment of transition from an earthly world of imperfect reality to a heavenly world of perfection. In colonial America the displacement of the settler society, characterised in the name New England and in the insistent mimetic naming of places, Plymouth, Portsmouth, New London and so on, was compensated by the puritan millenarianist project of creating America as the promised land. In this way the frontier took on a transcendental liminal quality.

In order to understand the myth of the promised land we have first to understand the myth of the frontier because the myth of the promised land depends on the myth of the frontier. The utopian promised land always existed in the mythical space of the frontier. With settlement came the loss of transcendence, the settled area became incorporated into earthly reality. As the frontier moved west New England became just a settler colony struggling to define its identity against the presence of Old England. When Frederick Jackson Turner read his paper 'The Significance of the Frontier in American History' to the American History Association in 1893, the mainland geographic frontier had been closed since the American acquisition of California from Mexico in the peace treaty of 1848. However, Turner was not in the first place concerned with national frontiers. He began his paper by quoting from an 1890 bulletin of the Superintendent of the Census. This quotation describes the end of the frontier in terms of the end of a line of settlement.

22. Thanks to Karl Neuenfeldt for pointing this ambiguity out to me.

What Turner's thesis did was to secularise the productive quality of the myth of the frontier. Where previously the frontier had marked the millenarian moment of heaven on earth, now the frontier was to be understood retrospectively as the site which produced all the distinguishing features of life in the United States. It is worth quoting the last two sentences of Turner's paper:

> What the Mediterranean Sea was to the Greeks, breaking the bond of custom, offering new experiences, calling out new institutions and activities, that, and more, the ever retreating frontier has been to the United States directly, and to the nations of Europe more remotely. And now, four centuries from the discovery of America, at the end of a hundred years of life under the Constitution, the frontier has gone, and with its going has closed the first period of American history.[23]

23. Frederick Jackson Turner, 'The Significance of the Frontier in American History,' in Frederick Jackson Turner, *The Frontier in American History*, Henry Holt & Company: New York 1950, p38.

Here, again, we have the puritan millenarian rhetoric. The closing of the frontier has led, Turner is telling us, to an end of history in history. The questionable comparison of the role of the Mediterranean for the ancient Greeks – it was after all a means of communication not a frontier – shows the need to reinforce the United States's identity through a comparison with the mythic historical founding nation of modern Europe. What is most interesting for our purposes, however, is that Turner describes the frontier as retreating not advancing.

Turner's paper constructs the secular importance of the frontier in opposition to the importance of Europe. In this way he asserts an identity for the United States outside of a mimetic relationship with Europe. At the same time he situates his paper within a United States from which the frontier retreats. In this reworking of the myth it is the moving frontier itself which creates the identity of the United States. The rhetorical slippage from the United States to America, whilst contextually justified, still prepares the way for the apocalyptic conclusion that, with the end of the frontier, the United States has been transformed into a country of place and identity.

It was the closing of the geographical frontier that gave rise to the secular construction of the last acquired part of the mainland as the promised land. It is this reconstruction which is echoed and legitimated in Turner's thesis. From now on the transcendental power of the frontier would flow inwards to the United States rather than outwards. Where the pioneers sought the promised land beyond the frontier, the closure of the frontier signalled an End to a spatial promised land beyond the kairotic frontier.[24] Instead the promised land began to be constructed within the frontier of the United States. In the context of the secular myth of American capitalism California acquired meaning as a land of unparalleled and easily accessible wealth. The discovery of gold at Sutter's Mill at the same time that the United States' Senate ratified the treaty with Mexico gave the myth a strong shove. With California constructed as the promised land, journeying within the United States gained its own

24. Frank Kermode in *The Sense of an Ending* Oxford University Press: Oxford 1966, discusses two different understandings of time which he distinguishes by use of the Greek words

transcendental quality as a journey to a post-apocalyptic world of wealth. In Chuck Berry's song, 'The Promised Land,' the poor boy starts on the East Coast in Norfolk, Virginia. He starts from a town bearing the name of an English county in the first state to be settled by the English. He travels by a variety of means of transport across the United States to Los Angeles, California. He ends up, then, in a city founded by the Spanish in a state named after a mythical land said to be very close to the terrestrial paradise. For the American traveller it is the promised land.

In the post-Second World War United States the movement from the East coast to the West was a movement away from an imperfect mundane reality that lacked the quality of identity into the more real world of the dream. It was also a movement away from the historically colonial land to the territory incorporated into the United States after the settler state became independent. The description of Hollywood as the dream factory signals the spatial and temporal movement away from the colonial northern East Coast to a southern West Coast which is closer to the last geographical frontier and closer to the greater reality of the dream. The fantasy of the realisation of the dream is the fantasy of colonial transcendence, the acquisition of a certainty of place in a promised land. In Berry's narrative the journey (with its historical Christian overtones of the pilgrimage) leads to a secular redemption in a promised land within the now unmoving frontier. This secular redemption is manifested in wealth. In the post-Second World War period the externalisation of the apocalypse and the narrative of the last days enabled not just California but the whole United States to take on the status of the promised land. This was the mythic inflection of the American attempt to construct a certainty of place, and of identity.

In his 1984 song 'Born in the USA' Bruce Springsteen articulates the same postcolonial crisis of identity we have found in *Apocalypse Now* and in Dylan's 'Blind Willie McTell'. In 'Born in the USA' the working class narrator describes how he was born 'in a dead man's town' and how he has ended up 'like a dog that's been beat too much.' He describes how he and his brother fought in Vietnam and how his brother died there. For the narrator the mythic America has become the real USA In the post-apocalyptic aftermath of the Vietnam war, there is no promised land anymore – not even in California:

> Down in the shadow of the penitentiary
> Out by the gas fires of the refinery
> I'm ten years burning down the road
> Nowhere to run ain't got nowhere to go.

In this new reality there is no redemption. For the narrator there is no longer a future because, in this post-apocalyptic demythologised world there is no longer a dream of a promised land, let alone a realised promised land in California.

On his 1978 album *Darkness on the Edge of Town* Springsteen included a song

chronos and *kairos*. Kermode writes that '*chronos* is "passing time" or "waiting time" – that which, according to Revelation, "shall be no more" – and *kairos* is the season, a point in time filled with significance, charged with a meaning derived from its relation to the end.' p47.

called 'The Promised Land'. This song forms a bitter commentary on Chuck Berry's earlier song. In Springsteen's song the worker now has a desperate belief in a promised land beyond the depressing mundanity of his life. The last line of the chorus is 'And I believe in a promised land', a line repeated without the 'and' at the end of the song. This narrator's image is of an apocalypse which will bring the promised land:

> There's a dark cloud rising from the desert floor
> I packed my bags and I'm heading straight into the storm
> Gonna be a twister to blow everything down
> That ain't got the faith to stand its ground
> Blow away the dreams that tear you apart
> Blow away the dreams that break your heart
> Blow away the lies that leave you nothing but lost and brokenhearted.

Whereas in Chuck Berry's song the promised land exists, in Springsteen's song it requires an American apocalypse to bring it into being. In the later 'Born in the USA' there is no longer a belief in a promised land. The narrator was born in the USA (not in the mythical America) but now has 'Nowhere to run ain't got nowhere to go.' The moral perspective which Baudrillard writes about as so necessary to the United States is to be found in the dream of a promised land. The loss of that dream is the loss of a unifying moral perspective and a return to the existential uncertainty which is the experience of a settler society.

V THE ROAD (TO NOWHERE)

Allied to the apocalyptic myth of the promised land is the myth of the road. The American road provides the site for the journey to identity. The road articulates the temporal movement to the apocalypse and the promised land as a spatial movement. When the frontier was moving, the mythic road led to the frontier. When the frontier stopped and the border was closed, the road led West, ultimately to California. The road movie of the late 1960s onwards has a pre-history in the wagon train Westerns of the 1940s and 1950s. These films restate the colonial experience of displacement in terms of a narrative journey to the unsettled land of the frontier. Constructed within the post-war eschatological myth of good versus evil, the righteousness of the settlers is always already undermined by the pre-existing aboriginal presence of the native Americans. In a seemingly endless retelling of the same story the wagon train Western attempted to instate a right of place through an apocalyptic story of a journey to the promised land at the frontier. By contrast, the road movies of the late 1960s and after increasingly described a personal redemptive journey through a diminished land of failed dreams, a world without an American promised land.

The first film to make clear the relation between the road and the promised land, and certainly the pre-war precursor of the late 1960s road movies, was

The Wizard of Oz. Made in 1939, it was based on a book published forty years earlier, in the same decade that Fredrick Jackson Turner helped to reconstruct the myth of the frontier. In this pre-'The Bomb' period the search is for a sense of place within the United States. Dorothy lives in rural Kansas with her aunt and uncle. She is already displaced then, not living with her parents.

Dorothy runs away from her home-which-is-not-quite home and has just returned to it when the twister hits. As in Springsteen's song the twister is used as an apocalyptic trope. The twister takes Dorothy's house along with Dorothy and her dog Toto and moves it to Oz. The narrative in Oz concerns Dorothy's attempts to return to Kansas. The scenes of Kansas at the beginning and end of the film are shot in black and white, whereas the bulk of the film, showing the land of Oz, is shot in colour using colours much brighter than normal. In this way we are led to accept that Kansas, the United States, is lacking whilst Oz is more real than real, having a post-apocalyptic super-plenitude of identity.

At this point it is instructive to compare *The Wizard of Oz* with Lewis Carroll's *Alice in Wonderland*. In important ways the narratives are similar. Both involve young girls visiting societies beyond their own where strange things happen. *The Wizard of Oz* can be read as a colonial rewriting of Carroll's story. Elsewhere I have analysed *Alice in Wonderland* as a colonialist story.[25] In general it is the story of a young English girl who visits Wonderland, behaves extremely rudely to the local people and attempts to impose her own, English, morals on them. It is a story written from the core. Like Marlow in *Heart of Darkness* Alice knows who she is and where she has come from and lives in Wonderland with the absolute knowledge of her superiority over the locals.

25. See Jon Stratton *Writing Sites*, Harvester-Wheatsheaf: Hemel Hempstead 1990.

The narrative of Dorothy in Oz is quite different. The film is preoccupied with the problem of home. The irony of the film is that when Dorothy is presented with a world more real than her own, she can not accept it as home. At the end of the film, when Dorothy has finally made it back to Kansas, all she can talk about is being home. The concern is so constant that the film betrays its insecurity about home precisely through Dorothy's claim that she is home. Alice would never have worried so much about being home. When Dorothy is talking with her aunt and uncle she insists that 'It wasn't a dream it was a place … Some of it wasn't very nice but most of it was beautiful. Just the same all I kept saying to everybody was that I wanted to go home.' In this statement Dorothy brings together the American apocalyptic trope of the dream with the American concern over place.

The film sets out to reassert Dorothy's aunt and uncle's house, Kansas, the United States, as home. However, as a film from a settler society, it constantly undermines this claim. What Dorothy discovers is that the post-apocalyptic world of the American dream is not home either. As a fantasy Oz serves to give meaning, and a moral perspective, to American experience but as a reality it turns out to be more alien than the world Dorothy has left behind. Dorothy is doomed always to experience her lack of a home. As if recognising this she reconstructs her fundamental experience of lack, the lesson she has learnt from her experience of Oz. Asked by the Good Witch of the North what she has learned from her experience Dorothy says: 'If I ever go looking for my heart's desire again I'll never look further than my own backyard because if it isn't there I never lost it in the first place.' If what Dorothy lacks most is a sense of place, a feeling of being home, then this must be her heart's nameless desire. Unlike Alice who enjoys her colonial adventuring Dorothy is so insecure about place that she never wants to leave her aunt and uncle's farm again. In order to get back to the Kansas farm the Good Witch instructs Dorothy to repeat, 'There's no place like home.' Dorothy keeps repeating, 'There is no place like home' as if to persuade herself that she really is home even after she has returned to her aunt and uncle's house.

In the promised land of Oz Dorothy has to travel the entire length of the Yellow Brick Road from Munchkinland to the Emerald City in order to meet the Wizard of Oz who, it is hoped, will get her back to Kansas. Along the road Dorothy meets up with the Scarecrow, the Tin Man and the Cowardly Lion. All three are transfigured characters from the Kansas farm, as is the Wicked Witch of the West. The three are all lacking something, brain, heart, courage, in this most complete of countries. Dorothy is lacking her home. In this road movie the road itself is already in the promised land. The journey to the Emerald City is the journey back to the lacking black and white world of Kansas. It turns out that the wizard is, in fact, another displaced person from Kansas. He, however, is quite happy with his lot having become a highly respected member of the community through the use of trickery to persuade the local population that he is a wizard. Here we have a version of the colonial experience quite different from that of Alice. The Wizard has used his American learnt trickery to attain a very powerful position in Oz for his own benefit. In Kansas he was a travelling salesman and entertainer. It seems as if he has learnt to accept the experience of displacement and make the most of his opportunities wherever he is. Dorothy and the revealed wizard are the only human beings in Oz. In the end it is not the Kansas charlatan but the Good Witch who sends Dorothy back to Kansas. The Good Witch is the only main character in Oz who has no counterpart in Kansas. She is, then, Other in a way the other main characters are not. She is a magical person, with religious overtones, who enables Dorothy to pass back through the frontier, over the rainbow, to Kansas.

The end of *The Wizard of Oz* is an attempt to invert the pre-'The Bomb' myth of apocalypse and of the promised land, to assert that the lived world of a displaced settler society is really home. In this case the journey down the road (with the Christian echoes of *Pilgrim's Progress*) leads to the revelation that Dorothy should never have tried to leave the reality of the Kansas farm, even if that meant accepting the killing of her dog. With all the insecurity of a settler society, the film attempts to assert the farm as home. Perhaps this reading helps us to understand the parochialism of small town values in the United States more generally.

In the 1950s and 1960s the prehistory of road movies involves films in which people travel to the promised land of California. In the main these films did not concentrate on the journey but on life in the secular and realised promised land, something easy to do when the Hollywood dream factory was built in the promised land. The song 'Route 66', popularised by the Rolling Stones on their first album (1964), is a post-war celebration of a road which leads from Chicago to Los Angeles listing the towns and cities on the way as if they are points on the journey to the promised land. As we have seen, by the early 1960s – by the time of Kennedy – the whole of the United States was coming to be thought of as the promised land.

Kerouac's *On the Road* was published in 1955. It chronicles the period from 1947 to 1955. The hero is named Sal Paradise and his first journey takes him from New York to San Francisco. However, Paradise does not find his promised land in California. As the narrator he writes, 'Here I was at the end of America – no more land – and now there was nowhere to go but back.' *On the Road* signals the early beginning of disillusionment with California as the promised land. The ironically named Paradise can not find his promised land and the rest of the novel chronicles his constant journeying. In *On The Road* the search is a male concern. Women, in the main, remain fixed to place and, in traditional American colonial terms, operate as a metaphor of the male experience of the land itself. It is not only the geographical end of the United States but the end of the myth of California as the promised land which is being suggested. At the conclusion of the novel Paradise is back in New York. He watches the sun go down. As he does so he sits 'on the old broken-down river pier watching the long, long skies over New Jersey and sense[s] all that raw land that rolls in one unbelievable huge bulge over to the West Coast, and all that road going, all that dreaming in the immensity of it.' The sentence goes on. The sun is setting on American dreams. The popularity of *On The Road* reflects the change in the American experience of the promised land and the road in the post-war period. Looking at its reprintings we see they pick up after 1965. The book was reprinted twice in 1968, 1970, 1971 and 1972. Even though *On the Road* was published in 1955, the American experience it expresses was that of the late 1960s and 1970s.

Another example of the new concern with the road in the early 1960s was the television series *Route 66*. *Route 66* began in October 1960 and finished in September 1964, spanning Kennedy's presidency. The series was based on the idea of two men travelling the United States in a car. Each episode recounts one adventure on their journey. The effect was to produce a celebration of travelling in the United States. Towards the end of the series the mood of the programme began to change. One of the lead actors left in March 1963. His replacement played a Vietnam War hero who had returned to the United States unsure of what he wanted from life. For him the road became a search for personal salvation.[26]

The late 1960s' loss of the promised land led to a fundamental transformation in the American experience of the road. As California, and the United States more generally, lost its eschatological claim to a sense of place so increasingly the road itself, the revelatory journey, was all that was left. On the 1968 Simon and Garfunkel album *Bookends* Paul Simon has a song called

26. This information comes from Tim Brooks and Earle Marsh, *The Complete Directory of Prime Time Network T.V. Shows*, Ballantine Books: New York 1981.

'America' in which the narrator has gone travelling across the United States 'to look for America.' At one point in the song he describes his sense of directionlessness to his travelling companion:

> "Kathy, I'm lost,' I said,
> Though I knew she was sleeping.
> 'I'm empty and aching and
> I don't know why."

From the late 1960s onwards the United States began to lose its claim to being the promised land, at the same time that the narrative of the global last days began to falter. Without an apocalypse the United States has no special history, no future and, worst for a settler society, no sense of identity. The narrator is metaphorically lost both in space and time.

Also in 1968 Dylan released 'The Ballad of Frankie Lee and Judas Priest' on his *John Wesley Hardin* album. In this ballad Judas Priest offers to lend Frankie Lee money. Judas Priest then goes to leave. When Frankie Lee asks him where he'll be:

> Judas pointed down the road
> And said, 'Eternity!'
> 'Eternity?' said Frankie Lee,
> With a voice as cold as ice.
> 'That's right,' said Judas Priest, 'Eternity,
> Though you might call it "Paradise".'

In this verse the promised land is troped as the post-kairotic timeless place of eternity, also known as paradise. The road leads there. Frankie Lee follows Judas down the road and finds Judas Priest in a house. When he asks Judas Priest about the house he is told: 'It's not a house ... it's a home' In this song the connection between the promised land and home is clearly made.

Judas, as we know from the New Testament, is a deceiver. For Frankie Lee this house turns out not to be home. He dies of thirst and Dylan ends the song with a moral:

> Well, the moral of this story,
> The moral of this song,
> Is simply that one should never be
> Where one does not belong.
> So when you see your neighbor carryin' somethin',
> Help him with his load,
> And don't go mistaking Paradise
> For that home across the road.

In this song, as in the Paul Simon song, we find a lack of certainty in home. This parallels the increasing loss of moral certainty which is a part of the crisis in the experience of the United States as the promised land. In the Dylan song the moral connects home with Paradise and suggests a further connection with Vietnam, 'the home across the road.' This further connection involves a conflation of Vietnam with the promised land, something made possible by the American post-war mission to save the Free World. The song implicitly signals the experience of the Vietnam War as an apocalyptic event and provides a commentary on it. Dylan's ballad articulates a search for home just as 'America' is, but my reading of 'The Ballad of Frankie Lee and Judas Priest' has a further implication: it suggests that the song makes a connection between the American search for identity and the Vietnam War as a colonial war.

Midnight Cowboy (1969), with its narrative of a journey to Florida through a threatening United States, was a transitional film between the view of the United States as the promised land and the new view of the United States as a mundane, imperfect reality. In *Easy Rider* (1969) the two main characters ride their Harleys through a threatening Southern United States. They are travelling to New Orleans to see the Mardi Gras, but when they get to New Orleans they spend the bulk of their time in a brothel and tripping on LSD in a cemetery with two prostitutes. At the end of this journey the promised land is debased, reduced from an ecstatic celebration of community and identity to a concern with carnality and capitalism. The American term for an LSD experience, a 'trip', signals the idea of a mental journey. After the two leave New Orleans Peter Fonda says 'We blew it.' He does not explain. The film ends with both characters being shot by rednecks. There is nowhere left to go. The journey of revelation reveals the loss of a future as it reveals the loss of a moral perspective.

Two films released in 1971 articulated the new understanding of the road: *Two Lane Blacktop* which focused on a race between two cars across the American South-West, and *Vanishing Point*. In both films the driving was what was important. With the loss of the United States as the promised land the road no longer leads anywhere. Rather, the road becomes the site for a travelling through a fallen world. The travelling itself becomes a narrative of personal salvation which often ends in death. The outlaw as hero, as in *Bonnie and Clyde* (1967) and *Badlands* (1973), is set against the experience of the United States as a fallen world. In addition to films there were a number of popular road songs such as Steppenwolf's 'Born to be Wild' and Canned Heat's 'On the Road Again' which celebrated the ideas of travelling and, often, of the outlaw who was wiser – and in a way morally superior – to the fallen world that had outlawed him (sic).

In Springsteen's lyrics the road becomes increasingly bleak. On the 1975 album *Born to Run*, the title track is a celebration of the road. The last verse begins:

> The highways jammed with broken heroes
> On a last chance power drive

and ends:

> Someday girl, I don't know when,
> We're gonna get to that place
> Where we really want to go
> And we'll walk in the sun
> But till then tramps like us
> Baby we were born to run

The road here still operates as a site of redemption. The American dream may be failing (in the first verse Springsteen sings about the 'runaway American dream') and Americans may now be broken heroes but the road still leads to the promised land. It is because the road still leads to the promised land that it is a site of redemption. However, the song does not celebrate travelling to the promised land, it celebrates running. The only redemption possible is now to be found in the driving itself. The promised land of the American Dream will never be reached. By *The River* (1980) the road is a place of rain, isolation and wrecks.

In 1985 Talking Heads released *Little Creatures*. The cover of the album is a primitivist painting, an apocalyptic vision. One of the most popular tracks on the album is 'Road to Nowhere.' The lyrics assert that:

> We're on a road to nowhere
>   Come on inside
> Takin' that road to nowhere
>   We'll take that ride
> *I'm feelin' okay this mornin'*
> *And you know,*
> *We're on the road to paradise*
> *Here we go, here we go*

Here nowhere and paradise are the same place. The lyrics work as a double vision. One part describes the road to paradise and the city of paradise that is approaching. The other part, which opens and closes the song, describes the road as going nowhere. Americans are being told that they have to get on the road, but the place the road goes to does not exist.

Against this background it is instructive to compare *Wild at Heart* (1989) with *The Wizard of Oz*. *Wild at Heart* recognises *The Wizard of Oz* as a road movie and makes constant allusions to it. In *The Wizard of Oz* Dorothy travels the Yellow Brick Road of Oz to return to her home in Kansas. In *Wild at Heart* Oz and the United States are conflated. The Wicked Witch and the Good Witch appear in the United States. Sailor and Lula are travelling from Cape Fear, near the border of North and South Carolina to California. They never reach the promised land. The road they travel tropes the Yellow Brick Road. The United States has become Oz but, in doing so, it has lost its moral perspective. This is

Springsteen's USA of 'Born in the USA.' It is also not home. At one point in the film Lula clicks her red shoes together and intones 'I want to go home,' just as Dorothy did. But Lula goes nowhere. She is home, but home is not home. The United States is once again, and this time in a more profound way, not home for the settler society. The end of *Wild at Heart* has a similar desperation to the end of *The Wizard of Oz*. The Good Witch visits Sailor and tells him, 'If you're truly wild at heart you won't turn away from your dreams. Don't turn away from love.' The only salvation the film can offer is an assertion of the personal myth of romantic love. Sailor returns to Lula and their son, and the film ends with a celebration of the nuclear family as home. They are, however, in a car stuck in a traffic jam.

The same point which is made in *Easy Rider* is also made in the 1991 film *Thelma and Louise*. Thelma and Louise find that outside of American patriarchal reality there is nowhere to go. They can not even leave the United States. The narrative closure of *Thelma and Louise* echoes that of *Easy Rider* and many other road movies. In *Thelma and Louise* the pair literally run out of road. Having been finally trapped by the patriarchal police of the Law of the Father at the end of a dirt track by the Grand Canyon, the two drive over the edge. The major difference between *Thelma and Louise* and earlier road movies is that, for the first time, the outlaws are women. Previously, as in both *Bonnie and Clyde* and *Badlands*, women outlaws were secondary to their male associates. As it was prefigured in *On the Road* the road movie was a white male genre, like the Western out of which it developed. *Thelma and Louise* appropriates the myth of the road, and the road movie, to make a point about the situation of women in patriarchy. The transformation of the myth which the film appropriates is that of the 1970s onwards.

VI   BEYOND THE MYTH OF THE APOCALYPSE

It seems that at the same time that the United States is articulating the post-apocalyptic utopian myth of the New World Order of global capitalism it is itself returned to a postcolonial search for identity. The myth of a global utopia is the externalised myth of the promised land. It is in this context that there can be an American claim to an end to history. The apocalyptic transformation of history in history leads to the claim that in the global promised land of global capitalism there is no more history. At this point there is a complex relation between the European myth of America, and subsequently the United States, as the promised land and the American myth of a global promised land. In 1960 (the year Kennedy was elected; his inauguration was in January 1961) Daniel Bell published a book entitled *The End of Ideology* which became very important in academic circles and precipitated what became known as 'The End of Ideology' debate.[27] The key idea of the book was that political ideologies no longer had any worth. The underlying assumption was that American politics was not ideological. At the end of the book Bell summed up his argument:

27. Daniel Bell, *The End of Ideology*, Free Press: New York 1960.

The problems which confront us at home and in the world are resistant to the old terms of ideological debate between 'left' and 'right', and if 'ideology' by now, and with good reason, is an irretrievably fallen word, it is not necessary that 'utopia' suffer the same fate. But it will if those who now call loudest for new utopias begin to justify degrading *means* in the name of some utopian or revolutionary *end*, and forget the simple lessons that if the old debates are meaningless, some old verities are not – the verities of free speech, free press, the right of opposition and of free inquiry.[28]

28. *Ibid.*, p406.

Here we can see clearly the claim that idealistic ideological utopianism is giving way to the real utopian society based on American liberal pluralism. The promised land is nigh. Bell's view, popularly held in the 1960s in the United States, was another articulation of the construction of the United States as the post-apocalyptic promised land.

In the 1990s the 'End of History' debate precipitated by Fukuyama's book *The End of History and the Last Man*[29] is one articulation of the claim to a post-apocalyptic New World Order. Fukuyama's work is self-consciously Hegelian. He makes use of Hegel's idea of recognition, arguing that 'In particular, [Man (sic)] wants to be recognised as a *human being*, that is, as a being with a certain worth or dignity.'[30] Fukuyama couples this interpretation of Hegel with Hegel's evolutionism in order to argue that the global spread of liberal democracy, which he claims best expresses the human need for recognition in political practice, represents the end of history. In one telling image Fukuyama writes that 'while modern natural science guides us to the gates of the Promised Land of liberal democracy, it does not deliver us to the Promised Land itself.' For Fukuyama the drive for this deliverance is an effect of the human need for recognition. In the image Fukuyama equates the promised land with the end of history. He makes the further equation of both these terms with the institution of liberal democracy in the first place in the United States and subsequently its global spread. Once more the United States takes upon itself the burden of the European utopian fantasy. It is enlightening to note, given what was said about Kojève at the beginning of this article, that the commentator on Hegel that Fukuyama uses most is Kojève. Given the similarities of their concerns, the one claiming the United States as the promised land whilst the other claims the world as the promised land, it is intriguing to note that Fukuyama does not reference Daniel Bell's *The End of Ideology*. What Fukuyama does is to appropriate the modern European idea of an End to history, epitomized in Hegel's work, and conflate it with the American idea of an apocalyptic consummation of history to produce an understanding of the New World Order. Here again, we see an illustration of Robinson's point, that the American dream is of an historical apocalypse, 'of a transformation *of* history *in* history that would consummate and so give meaning *to* history.'

In the post-Second World War period, whilst the Americans deployed eschatological rhetoric, the Europeans reworked the myth of the American

29. Francis Fukuyama, *The End of History and the Last Man*, Free Press: New York 1992.

30. *Ibid.*, pxvi.

'Wake Up' written by C. Neville, B. Stoltz, A. Hall, W. Green, © 1989 Neville Music. 'Wake Up' can be found on Neville Brothers *Yellow Moon* A. & M. 1989.

'Born in the U.S.A.' written by Bruce Springsteen, © 1984 Bruce Springsteen. 'Born in the U.S.A.' can be found on Bruce Springsteen *Born in the U.S.A.* CBS 1984.

'The Promised Land' written by Bruce Springsteen, © 1978 Bruce Springsteen. 'The Promised Land' can be found on Bruce Springsteen *Darkness on the Edge of Town* CBS 1978.

'America' written by Paul Simon © 1967, 1968 Paul Simon. 'America' can be found on Simon and Garfunkel *Bookends* CBS 1968.

promised land and fetishise the United States as the promised land of unlimited consumption possibilities. By the late 1980s there had occurred a fundamental transformation in the American myth of the apocalypse and its associated myths. From an American point of view the paradox of the American myth of a global utopia is that it places all countries on the same metaphysical footing. The effect of this is that the United States must lose its claim to having a special quality, a special status and therefore a special claim to identity. Most importantly it loses its apocalyptic claim to a unifying moral perspective. The effect is that the United States is forced to confront its own history as a settler society and to deal with the same problems of displacement, identity and the experience of living in an Other's land which are a part of the histories of other English speaking settler societies including Canada, New Zealand, South Africa and Australia. It may be that within the next fifty years we will begin to see the beginning of the political end for the last of the two super-powers produced out of European modernity.

I would like to thank Ien Ang for her help in editing what is an extremely dense article – and for her suggestions which have helped to make the article even denser!

'The Ballad of Frankie Lee and Judas Priest' written by Bob Dylan © 1968 Dwarf Music. 'The Ballad of Frankie Lee and Judas Priest' can be found on Bob Dylan *John Wesley Hardin* CBS 1968.

'Born to Run' written by Bruce Springsteen © 1974 Laurel Canyon Music Ltd. 'Born to Run' can be found on Bruce Springsteen *Born to Run* CBS 1975.

'Road to Nowhere' written by David Byrne © 1985 Warner Bros Music. 'Road to Nowhere' can be found on Talking Heads *Little Creatures* EMI 1985.

ENGULFED BY THE VECTOR

McKenzie Wark

I THE EVENT

Dateline: London, Friday August 24th, 1990. Television news around the world is showing videotape hijacked from Iraqi TV. President Saddam Hussein appears in a television studio surrounded by English children who were resident in Iraq and Kuwait when Iraq invaded its Gulf neighbour. Like an American 'Tonight Show' 'host' Saddam appears in a suit and tie with a little white handkerchief neatly folded in his left breast pocket. The foreigners are allowed to talk to their families while the rest of the world watches on. Or they are shown listening as Saddam explains that the western media have misrepresented the situation. They are not 'hostages' but 'peacekeepers', he says, and that their role is that of 'preventing war'. While the broadcast appeared on Iraqi television the program seemed entirely aimed at a western audience. The strange spectacle of the man the English press has dubbed the 'Butcher of Baghdad' stroking the hair of an English child on television was described by the British Foreign Secretary Douglas Hurd as the 'most sickening thing I have seen for some time.'

I was lying in bed with my partner, watching TV when this hostage thing spewed out of the TV at me. By one of those strange accidents of postmodern geography, NBC morning news programme is shown in Sydney, Australia around midnight. It's perfect media wallpaper for insomniacs and languid lovers. So there we were, a cosy domestic scene, lapping up the sweet with the bland, suddenly invaded by hostages and threats and urgency and Briant Gumble. Neither of us were really watching the set at the time. It just happened to be on, boring its weird interzone of happenings into our space. I think it was the word 'hostage' that tripped me into actually paying attention. I watched with an unwilling fascination, trying not to let myself submit to this ugly, uncanny image. The price of freedom from TV's montage of attractions is semiotic vigilance. At the next ad break, I pulled on an old track suit and headed out the bedroom door. 'Where are you going?' my lover asked. 'To work' I said, 'To work.'

So here I am, making coffee with the radio on in the middle of the night. Warming up the computer. Setting the video recorder rolling. Opening some new files. I put on some loud music – the radio and the TV are too distracting, too fascinating. A line from a song leaps into the interzone to comment, 'Radio birdman, up above. Beautiful baby, feed my love....' I need loud music to drown out the silence and the war. I turn on the heater in the study – it gets cold in Sydney in August. I could smell trouble. I could sense an event coming on ... I should know, I've been studying them for years.[1]

1. McKenzie Wark, 'On Technological Time', *Arena*, no.83, 1987, pp82-100.

Months later, I could close the door to this study, with its mountains of old newspapers, videotapes, photocopies with coffee cup rings all over them. By then, this private zone of disorder would look like a pathetic tribute to the carnage in Baghdad. This little room would become a monument made out of trashed information, jerry-built concepts and emergency rations of toxic expresso and vodka, neat. By then the endless series of books on the Gulf War by American academics would start to roll off the press, engulfing us in a forest of critical print as dense and misty as CNN. From what I've seen of this literature, a lot of it goes off like unguided missiles because it treats the Gulf War as something new rather than as the latest installment in a wider process – the process of incremental abstraction by which the globe becomes a traversable space.

This techno-cultural process intersects with a political one – the decline of American power, or what I have called elsewhere the passage from 'Fordism to Sonyism'.[2] While it was not clear during the Gulf War that American power *was* in decline, it is a lot clearer now, following President Bush's failure to get himself re-elected. This is a separate problem which only confuses matters if it is lumped in together with the unfolding of the abstract space of the vector, and prevents the latter from being properly theorised. This essay is a reader-friendly attempt to do just that.

Let's go back to that cold August night, before any of this was clear, even though the media spectacle of the hostage crisis already had a strange familiarity about it all. With the unfolding of the hostage-crisis the Gulf War as an *event* can be said to begin. Since media events of this kind are one of the most fascinating clues as to the kind of postmodern media world we are now living in, it seems as good a place as any to start describing what an event is like and conceptualizing what they are and how they happen. It is a difficult thing deciding the start and end of a media event. It is even more difficult still distinguishing the features of events that are purely media-effect from those that are to do with the politics and conflicts of other places, other times. Indeed, if there is a defining characteristic of these media events and of postmodern times in general it is the way the kind of politics which used to be specific to particular places, particular cultures, all get caught up in each other and caught up in the global media.

'With the unfolding of the hostage-crisis the Gulf War as an *event* can be said to begin.' The event as I will define it is something which unfolds within the media vectors which connect the site at which a crisis appears with the sites where its image is managed and interpreted and the sites to which it is disseminated. In this instance this connects together a bewildering array of sites: Baghdad, Riyadh, Washington, London, Paris, New York and some less familiar places were montaged together into the seamless space and staccato time of the vector. The terminal site of this media vector, needless to say, is the terminal up in my bedroom – the TV terminal that since the 50s has become a standard feature of everyday life for those who can afford it.[3]

Watching the hostage crisis on TV, the news reporters and producers go out

2. See McKenzie Wark, 'From Fordism to Sonyism: Perverse Readings of the New World Order', *New Formations*, Winter 1991, pp43-54.

3. Lynn Spigel, *Make Room For TV: Television and Family Life in Postwar America*, Chicago University Press, Chicago 1992.

of their way to pretend that they are just objective reporters, that all this happens someplace else, independently of anything they do. The fact is though, that once a political situation, particularly a crisis situation, gets into the media, the media can affect the way it will turn out. The event really takes place in a media space, where the media is the vector, the conduit, the trajectory connecting places and powers together. TV news gives the appearance of merely *reflecting* a 'naturally occurring' moment outside of all such apparatus, but it seems that in the postmodern world, the media are rapidly becoming the site of politics itself.

This may sound a little counter-intuitive, since we all tend to take it for granted that events which occur in the media do so because the media is reporting something outside of itself. While not disputing the fact that violent and momentous situations arise regardless of whether the media report them or not, my point is that once such situations are taken up within the media apparatus they assume a quite different character. Wherever there is a relationship of power between people, there is politics – and isn't that everywhere? Nevertheless, the increasing mobility and flexibility of the media and its now almost saturation coverage of the globe means that what were once local political crises become the spectacle for a global grandstand of spectators, all sitting in fascination, or yelling to the emperor to give the thumbs up – or thumbs down.

The 'emperor' in this metaphor might be the United Nations. It might be the great imperial powers, particularly the United States. When Saddam Hussein took hostages before a global media audience, he stepped into this arena. When the Chinese government sent the tanks into Tiananmen Square, so did they.[4] When white LA police beat the shit out of a black man, Rodney King, they stepped into the arena. When the Serbian concentration camps became public knowledge during the civil war in Bosnia, it was their turn to face the crowd. Sometimes the crowd yells 'thumbs up!'. Sometimes 'thumbs down!' Sometimes they sit mute, mouths open. Sometimes the imperial powers act, as in the Gulf War. Sometimes they don't, as in the Tiananmen Square and Bosnian crises. Either way, a particular form of politics, that I call the media event, has come into being. What makes it possible is the technology of global, simultaneous media vectors. What makes it dangerous is that no-one yet has the damndest idea how it all works.

The hostages Saddam Hussein held in Iraq connected Baghdad to practically all points in the western world. The fact that the media vector out of Iraq showed hostages from the over-developed countries of the west was the point at which the event became global and directly engaged the interest of many millions of viewers, readers, listeners. The hostages were 'ours' and 'they' were holding them. 'They' had invaded some little country and 'they' were threatening 'us' to prevent 'us' from retaliating against 'them'. Hence the principle focus was on an aspect which emotionally involved people in the event.

Global politics is a tricky thing that most people don't even pretend to

4. See McKenzie Wark, 'Vectors of Memory ... Seeds of Fire: the Western Media and the Beijing Demonstrations', *New Formations*, Spring 1990, pp1-12.

understand. The media make no effort to explain it. They expect that as soon as it all gets too difficult, viewers will switch off *en masse*. The NBC 'Today' show is in the entertainment business as far as NBC executives are concerned.[5] But when the news takes a turn that people can understand, like a picture of a child hostage, or a starving man in a Serbian concentration camp, or the faces of skinny students in their ramshackle tents in Tiananmen Square, then the global media can zoom in, knowing full well that these images will trigger the emotional reflexes of their audience even as the rational analysis of why this happened leaves them – us – cold. This is the curious thing about global media vectors. They can make events which connect the most disparate sites of public action appear simultaneously as a private drama filled with familiar characters and moving stories.

5. Edwin Diamond, *The Media Show*, MIT Press, Massachusetts, 1991.

The vector crosses the thin line between political crisis and media sensation; it crosses the geographical barriers separating distinct cultural and political entities; and it transgresses the borders between public and private spheres both on the home front and the front line. Moreover, it constructs the 'us' and the 'them' as the key to the story line within the event in the process of threading its way across all of these other boundaries. In breaking down old boundaries, new distinctions are created. This is part of the postmodern condition: flexible, narrative distinctions within flows of information replace the old walls and barriers which compartmentalised information in days when vectors were less rapid and less effective.

Events are curiously fractal things. They have no particular scale, duration or place. A tiny gesture or a major battle can be rendered equivalent in the media vector. Television frequently performs this extreme relativity of scale, time and place. The Gulf War was at times a matter of eyeball-to-eyeball close-ups, at times a matter of vast maps and bespectacled experts with pointers. Some pundits would date the start of the event from the invasion of Kuwait, some would trace it back to imperialist legacies, others to the misty dawning of 'Islamicism'. The site of the event also shifted from time to time. Did the Gulf War take place in Kuwait, Baghdad, or Washington? Was the site the middle east or the whole globe?

This is a particularly vexing point. If Iraqi commanders order a SCUD missile launch via radio-telephone from Baghdad, the signal may be intercepted by orbiting US satellites. Another satellite detects the launch using infra-red sensors. Information from both will be down-linked at Nurrungar in South Australia. From there it will be relayed via satellite to the Pentagon, then it is relayed again to US command HQ in Saudi Arabia and to Patriot missile bases in Saudi Arabia and Israel.[6] This is not the only vector involved which crosses borders – the traditional stake in geopolitical struggles. A journalist who files a report via a Satellite News Gatherer (SNG) from Baghdad will also be sending a signal bouncing around the globe, via satellite back to Cable News Network (CNN) headquarters in Atlanta, and from there back to Europe, America and Australia via cable, landline and satellite. Events, then, are a product of competing vectors which cross borders with impunity. The volume

6. Brian Toohey, 'Bases Play a Crucial Role', the *Age*, 3 February, 1991.

and velocity of information it generates may bear no relation to the significance or scale of the event.

Underlying the various constructions of the event there are, needless to say, 'real' actions and forces at work. Arguing that the media space is becoming increasingly important and a site of power and struggle is not the same thing as saying that power has vanished or that the simulated world is everything. These ideas, which come from a rather literal reading of the popular writings of Jean Baudrillard, are not particularly helpful.[7] Nor are they the only way of thinking about the postmodern. Arguing that politics is now infected with the media virus and that politics and the media are inseparable is quite a different way of thinking to 'end of politics, power, history, everything' rhetoric that was popular in the 1980s. That rhetoric at least got issues about the mediated form of today's politics and culture on the agenda. Now we have to figure out how it all ticks.

The basic point is that political crises are not independent of the processes of media representation which they give rise to. Where the crisis gets so caught up in the media that the media starts to effect how the political crisis works out, there exists what I call an *event*. In the case of the Tiananmen Square massacre in 1989, this event took the form of a positive feedback loop. The stories about the event made by foreign journalists were fed back into the event itself via a global feedback loop encompassing radio, telephone and fax vectors and impacted upon the further unfolding of the event itself. The democracy movement were turned into this global media because they couldn't trust the government's propaganda. (Whether they were any better served by the global flows of the western news agencies is of course questionable). Information which is available 'live' from the other side of the world can flow straight back there, just as fast and just as 'live'. Hence extremely volatile interactions between constructions of events where and when they occur and in international news vectors elsewhere are possible, and indeed increasingly common.

The event, then, is very much a problem of *movement*. It is a complex of *doubled* movement, wherein the political movements intrinsic to a situation at a particular site, be it Baghdad or Beijing, are caught up in international media vectors. A 'vector' is a term from geometry meaning a line of fixed length and direction but no fixed position. The French writer Paul Virilio employs it to mean any trajectory along which bodies, information or warheads can potentially pass.[8] As vectors proliferate, events appear more suddenly and connect quite disparate sites together in tightly coupled form. This has not made events any easier to understand or any clearer. Paradoxically, the more quickly the media get to the scene of an event and the more rapidly they transmit information about it to the rest of the world, the more impossible it becomes to disentangle the situation itself from the vectors into which it is inexorably drawn. Added to this is the fact that the media are not the only institutions which have access to fast and flexible vectors. In this war of vectors, the indigenous roots of the crisis can become captivated by the spectacular doubling of the crisis in a new, vastly expanded media terrain.

As such, the event is something quite elusive, something quite singular. Thus

7. Jean Baudrillard, *Selected Writings*, Polity Press, Cambridge, 1988.

8. Paul Virilio, *Pure War*, Semiotext(e), New York, 1983; *Lost Dimension*, Semiotext(e), New York, 1991.

not all news is an event. Much of what constitutes the news is routine and in no way singular. The event irrupts through the routine occurrence of news, always a little quicker than news professionals can stuff it back into acceptable formats. As news vectors become faster and more flexible, the potential for such irruptions increases. The speed of the event triggers endless series of little crises in the production of the news as 'stories'. There were plenty of irruptions within the over-all event-horizon of the Gulf crisis, as we shall see.

II TELEVISION HOSTAGES: FULL STORY

Let us return to the hostage crisis that unfolded before my eyes that cold night back in August 1990. The moment Saddam Hussein took hostages, an added moral dimension was inevitable in this event. Holding hostages at strategic sites was clearly a terrible kind of weapon. This weapon was given added force by coupling it with another. That weapon was and remains – television. The message that some of 'our' people were being held close in his domain was inserted as close to home in the west as it is possible to go: right into the living rooms of millions. With few weapons with which to take the conflict to the western powers, Saddam found a way to lob a logic bomb directly into every news-watching home in the western world. While thousands of third world refugees fought for food in Jordan, a few western women and children, released with impeccable public relations timing, captured the attention of the world media. A cynical business all round.

Here television was the trigger for yet another weapon – public opinion. Those poor people being held in Iraq were not exactly hostages, they were prisoners of war. The news bite has eliminated the distance between the battle and the home front as effectively as has the vector of nuclear missiles. Saddam fought with missives where he has no missiles; fighting on the western home front with the weapon of public opinion. Hence the media were not exactly in a position to stand back and take a moral stand against the hostage taking when they were at the same time competing to present the hostage spectacle and thus implicate themselves in the semiotic violence.

The taking of hostages is immediately associated in the western imagination with the 'evil' that is the stock perception of the middle east. Newspaper reports haul out long strings of stories which encourage their readers to remember the middle east as a place always associated with hostage-taking, where presumably it is an 'ancient custom'. They rewrite this present hostage scenario as the latest instalment in a long-unfolding event, including hostages held by pro-Iranian groups at the time when tension between Iran and the west were at flash point. The fact that Iraq received 'our' support at the time; the fact that the US is making overtures to Iran now are blithely ignored as the media attempt to sort out who the bad guys are.[9] The fact that the Cold War was nothing but a global hostage crisis, where the American and Russian empires held each other's populations hostage to nuclear terror, is of course not mentioned. This byzantine hostage-taking was called deterrence. Taking hostages is something

9. On America's manipulative 'realpolitik' in the Gulf see Christopher Hitchens, 'Why We Are Stuck in the Sand', *Harper's*, January 1991.

Arabs do, not the 'free world'. Not our new-found friends in the former USSR.

As we watch the wheels of television's supple if obtuse imagination turn, we are watching what the Palestinian-American writer Edward Said calls 'Orientalism' at work. As Said says: 'One aspect of the electronic, postmodern world is that there has been a reinforcement of the stereotypes by which the Orient is viewed. Television has forced information into a more and more standardized mould.'[10] The stereotypes built up during the western conquest of the middle eastern edge of the Orient in their imperial writings and reports are at one and the same time a powerful knowledge through which western power is still asserted in the region, and a misleading discourse which gives us demonically simple images of the complex reality of the middle east. What Said does not supply here is an explanation for why television should have truck with orientalist cliches. Part of the answer, it seems to me, is that the speed with which television brings the force of events to bear on public consciousness requires simple but subtle, standardized but interchangeable stories to prevent the event from rupturing the seamlessness of televisual discourse. Thus the Saddam Hussein who strokes the hair of the child hostage on television is at once the devious pederast which the orientalist imagination deems this behaviour to signal.

For the media, difficult events have to be handled quickly and in such a way as to preserve the distance between it and us. The professional media manager of the event needs to stand on 'our' side of the event in order to project it as belonging to the bad guys. At the same time the event has to engage 'us' at some fundamental level of belief or motivation – when Saddam touches that child we know, we just know, that something is wrong with this picture. When events blast through the routine of information, they must be quickly captured and interpreted in an acceptable narrative framework. The difficulty is that the very pertinence of an event frequently derives from its uninterpretability, from its resistance to existing narrative frameworks. The critical task for a writer on the left who wants to engage with this postmodern media event is to show that the media are not a transparent 'window on the world' – they affect what is happening. The task is to show how the media and politics are threaded together and affect each other.

The work of repairing the holes rent in the narrative fabric of public discourse by events rarely takes place in the electronic media, but in media which work at slower rhythms, so it is necessary for criticism to follow the trace of events through these too. As Saddam's western hostages were released with a wave of yellow ribbons, as the US moved troops to the Persian Gulf and George Bush put together the UN resolutions and the new 'Delian League' in a matter of days, the Gulf became a military theatre of operation. Yet there was another theatre of operation working overtime attempting to furnish narrations to the media vectors which would accommodate this twist of events. The invocation of orientalist images is the popular edge of the narrators' task. These have to parallel more complex invocations of the 'shifting sands' of vested interest.

10. Edward Said, *Orientalism*, Harmondsworth: Penguin, 1985, p28.

This is a particular challenge when events stretch like explosive chain reactions back through time – as in the middle east. Or where once rock-solid media stories are at stake – as in the end of the cold war.

The Gulf crisis thus comes piled up on top of any number of crisis events. There appears indeed to be a 'storm blowing from paradise', as Walter Benjamin said during the previous great shake-out of politics and communications – the 1930s.[11] Consider the recent wreckage added to the pile of progress: the Tiananmen Square massacre gave the lie to the myth of Deng Xiaoping the 'liberal reformer'. On the other hand the fall of the Berlin Wall flatly contradicted the conservative's story about how totalitarian regimes had a total ideological domination over their populations in contrast to merely despotic or dictatorial ones.[12] In short, the narrative structure of the cold war was unraveling event by event.

The invasion of Kuwait was perhaps not such a shock. Despite the political pressure which had been exerted on journalists who wrote critically of Saddam Hussein's regime, the prevailing view is best summed up by Geoffrey Kemp, who headed the middle east section of the National Security Council under the Reagan administration: 'We really weren't that naive. We knew he was an SOB, but he was our SOB.'[13] Nevertheless, the Gulf crisis stands as an event of considerable significance for the number of layers of the media's stories about the world which were at risk and the sure but shallow resolution the interwoven vectors of the military and the media were able to fabricate.

The Gulf War closed a gap in narrative space. As Michael T. Klare argues, the argument in the ruling circles of the United States pitted a geo-economic story about the future of American power against a geo-strategic one. Klare summarises the issues underlying the divergent narrative lines thus: 'At issue are such questions as (1) who will control America's foreign policy establishment in the years ahead; (2) which of the giant federal bureaucracies will prosper and which will fall into decline; (3) which of our states and communities will be the beneficiaries of government spending and which will be deprived; and, likewise, (4) which giant corporations will receive lucrative government contracts and which will not.'[14] The Gulf War seemed to give the geo-strategic line the upper hand. Two years later, when George Bush faced re-election, this version of the story was in crisis again, and a new struggle to fashion the storm blowing from paradise into intelligible stories is on the agenda once again. Emperor Bush, by this time, appeared a pretty threadbare media figure, perhaps an emperor with no clothes.

Even during the Gulf War, the theme of the 'new world order', the ongoing drama of Pax Americana, seemed a little too incredible to believe. Like the shaky alibi that it was, it held up for the few short months needed to go to war. At a time when Japanese and German corporations were decimating American machine tool firms and semi-conductor manufacturers, even buying out famous Hollywood studios, a geo-economic focus on investing in research, development and industrial recovery had powerful advocates. Its acceptance as a post Cold War story was thwarted by other forces turning to good profit the

11. Walter Benjamin, 'Theses on the Philosophy of History', in *Illuminations*, Shocken Books, New York, 1989.

12. McKenzie Wark, 'Europe's Masked Ball: East Meets West at the Wall', *New Formations*, Winter 1990, pp33-42.

13. Cited in Adel Darwish and Gregory Alexander, *Unholy Babylon: The Secret History of Saddam's War*, Victor Gollancz, London, 1991, p63.

14. Michael T. Klare, 'Policing the Gulf – and the World', *The Nation*, 15 October, 1990.

Gulf events. 'Recent events have surely proven that there is no substitute for American leadership' as Bush told a global television audience in September. Or as General Colin Powell put it some time earlier in the debate, 'We have to put a shingle outside our door saying "Superpower Lives Here".'[15]

15. Both quotes are from Klare, *op. cit.*

The projection of American forces in the Gulf becomes a model for the post-cold war style for the 'spin control' of events themselves. After a brief period of confusion and bet-hedging, the networks trooped into the fray with a geo-strategic understanding of the future as well. Having extracted themselves from the debris of Cold War storytelling, political power and media vectors had to concoct a new story which would correspond to American and allied intentions in the new events in the Gulf. Curiously, this took on the appearance of a relation between two kinds of *television*.

III DESPOTIC TELEVISION

Saddam Hussein has TV charisma, as Samir al-Khalil points out in his dissident critique of Iraq, *Republic of Fear*.[16] His authority is not based on attributes like heroism, oratory and prophecy – the classical sources of charismatic power.[17] His is an administered charisma, elaborately rehearsed, staged and edited:

16. Samir al-Khalil, *Republic of Fear: The Politics of Modern Iraq*, Hutchinson Radius, London, 1989, pp82-88.

17. Max Weber, 'The Sociology of Charismatic Authority', in Hans Gerth and C. Wright Mills (eds), *From Max Weber* RKP, London, 1982.

18. Samir al-Khalil, *op. cit.*, pp114–115.

> 'Saddam's appearances on television lasting several hours a day in various guises are masterpieces of calculated duplicity.... The propaganda is so 'bad' that even some Iraqis will pretend to dismiss it; yet they bring their children up to applaud it. Imagine endlessly varied film clips of Saddam Hussein in local Arab attire one day and Kurdish dress the next. Picture him crouching around trenches in camouflage fatigues, standing erect in full parade uniform, embracing foreign dignitaries at the airport in the latest Pierre Cardin suit, handling machinery....'[18]

Now, thanks to the Gulf War and CNN, we have all seen a little of this. The morning after the first bombing run on Baghdad, Iraqi TV staged a 'Saddam at large' programme. In casual battle dress, Saddam walked around a seemingly deserted city, hopping out of a sedan car to shake hands. It was a poignant counterpoint to the excerpt from the day before, showing a mass of Iraqi soldiers marching beneath the huge crossed swords of the Victory Arch to the theme music from *Star Wars*.[19]

19. Samir al-Khalil, *The Monument: Art, Vulgarity and Responsibility in Iraq*, Andre Deutsch, London, 1991.

The curious thing is that television vectors could send an image across the battle line with ease, but once through to the media space on the other side, that image lost its resonance with the usual associations it would connect with in its 'home' discourse. Thus the Iraqi TV pictures of Saddam served perfectly as images of a vain, treacherous, oriental enemy in the context of western news television. The shots of Iraqi crowds shouting and waving guns in the streets could easily be contextualised as a synthetic frenzy whipped up by a totalitarian regime. On the other hand, Iraqi TV could broadcast images of western demonstrations against the war, but these tokens of the strength of western pluralism (as western commentators would insist) were recontextualised to show a lack of resolve to fight.

CNN's bombastic owner Ted Turner launched the now famous station by saying to his employees 'See, we're gonna take the news and put it on the satellite, and then we're gonna beam it down into Russia, and we're gonna bring world peace, and we're gonna get rich in the process! Thank you very much! Good Luck!'[20] But in the crisis atmosphere of the event, the international news vector is not a form of *communication*. No mutually accepted 'messages' passed through this channel from one community to another. There was no commonality between encoding and decoding practices at either end. Rather, the vector allows each side to exploit images which come from the other side within their own interpretive framework. The fact that the image is an authentic product of 'their' media merely legitimates a construction of the other which is entirely 'our' doing. This magical 'us' which appears as the central thing threatened by the Iraqis is itself a product of our media's projection of an image of them. So while the images of Saddam, his army, the Iraqi people, actually come from Iraq, the stories we see these images in are fabricated on our side of the line. These pictures of the bad guy are all the more powerful, all the more legitimate-looking because they really do come from the place of the enemy. This authentic quality to the image bolsters the credibility of the stories they illustrate. The vector makes this image of the bad guys possible, and makes an 'us' possible. Who are we? We are the good guys opposed to the bad guys.

20. Hank Wittemore, *CNN: The Inside Story*, Little, Brown & Co., Boston, 1990, p124.

This definition of who 'we' are that the vector creates in a crisis is largely negative. We are defined solely in opposition to them, their dialectical opposite. Because this dialectical relationship is imaginary, total and negative, it will lead formerly tolerant people to rash acts. Arab-Australians were attacked in horrible acts of senseless victimisation. When the event bursts on the scene and the vector implicates us directly in this totally negative identity, all the rational, positive, incremental work that has gone into making the uniquely Australian version of a multicultural society goes out the window as the vector pours in through the TV. That the vector can be dangerously divisive in times of crisis is one of the more disturbing aspects of postmodern culture, and something rarely discussed in the 'don't worry-be happy' version of the postmodern pluralist rhetoric.

This negative identity formed in relation to the bad other can appear quickly and dramatically. Hence the phenomenon of a George Bush supported by 90 per cent of Americans surveyed, at that triumphal moment when he appeared before congress to make his victory speech. Interestingly enough, he referred in that speech to television, and the televised repeats of the speech were able to montage the speech together with the television images he referred to. Bush spoke of a moment which brought tears to his eyes, the moment when Iraqi troops were hauled out of hiding and an American soldier said to them, 'It's OK now. You're all right.' Here the public and private merge totally in the detail of the public performance of the President's private tear. Here 'we' come together as witness to the image of the vanquished other, and the television vector assumes its place as the centre of the construction of the event. After the moment of triumph, the negative relation which held 'us' together vanishes as swiftly as it materialised, leaving the Bush re-election campaign, as he would say, 'in deep doo-doo'.

Regardless of whether Ted Turner gets rich off it, media events like the Gulf War are not communication. The symbiosis of the vector with power creates a movement of information, but one which legitimates a *non-communication*, not one which creates an exchange. The real winner here is the power of the vector, a power which appeared to have vanquished the Iraqis and did; which appeared under the control of the President but was not; which appeared to serve a vast televisual audience which was in fact trapped as the deadly poll of 'public opinion' within its vast and instant reach. No longer an innocent bystander, television is forced onto the frontline, and forces the frontline into our living rooms for nightly salvoes. The old cold war might be over, but television is still sharpening its teeth.

IV FROM CNN TV TO WAR TV

It was the instant, continuous, global news bite of CNN that won this war. While the ordinary people of Iraq buried their dead and George Bush lumbered on into the LA riots, CNN emerged as the world's leading news vector. This was clear even as the event unfolded. By the third day after the passing of the UN deadline of 15 January, the media had woken up to the fact that this was 'the first war ever to begin on live TV'. It established once and for all the supremacy of CNN's style of coverage, forcing the other US networks to imitate it. President Bush, Defence Secretary Chaney, Egyptian President Mubarak were all reported to be avid CNN watchers. Even Saddam Hussein had a private receiving dish.

CNN has certainly had a considerable effect on television news. It has taken advantage of satellite vectors to break the transmission monopoly of the American television networks. Being a 24-hour service, it does not have the luxury of collecting evidence of an event for hours before the nightly newscast and compressing the available data into conventional narrative form. CNN has introduced the concept of 'live' news coverage – an instant audiovisual presence on the site of an event. In seeking to speed up the audiovisual news vector, the station has dispensed as much as possible with the narrative strategies of American network news practice if not with its visual conventions. CNN concentrates on attempting to establish a news vector hours or even minutes before the competition. Being based on satellite linkages, CNN can base itself in Atlanta without too much disadvantage compared to the New York based networks. In fact, it enjoyed a considerable advantage, being able to set up business paying rates far below the relevant awards with non-union labour.

On the American TV current affairs talkback show *Donahue*, CNN had to defend its coverage in front of a hostile audience, many of whom quite candidly expressed a preference for news managed and censored by the military to any attempt at open and critical journalism. CNN's Ted Turner tried to defend the station's approach in terms of the liberal understanding of the freedom of the press and the distinction between propaganda and information. His respondents, like the opinion polls, seemed to want propaganda. This is a curious aspect to the whole event. It seems that TV viewers are even more aware than CNN that the vector does not communicate, and resented the station's feeble attempts to make it do so. They preferred to view the other through the slogans of the President and the bloodless diagrams of the military briefings. Television has a narrative function and exists in the private domain of the living room. In the throes of a media event which links people to the other as graphically as a hostage crisis, in a dialectical relation to evil, there is no room for liberal common sense. CNN were victims of their own creation: having used the vector to create this relation to the other, they were inevitably under pressure to sever the relationship itself. What CNN (and no doubt the Bush camp) knew, was that CNN's Baghdad reporters and the satellite feed pictures of Saddam and his henchmen were essential to the 'war effort' precisely because they showed images of the other.

This put CNN in a double bind. They were knee deep in creating a relationship of mythic otherness across the globe, yet they wanted to talk about their media policies like nice liberals. CNN were trying to give the news vector an information function in the style of the liberal understanding of the role and rights of the public sphere. The vector has already crossed the boundary between public and private sphere, and the event has already taken on a narrative form linked to the projection of the other. So while CNN was popular because it raised the vector to a new velocity, it met resistance too for attempting to preserve an understanding of news from an era before the volume and speed of media vectors broke down the flimsy partitions of the liberal imagination.

Like everyone else, I watched all this in the first few days of the war with morbid fascination. Sitting in the living room with the remote control in my hand, I felt powerless, yet I could direct streams of global media flow with the touch of a tiny button. I turn the TV on. The NBC reporter announces that heavily laden F-15 bombers are leaving Saudi Arabia. I flip channels idly to CNN, just in time to see White House Press Secretary Marlin Fitzwater declare that 'the liberation of Kuwait has begun'. CNN then teleports me thousands of miles across space to Baghdad where CNN's former gardening correspondent describes the sound of a US attack beginning on the city. Flip again and an expert on NBC is pointing to a map drawn up in the conventions of a weather report, only the lines on it are not cold fronts but troop fronts. The aim of the map and pointer exercise seems to be to make a rather mundane exercise seem truly bizarre. I flip again to a satellite feed from Britain's Channel 4 and gaze at elaborate computer graphic images chroma-keyed onto a simulated map of the front line. Little digital images of tanks and troops glide about.

Yet not even colour graphics could prevent the war from sagging as the sheer lack of pictures or hard information blocked the unfolding of a tellable *story*. The media filled in the dull patches by reporting about *itself* reporting the war. At this point in the programme we are entitled to ask whether the usual liberal soul searching about war, censorship and the media really goes far enough. As television entertained us with the Pentagon-controlled pool footage, explained it all in Pentagon doublespeak terms, and showed us how a weapon worked with a video simulation supplied by the manufacturer, perhaps we should entertain the hypothesis that the media have become a dangerous weapon in war rather than its liberal conscience. As Bernard Shaw, CNN reporter in Baghdad asks: 'Wherever you are in the world, ask yourself, why are the governments of Iraq and the US allowing this report from Baghdad to get out of here to you?' He should know. He was the CNN reporter who was cut off air 'live' in Beijing as Deng's troops cut out the media feedback loop before going in to violently retake the city.

TV was implicated in the process which led to war. In competing with each other the US networks fought to implicate themselves in the diplomatic endgame. As Alexander Cockburn wryly commented on the early days of the story, 'in the absence of military conflict most Americans have settled back to enjoy the war of position and manoeuvre being fought by the television networks on the edge of the fall season and facing a declining share of the market.'[21] ABC's Ted Koppel dined with the Jordanian royal family, then secured an exclusive briefing with the Iraqi foreign minister to pass on the message he had elicited from Jordan. Not to be outdone, Dan Rather went after and got an exclusive interview with Saddam for CBS. The political talking heads followed news-anchor celebrities into the fray. Bush sent Iraqi TV an eight minute video tape putting the US position. Saddam replied by sending US TV networks a 90 minute videotaped reply – which adds a whole new dimension to the concept of military escalation. On the eve of the US ,counter-invasion of Kuwait, James Baker, George Bush and Iraq Foreign Minister Tariq Aziz all appeared live, while pre-recorded Saddam beamed in from Iraqi TV.[22]

While the networks fight each other to get into the fray, the politicos and the military fight to present their chosen images. The Bush campaign was stage-managed by Sig Rogich, a former Las Vegas advertising man with interests in property and casinos. Rogich had a set specially built at Dharan for Bush's pre-war warm up visit, complete with neat rows of F-15 and F-16 warplanes lined up in shot as a backdrop. Rogich stage-managed images of Bush walking tall against desert sunsets, Bush the war veteran talking man-to-man with the troops. The purpose of these images was to narrate the war and cement a collective subjective response to it as an event – and it worked.

Of course, to anyone who has been reading their Noam Chomsky, none of this would come as any surprise.[23] I don't think it was any surprise to the general public either, when the newspapers revealed that the Kuwaiti

21. Alexander Cockburn, 'Hawks and Doves', *New Statesman*, 7 September 1990.

22. Phillip McCarthy, 'Big Shots look to Small Screen to Get the Message', *Sydney Morning Herald*, 12 January 1991.

23. Noam Chomsky, *Deterring Democracy*,

government hired a public relations firm to cook up stories about babies being tossed out of their incubators by those Iraqi devils, plundering and looting their captured city.[24] The kind of thing that needs explaining is how people who don't actually believe what they see on TV can nevertheless get caught up in the logic of the story and the intense negative feeling that there are bad guys at large, not just next door or someplace else in the country, but on the *other side of the world* in places people never used to even hear about. What needs explaining too is how volatile these reactions are. How people who were so gung-ho for Bush and war won't even vote for him a year later. There may be manipulators of the media, but the vector is a force powerful enough to detonate a logic bomb under even the best laid plans of Bush and Baker.

Then there are the wars we do not see. The Pentagon has greatly restricted media access to its dirty little wars – not to mention the complete lack of coverage of those fought by the CIA. Given the multinational nature of the anti-Iraq force, an office called the Joint Information Bureau (JIB) co-ordinated the manipulation of what we saw from the Gulf.[25] In going in to battle with each other for ratings, the media happily surrender to the demands placed on them by the military machine. This deference on the part of television to the military stems in part from the ability of the military to block news vectors out of territory it controls and operates. Military secrecy creates gaps and blanks in the illusion of televisual ubiquity. In order to extend its vectoral potential into military zones, television has to reach a *modus vivendi* with the war machine. Here the competitive imperative towards a global vectoral system on the part of television, a desire for the potential to put a vector between any and every event, anywhere in the world and the massed living rooms of the target audience, takes precedence over the professional ethics of journalistic propriety.

Not surprisingly, print journalists, saddled with yesterday's vector, with no other advantage left to them beside time to pause and reflect, frequently criticise television coverage. Academics, with not even the instant media flows of the newsroom wire service, content themselves with writing books about it afterwards. Yet even television cannot compete with the effectiveness of military communications vectors. This is the other reason why television finds itself deferring to the military. The military are specialists in the development and implementation of communication vectors.[26] Indeed, most of the technology now accessible to television, including satellites and SNGs are the downstream, civilian progeny of technological developments which have their headwaters in research for military applications. Portable video is a spin-off from military needs, as are the new cameras which incorporate gyroscopes to prevent wobble. These arose out of the need for stable images shot from moving vehicles or aircraft which generate a lot of vibration. The little charge-coupled devices (CCD) used in contemporary video cameras have an even more spectacular origin. They were designed for real-time satellite reconnaissance of the type performed by Keyhole satellites over Iraq. During the war television began to make extensive use of night-vision lenses. These are

Verso: London, 1991; Edward Herman and Noam Chomsky, *Manufacturing Consent*, Pantheon: New York, 1988.

24. Phillip McCarthy, 'America's Tattered Triumph in High-Tech War Against Saddam', *Sydney Morning Herald*, 10 August, 1992.

25. John Pilger, 'Myth Makers of the Gulf War' *Guardian Weekly*, 13 January 1991.

26. McKenzie Wark, 'The Logistics of Perception', in *Meanjin*, Autumn 1990.

used for night fighting, and during the Gulf War were used to show artillery barrages both from the Kuwait border and over Baghdad itself.

V MISSILE-CAM

Even so, television cannot compete with some of the more extraordinary vectors the military can effect, and thus must defer to them. Only the military can produce reconnaissance pictures showing the aerial bombing of strategic sites in Baghdad. Grainy, black and white images show the bomb falling earthwards, dropping through the lift well of the building, exploding several storeys further down, blowing out the side of the building. Even more extraordinary, pictures from the nose cone of a missile, homing in on the target. Television has for some time being trying to capture images of extremely fast vectors. Race-cam pictures from the cockpit of sports cars and similar images from skiing and surfing prepared us for the ultimate vertigo of 'missile-cam'.

With missile-cam the vectors of destruction and information become almost completely synonymous. Only at the point of impact does the information vector fail, the screen turning to white noise as the warhead hits its target; the interruption of the arc coinciding with the violence of impact. Television cannot match such a trajectory, so becomes complicit with it. Television gives the armchair viewer a missile-eye view of the vector itself, suturing spectator and weapon together up until the last moment. This one missile becomes also the million viewers stitched, eyeball to eyeball with its line of flight into enemy territory, and we become complicit with its violation of that territory. The beautiful, historic city of Baghdad, home of so many architectural treasures of the middle east, becomes a site of pure, naked targets – rather like bombing Venice.[27] The vector has so overwhelmed territory and its defences that recording the rape of territory by the projectile is not only technically feasible but publicly celebrated as an emblem of American sophistication and triumphalism.

All wars are wars of the vector. Military competition has for some time been a matter of states attempting to acquire missiles with longer and longer ranges. Some, including Iraq, were attempting to develop satellite reconnaissance to add a vector of vision and precision to the random trajectories of their missiles.[28] The media war has accustomed us to the image of war as something always ever-faster, ever more destructive. From the saturation bombing of Tokyo or Dresden to the threat of instant nuclear extermination, war gets bigger and faster, exponentially. The Gulf War showed another side of this. It showed that flexibility and precision are as much a part of the proliferation of vectors. During the Second World War, the saturation bombing runs were lucky to hit the right city, let alone the right target. In the Gulf War, precision became an almost aesthetic fetish. Actually, the satellite surveillance was not nearly as complete or as useful as technofetishist stories in the media might lead us to believe.[29] Completion of the global surveillance vector of Keyhole

27. Only Edward Said mentioned the historic significance of the city, see 'Arabesque', *New Statesman*, 7 September 1990.

28. Adel Darwish and Gregory Alexander, *op.cit.*

29. Jeffrey Richelson, 'Eye in Space is Not All

satellites will, no doubt, be a high priority as well. The capacity to see the enemy is equivalent to the capacity to kill, so we can expect nothing but the perfection of more flexible trajectories of death.

Missile-cam is the *reductio ad absurdum* of this coupling, given that not only is the vision of the target connected in real-time to its destruction, but an international audience gets to see the event later the same day on television. We can only await with dread the event which features live missile-cam attacks.

Against this the best the Iraqis could manage was a display of western prisoners of war on television. This raised the ire of the western press, leading a Murdoch tabloid to the considered opinion that we should 'hang Saddam long and slow'. Yet the missile-eye view of destruction is surely just as much an expression of the horror-show which television becomes in war. More chilling than the human tragedy of capture, the pure, disembodied vector turns war into a pure violation of the spatial integrity of the other. Any human dimension is denied in the simple geometry of the blowing up of block-houses.

As John Pilger points out, the US deployed many anti-personnel weapons it perfected in Vietnam against Iraq, but no mention was made of this amid the rhetoric of 'surgical' precision and the avoidance of civilian casualties or 'collateral damage', to use an expression coined at the time of Vietnam.[30] The human becomes simply an appendage, hidden from view of the vector. The vector appears as a power over and against the human, even against the social relations which built and guided it. The vector makes an appendage of the spectators at either end: the televiewer at home, sucked along in the slip stream; the poor spectator down below, who sees only her or his death as an imminent, inexplicable terror. The irony of missile-cam is that while it appears to aim the vector at the other, in reality it aims it at us. As we watch the block-house come closer and closer, it is our house as much as that block-house which is engulfed by the vector's gaze and deadly power. As the screen turns to pure white noise on impact, communication ends, but the channel remains open, broadcasting the white noise of events on the threshold of control.

Seeing', *Sydney Morning Herald*, 19 February, 1991.

30. John Pilger, 'The True Nature of the Gulf is Civilian Slaughter', in *Arena*, Autumn 1991.

THE POLITICS OF SILENCE: THE MEANING OF COMMUNITY AND THE USES OF MEDIA IN THE NEW EUROPE

Kevin Robins

A group is a collection of people who are resolved to keep silent about the same thing: a thing that then becomes a secret. This 'point of silence' holds the group together, sustains it, and even structures it. To violate it is to violate a taboo, to re-open a great wound. It is to risk driving the group to despair because it has absorbed and digested this silence to ensure its very survival.[1]

1. Daniel Sibony, 'Bosnie: le Point de Silence', *Libération*, 7 June 1993, p6.

The media industries have been assigned a leading role in the cultural community of Europe: they are supposed to articulate the 'deep solidarity' of our collective consciousness and our common culture; and, at the same time, they are asked to reflect the rich variety and diversity of the European nations and regions. There is the belief, or hope, that this cultural project will help to create the sense of community necessary for Europe to confront the New World Order. But in as much as Europe can imagine itself as a community, it seems that it is an unimaginable community that is being imagined.

Over the past ten years or so, there has been concerted series of initiatives across Europe, aimed at the transformation of the broadcasting and media industries. A new media order is being shaped, reflecting 'the dreams and the aspirations of the politicians and the bureaucrats for these industries which produce the dreams and desires of us all.'[2] What the politicians and the bureaucrats hope, of course, is that media industries and technologies will support and sustain the project for European integration and unity. With the implementation of the EC Television Directive in October 1991, they took a big step in the elaboration of a legislative programme designed to extend the organisation and regulation of broadcasting beyond the confines of national boundaries. 'Television without frontiers' is about creating a broadcasting industry and culture that will serve the needs of the European Community into the next century.

2. Vincent Porter, 'Film and Television in the Single European Market – Dreams and Delusions', *Journal of Media Law and Practice*, vol.13, no.1, April 1992, p148.

What is at issue, then, is the question of media and community. It has been frequently observed that mass communications have played a fundamental part in the historical development of national cultures and identities. Print and then broadcast media brought into being mass publics who began to imagine the community of the nation and nationalism. On the basis of this historical experience, it is now being widely assumed that the media are destined to play an equally significant part in the development of European culture and identity. The inference is that transnational media will give rise to transnational publics, who will then begin to imagine the new community of Europe. What the politicians and bureaucrats assume is that, in creating the economic community of the single market, they are at the same time creating the basis for a future political and cultural community at a European scale.

I want to question these inferences and assumptions about what the media can do for the European project. If we look at contemporary developments, particularly in the period since the idealism of '1992' has been exploded by the realities of 1989, the prospects for building a transnational community look bleak. If there are tendencies towards integration at the economic level, what we are seeing in the political and cultural life of the continent are dynamics of fragmentation and division. Europe is 'caught in the clash between two opposing forces: the logic of economics and interdependence that spells community, and the logic of ethnicity and nationality that demands separation.'[3] The great danger is that, as it is caught between these contradictory logics, Europe lacks the political resources to address the problems that confront it. 'We now have an essentially, economic vision of the state and an essentially cultural vision of society,' Alan Touraine observes, and 'we have a great need for properly political categories to mediate between the world of the economy and the world of cultures.'[4] It is this political silence, this crisis of political will, that forecloses any meaningful sense of post-national community in the new Europe.

This is the context in which a new media order is being evolved in Europe, and in which expectations are being raised about its capacity to promote integration and cohesion. What I shall argue is that these expectations of the politicians, the bureaucrats and whoever, cannot be met: the media will not be the means to create the imagined community of Europe. I am inclined to agree with Philip Schlesinger when he argues that the case of Europe in fact 'illuminates the *limitations* of what we may expect a communications policy to do and causes us to think again about the relations between the social and the communicative.'[5] What we are now seeing is the inability to achieve any congruence between the economic space of the large market and the political and cultural spaces of European community. Particularly disturbing is the difficulty of building a political public sphere across national boundaries.

These limitations in the development of a European media culture reflect the broader tensions and contradictions in the European project, but there are also limitations that derive from the changing nature of the broadcast media themselves. François Brune has argued that the contemporary media have brought about a kind of devalorisation of reality, a 'dispossession of the real', which serves to disorientate viewers and to inhibit their access to political consciousness. What they do is to 'make us purely spectators, that is to say

3. Josef Joffe, 'The New Europe: Yesterday's Ghosts', *Foreign Affairs*, vol.72, no.1, 1993, p43.

4. 'Républicains ou Démocrates? Débat entre Paul Thibaud et Alain Touraine', *Projet*, no.233, Spring 1993, pp28-29.

5. Philip Schlesinger, 'Wishful Thinking: Cultural Politics, Media and Collective Identities in Europe', *Journal of Communication*, vol.43, no.2, Spring 1993, p7.

powerless ... In the face of what is presented as the order of things, we can only listen, watch and keep silent.'[6] In thinking about 'the dreams and desires of us all' – and about why they do not correspond to the 'official' dreams and aspirations of the politicians and the bureaucrats – I want to pursue this line of argument. What *are* our dreams and desires? To which of our desires do the media most fully respond?

6. François Brune, 'Néfastes Effets de l'Idéologie Politico-Médiatique', *Le Monde Diplomatique*, May 1993, p4.

I MEDIA AND COMMUNITY

What we are seeing in the European media industries is the emergence of a new supra-national regulatory environment in which the emphasis has shifted dramatically towards questions of economic, industrial and competition policy, and away from the political concerns that characterised the old public service system. Now the emphasis is on the creation of a large European audiovisual market that will eliminate barriers to the buying and selling of programmes and to their transmission and reception in the Community. New media technologies and markets seem to make a mockery of borders and frontiers; the order of the day is the 'free circulation' of media products and services. In the broadcasting industry, it is felt, 'the continuation of national barriers and of the fragmentation they cause prevents European producers from taking up the challenge presented by external competitors. They are a major handicap for Europe's industry and cultural identity.'[7] European media must move rapidly from their old state of fragmentation to a new condition of integration and cohesion.

7. 'Television and the Audiovisual Sector: Towards a European Policy,' *European File*, 14/86, August-September 1986, p6.

What we are seeing is the transition from a model of regulation which required broadcasters to provide a diverse and balanced range of programmes (education, information and entertainment) for citizen viewers, to a successor model in which the imperative is to maximise the competitive position of European media businesses aiming to satisfy the needs of consumers in global markets. That is to offer a stark, and therefore somewhat reductionist, account of the changes we are seeing in European broadcasting, and I will qualify it in a moment. The stark version has the merit, however, of highlighting the economistic logic that is such a powerful force in the project of European transformation. J.G.A. Pocock describes the new European order as an 'empire of the market'. What is being constructed, he argues, is an economic community based on

> a set of arrangements for ensuring the surrender by states of their power to control the movement of economic forces which exercise the ultimate authority in human affairs. The institutions jointly operated, and/or obeyed, by member states would then not be political institutions bringing about a redistribution of sovereignty, but administrative or entrepreneurial institutions designed to ensure that no sovereign authority can interfere with the omnipotence of a market exercising 'sovereignty' in a metaphorical because non-political sense.[8]

8. J.G.A. Pocock, 'Deconstructing Europe', *London Review of Books*, 19 December 1991, p9.

This might mean that Europe can only aspire to be an economic-administrative union, committed to the inhibition and containment of the political forces that perpetually threaten its fragmentation or dissolution. It is no doubt possible, though deeply problematical, to go further and maintain that the hegemony of the economic and technocratic is essential in the immediate future to create the cohesion and integration that would, in the longer term, sustain a supra-national community that is more than economic. Whichever, the present reality is that the political is subordinated to the economic. In the sphere of broadcasting, the present reality is that the cause of private media and advertisers prevails over concerns of public service and media democracy.

Of course, it is all a great deal more difficult, and constructing an empire of the market cannot be just an economic matter. Culture and politics insist on complicating the Euro-media business; the creation of a European media market inevitably comes up against the problem of cultural preferences, tastes and desires. Some twenty years ago, Thomas Guback identified an economic logic struggling to express itself through the European project. The creation of an economically integrated Europe, he argued, 'favours the enlargement of firms to international stature, with concomitant trends toward standardisation, at the expense of small enterprises and a great deal of variety.' And if this is the case, he went on,

> then it is obvious that the major emphasis is not upon *preserving* a variety of cultural heritages, but rather upon drawing up a new one which will be in tune with supranational economic considerations. In that case, we had better forget about the past and concentrate upon seeing the creation ... or fabrication – of a new economic European consumer whose needs will be catered to – if not formed – by international companies probably operating with American management and advertising techniques.[9]

This logic is still at work. There is still the belief, or maybe hope, that it will be possible to fabricate the new model European consumer who will consume new model European programmes.

If it is an economic logic that drives this project, it is also the case that it carries with it a certain 'vision' through the expectation that the single market in broadcasting will help to promote the reimagination of community and identity in Europe. As the free circulation of programmes throughout the Community reinforces Europe's production and transmission capacity, it is argued, so will it come to promote the ideals of the 'Europe of culture' and the 'citizens' Europe'. For the vision of 'television without frontiers' to become a reality, there must be congruence between the economic space of the Community and its cultural space. 'Programmes intended, from the beginning, for all of Europe', the Commission believes, 'could count on an audience and resources that would never be available at a national level; they would help to strengthen the feeling of belonging to a Community of countries at once different and deeply united.'[10] Pan-European television will help in improving

9. Thomas H. Guback, 'Cultural Identity and Film in the European Economic Community', *Cinema Journal*, vol.14, no.1, 1974, pp10-11.

10. 'Television and the Audiovisual Sector', *op.cit.*, p9.

mutual knowledge among the peoples of Europe and will increase their consciousness of the values and the destiny they have in common. It is a deeply problematical vision, but its existence seems to have some kind of necessity. It constitutes an ideal of a sort for the future of European culture, perhaps the only sort of ideal that a market technocracy is capable of coming up with.

What the European Community is struggling to create is, in fact, an expanded version of the national broadcasting model; one that seeks to maintain, at a higher level, the congruence between economic and cultural spaces of broadcasting. It aims to persuade us that a European audience might come to enjoy the imagined community and solidarity of some kind of supra-national identification. In the era of public service broadcasting, coherence and integrity were conserved over decades, in the face of both regionalist and internationalist pressures, through the national compromise. The possibility that this could now be succeeded by the similar coherence of a European compromise seems unlikely even while the idea is still on the drawing board. It was the correspondence of economic, political and cultural spaces that gave national broadcasting its resonance and vitality. This is difficult to replicate at the larger, continental scale. But, above all, the processes of globalisation have stirred up forces that now seem to make such correspondence difficult to sustain at any level.

What is also problematical about this European media project is that it is based on a very thin and abstract condition of unity. It risks the contempt of a reality whose complexities are indifferent and resistant to such imaginings. The integrity of this European cultural area is threatened by forces both outside and within it. From outside, the challenge to Europe's fragile integrity comes from those who take very seriously the idea of 'free circulation' – so seriously that they believe products and programmes should be flowing freely on a global scale. For them, the idea of constructing a European cultural area, based as it must be on cultural protectionism and defensiveness, is an anachronism and an absurdity. 'Is the culture in any of these European countries so flimsily anchored that European consumers must be caged and blinded else their links with their past, like an exploding star, vanish?' asks Jack Valenti, president of the Motion Picture Association of America.[11] These interests aim to use what they see as their GATT rights to make sure that 'television without frontiers' means a great deal more than the small European affair that the European Community intends.

Inside Europe, this ideal of unity is contested by those who assert a contrary ideal, one that celebrates the diversity and difference of identities in Europe. Against the principle of a cultural melting pot, the advocates of European nationalism and regionalism struggle to sustain the image of a continent that is really and essentially a cultural mosaic. Here the emphasis is precisely on the preservation of a variety of cultural heritages, both national and regional. The evidence from audience behaviour suggests that television remains very much a national medium, and that national television cultures remain a force to be reckoned with. It is difficult, at the present time, to see what other kind of

11. Quoted in Fred H. Cate, 'The European Broadcasting Directive', American Bar Association, Communications Committee Monograph Series 1990/1, Washington DC, 1990, p4.

identification there is to compete, and hard to see why national cultures of television will not continue as the fundamental points of reference well into the future. There is at the same time an excitement about the possibilities opened up by broadcasting at the sub-national and small national scale. For the protagonists of this cause, these possibilities are about the revitalisation of identity and community in the face of those forces that are seen to have promoted centralisation and homogenization. Regional and local media are seen as fundamental resources of both democracy and identity. What we have here is an appeal to the kind of situated meaning and emotional belonging that seem to have been eroded by the forces of internationalisation and globalisation. What is invoked in the rich diversity of a Europe of the regions and small nations is a new particularism for our times.

In the evolution of European Community broadcasting policy both integrationist and particularist strategies have figured. In the 1980s, what prevailed was the strategy to create a large audiovisual market, which could sustain an equally large audiovisual industry, competitive on a global scale with US and Japanese interests. Here, as Richard Collins argues, 'unity through a common European television channel and common European programming ... was advocated for the integrative effects on European culture and consciousness it promised.' More recently, however, there has been an apparently contrasting emphasis on diversity over unity, for example in the European Community's MEDIA programme. In this case, the emphasis has been on the need for recognition of, and sensitivity towards, cultural difference. 'We have no interest in promoting a melting pot', as one EC policy maker recently put it, 'we want to preserve European identities.'[12] And, of course, this question of diversity and differences is mixed up with the still significant and salient question of national broadcasting industries and policies. In the view of a French observer, 'aesthetic and cultural differences, which make up the richness of European nations, are incompatible with cultural unification ... Culture, and particularly audiovisual culture, touches the very heart of nationalism.'[13]

What seems necessary is some kind of accommodation between the aspirations for a common European culture and the more comfortable certainties of national or regional attachments. In the formulation of European audiovisual and communications policy, a 'Cultural Europe' is being fashioned, or rather re-fashioned, for us to belong to and identify with:

> Europe's cultural dimension is there in the collective consciousness of its people: their values are a joint cultural asset, characterised by a pluralist humanism based on democracy, justice and liberty ... It also involves new kinds of solidarity based on belonging to European culture and greater participation of the people in cultural life, as well as new possibilities for exchange and cooperation which enrich the diversity of our local, regional and national cultures.[14]

12. Richard Collins, 'Unity in Diversity? The European Single Market in Broadcasting and the Audiovisual 1982-1992', Paper presented to the PICT National Conference, 1992, pp10, 14.

13. Jean Cluzel, 'L'Audiovisuel à la Veille du Marché Unique', *Revue Politique et Parlementaire*, no.959, 1992, p46.

14. 'The European Community and Culture', *European File*, 10/88, May 1988, p3.

What is asserted here is the continuing relevance and vitality of the European idea. It is the idea of a historical continent which is sufficient to itself, but which contains within itself rich and varied resources of belonging and identity; to be European now is to enjoy a complexity and plurality of allegiances.

There are two observations that should be made here about this association of media and community in the new Europe. The first is that what is presented in terms of richness, complexity and choice might better be seen in terms of tension and stress in identities. To be within an integrated Europe seems desirable, and yet such a way of belonging is also rather abstract and is associated with fears that something about who we are is being lost or damaged in the process. And if the alternative of cultural nationalism represents a way of reasserting that something, there is also sufficient awareness of the limitations of parochial and restrictive attachments. What we see is, in fact, a condition of suspension between identities in which none of the alternatives seems entirely satisfactory. This, as Julia Kristeva argues, can easily translate into an identity crisis 'where people no longer know what their values are, what their future can be, and refuse all projects of community which they consider threatening.'[15] What is there of this complexity in the European broadcasting directives, or in the Maastricht Treaty with its commitment to 'contribute to the flowering of the cultures of the Member States'?

The second observation is that the emphasis of European broadcasting policy is on questions of cultural community at the expense of those of political community. Under the old public service regimes in Europe, broadcasting assumed a dual political role, serving as both the focus of national or nationalist culture, and as the basis for the political public sphere and democratic politics of the nation state. How successfully or unsuccessfully this was accomplished is a matter of opinion and debate: the point is that within the national compromise both functions were, in principle at least, held together at the same territorial scale. In the context of the new European media this kind of accommodation looks highly problematical. The European Community has so far failed to develop an adequate political culture or a basis for European citizenship.[16] The emphasis on cultural community in Europe then compensates for, and deflects attention from, this political absence. The danger is that, within the European audiovisual space, the compensations of cultural identification will prevail over the political objectives of public debate and citizen rights.

15. Julia Kristeva, 'Le Temps de la Dépression', *Le Monde des Débats*, October 1992, p1.

16. Blandine Barret-Kriegel, 'La Citoyenneté en Europe', *Raison Présente*, no.103, 1992.

II COMMUNITY IN THE NEW EUROPE

Historically, the mass media have played a fundamental part in the political life of modern Europe. Not only were the media born with the bourgeois democracies, but they have been inseparable from them and have evolved in concert with them. These democracies have developed on the basis of the political legitimacy of the nation state and the political space of national cultures. In the post-war period particularly, it has been broadcasting that has played the most powerful integrative role, becoming one of the paramount institutions through which social collectivities have constituted and known themselves as national. Broadcasting has functioned as the space in which the *imaginaire* of a national community is reflected and shaped, and as the preeminent forum through which the democratic life of the nation-state has been represented.

In the context of increasing European integration, however, important issues are being raised about the future role of the media in the constitution of political and cultural community. If it has been suggested that the new media will help to construct a democratic public sphere on a European scale, there is as yet little sense of what political community might mean on this transnational basis. The 'official' policy of the European Community in effect represents the transposition of the national conception of broadcasting to the supra-national level. 'This', as Philip Schlesinger observes, 'immediately raises questions about its plausibility in circumstances where no single politico-cultural community is confronted by television, but rather that television faces cultural, linguistic, and political diversity.'[17] To understand the contribution of broadcasting to the reconstruction of European identity, to consider whether European broadcasting can come to terms with this diversity, we must first understand something of the nature of the community that is being constructed.

17. Philip Schlesinger, *op.cit.*, p10.

It is through some sense of community that people have felt they can belong to, and identify with, a particular territory. Community has been about social integration, about achieving a sense of coherence and cohesion within a social group; it should be seen as a kind of compromise, a way of holding conflicting forces in tension. In modern societies, of course, the scale and complexity of social processes ensure that the meaning of community is no straightforward matter. Eileen and Stephen Yeo have distinguished competing meanings of community. At one level, they suggest, community is a positive quality of relationship, 'the characteristic of holding something in common, a feeling of common identity and, most positively of all, a quality of mutual caring in human relations.' It is 'community made *by* people *for* themselves.' At another level, community is associated with state and nation. In this area of meaning, 'the community *already exists*, has perhaps existed from time out of mind. It certainly pre-dates and does not depend upon the activity of the inhabitants for whom it is supplied, from above; it is made for people, not by them.'[18] Here it is a formal and abstract relationship, a social contract which, at its most democratic, reflects public opinion and is concerned with the public good (but which, of course, is not always democratic).

18. Eileen Yeo and Stephen Yeo, 'On the Uses of "Community": From Owenism to the Present', in Stephen Yeo (ed), *New Views of Cooperation*, Routledge: London, 1988, pp230-231.

The nature and the scope of community have, over the past century and a half, been contested around these competing meanings. It has been a contestation between 'community from below' and 'community from above': the struggle between a more particular and localised sense of community, a sense of community created from inside, with its more ethical and human relations, and the more abstract and transcendent sense of community associated with system integration across the extended territory of modern societies. What is significant, however, is the success which national communities have had in holding these contrary dynamics in tension. As the Yeos put it, there has been an aim 'to fuse or to confuse the two opposites and to attach warm feelings about mutuality and fellowship to unequal social relationships which are structured from above and which often involve the state.'[19] In modern societies, social integration and cohesion has been most effective when there has been a complementary, or perhaps compensatory, balance of power between the enchantment of mutuality and the more formal and contractual relations of the enlarged political community.

It is, of course, at the level of the nation-state that this compromise between mutualist and contractual senses of community has been held in tension. Through its sovereign state, the national community has, in principle at least, disposed of the political resources to both represent the collective interests of its citizens and to act as arbitrator or regulator in the event of conflicts of interest. Through the mechanisms of the nation state, internal conflicts have been managed and external conflicts and threats have been absorbed or deflected. But more than this, the nation has been the 'place' in which its citizens feel they have their roots. It evinces a direct and even visceral experience of belonging. In Slavoj Žižek's psychoanalytical terminology, the nation has functioned as 'our Thing':

> as something accessible only to us, as something 'they', the others, cannot grasp, but which is nonetheless constantly menaced by 'them'. It appears as what gives plentitude and vivacity to our life ... If we are asked how we can recognise the presence of this Thing, the only consistent answer is that the Thing is present in that elusive entity called 'our way of life'.[20]

The national 'Thing' is about the unique way a community 'organises its enjoyment'. Or, in Edgar Morin's terms, nationalism represents the 'projection onto the national of infantile feelings that were once felt towards the family'; the nation is the 'homeland', the 'motherland' or 'fatherland'.[21] The national community in this sense is about the way a community organises its collective need for both affirmation and security.

It seems now, however, that something has happened, or is happening, to the enjoyment and security of members of national communities. There is the feeling that we are in a period when the authority of the nation-state is being undermined, when the state can no longer guarantee economic and political integration, and when the idea of a 'national community of fate' is problematical. Eric Hobsbawm makes the point in its strongest form when he argues that the nation-state is in retreat, and that any future history of the world

> will inevitably have to be written as the history of a world which can no longer be contained within the limits of 'nations' and 'nation-states' as these used to be defined, either politically, or economically, or culturally, or even

19. *Ibid.*, p231.

20. Slavoj Žižek, 'Eastern Europe's Republics of Gilead', *New Left Review*, no.183, 1990, p52.

21. Edgar Morin, 'Formation et Composantes du Sentiment National', *Cosmopolitiques*, no.16, 1990, p30.

linguistically. It will see 'nation-states' and 'nations' or ethnic/linguistic groups primarily as retreating before, resisting, adapting to, being absorbed or dislocated by, the new supranational restructuring of the globe.'[22]

This process of change can be seen as a reflection of the forces of globalisation that are overcoming national boundaries, undermining national states, and, it is said, creating a new kind of global civil society. 'At the end of the twentieth century', argues Ronnie Lipschutz, 'we are seeing the leaking away of sovereignty from the state both upwards, to supra-national institutions, and downwards, to subnational ones', and in the process we are seeing the growth of a 'global civil society [which] represents an ongoing project of civil society to reconstruct, re-imagine, or re-map world politics.'[23] This global civil society mirrors the type of supra-national society that existed before the seventeenth century, Lipschutz suggests, when 'prior to the Treaty of Westphalia and the emergence of the state system, there existed a relatively vibrant trans-European civil society, linked to territories but not restricted to territory.'[24]

Does this period of transformation then mark the beginning of the end for the 'Westphalian model' of sovereign state power? Does the idea of Europe and European Community represent a next, and a more cosmopolitan, stage in the political and cultural life of this continent? When we look at the aspirations and the inspirations of the politicians and the bureaucrats we are likely to doubt this. What we are in fact seeing in the project to construct a European Community seems to be more about trying to re-create the conditions of national community at a higher order – the construction of a kind of European nation-state.[25] Europe is invoked as a new basis for integrating and unifying contradictory and conflicting forces. The expectation is that the relation between mutuality and political community might be re-negotiated and held in compromise at this higher level. What we see, then, is a kind of transfer or displacement of nationalisms to bring into existence a new and enlarged community, with the same objective and aspiration as the national community of achieving correspondence between state, people and territory.

But if Europe has begun to emerge as a market and as a power bloc, it is more difficult to see the construction of a common and unitary political culture comparable with that which was historically achieved by the nation-state. Whatever else we might say about it, the nation-state was able to hold in balance the mutualist and political senses of community, and thereby to achieve some compromise between cultural belonging and political life. What is problematical at the scale of Europe is to combine community as mutuality with community as democratic state; to reconcile the idea of a 'community of culture' with that of 'political community'. What seems to be happening, as a consequence, is that questions of citizenship and questions of identity are becoming dissociated.

Most critical, in the light of what is happening to the powers of the nation-state, is the question of political culture and citizenship at the European level. In a discussion of what it might mean to move from a national to a

22. E.J. Hobsbawm, *Nations and Nationalism Since 1870*, Cambridge University Press: Cambridge, 1990, p182.

23. Ronnie D. Lipschutz, 'Reconstructing World Politics: The Emergence of Global Civil Society', *Millenium: Journal of International Studies*, vol.21, no.3, 1992, pp 399, 391.

24. *Ibid.*, p400.

25. Philip Schlesinger, ' "Europeanness": A New Cultural Battlefield?', *Innovation*, vol.5, no.1, 1992, p15.

continental political space and public sphere, Stig Hjarvard recognises that 'at the European level there is no public with the ability to perform a critical function or represent alternative interpretations or definitions of the political agenda.' The deficiences of the European public sphere, he goes on, are 'the effect of an unequal development in which the internationalisation of capital and formation of a supra-state administration and regulation have grown rapidly but have not been accompanied by a parallel development of public knowledge.'[26] Hjarvard seems to imply that the 'democratic deficit' in European can be corrected. As yet, he suggests, 'a European public sphere is only in its beginning', and we still have some way to go in elaborating the appropriate mechanisms for effective publicity and debate across the continent.

But is it just a question of the appropriate mechanisms? Or are there more profound obstacles to the development of a European political culture? We must be concerned, Étienne Balibar suggests, with 'what the state is tending to become, how it is behaving, and what functions it is fulfilling in the European space ... a space which, in particular, cannot simply be reduced to the figure of a "territory".'[27] The problem he identifies is the apparent inability to develop a political culture and citizenship appropriate to times of transnational community. Europe is caught between the limits of the nation-state and non-existence of a supra-national alternative. If the European Community has developed certain administrative (and repressive) apparatuses – that is to say, a certain kind of *statism* – it has not managed to constituted itself as a *Rechtstaat*, a state through which Europeans are represented as citizens. Under this reign of 'statism without a true state', all the conditions are in place, Balibar argues, 'for a collective sense of *identity panic* to be produced and maintained. For individuals fear the state ... but they fear still more its disappearance and decomposition.'[28] What this points to is a crisis of politics and of the political in contemporary Europe.

If the European Community is in one respect an attempt to create the conditions of national community at a higher level, it might also turn out to be a mechanism for sustaining nations and nationalisms in a world that is increasingly shaped by the forces of globalisation. We could see the Community as offering a way for member states to pool certain aspects of their sovereignty in order to hold on to others which have greater significance – real or symbolic – for them. We might, for example, see the principle of subsidiarity as a mechanism for the 're-nationalisation' of what had been achieved through the existence of the Community.[29] But it is not just a question of the preservation of the European nation-states. What we are also seeing is the proliferation of a whole array of new nationalist, regionalist and ethnic aspirations. What this reflects is the persistent appeal of nationalist sentiments and attachments in a Europe that is being re-shaped within the New World Order. 'Why', asks Tom Nairn, 'has the End of History carried us forward into a more nationalist world?'[30] Even as he argues for the declining historical significance of nationalism, Hobsbawm, too, has to recognise that it is still a prominent force in the world, and that there is still as much of it in the world as

26. Stig Hjarvard, 'Pan-European Television News: Towards a European Political Public Sphere', in Phillip Drummond, Richard Paterson, Janet Willis (eds), *National Identity and Europe*, British Film Institute, London, 1993, p90.

27. Étienne Balibar, '*Es Gibt Keinen Staat in Europa*: Racism and Politics in Europe Today', *New Left Review*, no.186, 1991, p16.

28. *Ibid.*, p17.

29. André Riche, 'L'Élargissement de la Communauté en Question', *Le Monde Diplomatique*, June 1993, p3.

30. Tom Nairn, 'Demonising Nationalism', *London*

there ever was. Nationalist sentiments and attachments are set to play a significant role in the future of European life – but they will do so in an altered context in which our relation to the national community is different.

Review of Books, 25 February 1993, p6.

This resurgent spirit of nationalism is a complex and a contradictory phenomenon. In one respect, it can be seen as an expression of the revitalisation of civil society, an assertion of more meaningful collective identities against the bureaucratic and technocratic vision of Europe emanating from Brussels. Julia Kristeva points to the search for new forms of democratic participation, and suggests that these new kinds of particularistic attachment represent 'attempts to close the gap between government and the man in the street, between politics and the hands-on exercise of responsibility.'[31] But there can also be a dangerously narrow and parochial quality in these attachments. They mobilise warm feelings of mutuality and ideals of community created from within and sustaining familial or kinship relations. The danger in this neo-nationalism is that questions of identity eclipse those of citizenship and democracy. Jonathan Friedman observes

31. Julia Kristeva, *op.cit.*

> the weakening of former national identities and the emergence of new identities, especially the dissolution of a kind of membership known as 'citizenship' in the abstract meaning of membership in territorially defined, state-governed society, and its replacement by an identity based on 'primordial loyalties', ethnicity, 'race', local community, language and other culturally concrete forms.[32]

32. Jonathan Friedman, 'Culture, Identity and World Process', *Review*, vol.12, no.1, 1989, pp61-62.

Where people once turned to the state to represent their interests and guarantee their rights, the danger is that they will now turn to group solidarities for protection. The weakening of political life at the local level opens the way for cultural identity to become both refuge and solace. At this level, too, the compromise between the political and cultural aspects of community is destabilised.

What is at issue is the question of community in Europe now. I have suggested that there are contradictory strategies at work in the continent: on the one hand, there is the project to create the supra-national entity of the European Community; on the other, there is the reassertion of the particularistic and emotional communities of the European nations and regions. The resolution – which is in fact a perpetual deferral or quasi-resolution – appears to be the acceptance of some kind of schizophrenic compromise between the conditions of integration and fragmentation. The problem is that neither in itself seems to represent an acceptable or a meaningful choice. Jacques Derrida identifies the acute dilemma: on the one hand, the European cultural entity 'cannot and must not accept the capital of a centralising authority', and yet, on the other, it 'cannot and must not be dispersed into a myriad of provinces.' 'Neither monopoly nor dispersion, therefore. This is, of course, an aporia,' Derrida observes.[33] It is this that makes the experience of community both frustrating and discomforting.

33. Jacques Derrida, *The Other Heading*, Indiana University Press: Bloomington, 1992, pp39, 41.

In one sense, the issue is about how Europe might move beyond the Westphalian model of sovereign power. This model 'depicts the development of a world community consisting of sovereign states which settle their differences privately and often by force; which engage in diplomatic relations but otherwise demonstrate minimal cooperation; [and] which seek to place their own national interests above all others.'[34] Within this perspective, the political culture of citizenship is concerned almost exclusively with domestic issues – 'our' community – and citizens are not concerned with, or involved in, the foreign affairs that go on beyond the boundaries of their sovereign state. The national community includes 'our' people, over whom 'our' state has jurisdiction, and at the same time it excludes strangers and aliens, from whom we differentiate ourselves, and towards whom we have minimal responsibilities and obligations. What is now called for, and what is indeed recognised in the more ambitious expressions of Europeanism, is the need to come to terms with other cultures, communities and nations. In the context of the changing world order, there is the need to recognise that a community's obligations extend beyond itself; that a community can no longer simply follow the self-interest of its own members, but must acknowledge the increasing interdependence of cultures and the consequent obligations to 'foreign' citizens, both beyond and within its frontiers.[35] If the European project is to mean anything, if the Westphalian model is ever to be replaced by a more open and ecumenical political culture, then these obligations must find expression in and through the creation of political and cultural institutions.

What is happening in Europe now is, however, a far cry from this aspiration. What we see, in both the resurgence of nationalist sentiments and the apparent inability to imagine Europe as anything other than a national community writ large, is the powerful hold that the 'Westphalian model' has in European culture. In the face of uncertainties and instabilities, the spontaneous political culture of Europe – both the European Community and the national communities – is one of closure and introversion. In Europe now, 'the great temptation is that of withdrawal, whether it be at the local, regional, national or continental level, and whether it assumes an economic, political, religious or racial aspect.' The most general problem is that of 'the contrast between the search for economic progress and the fear of insecurity, between the opening up of frontiers and nostalgia for closed and stable communities.'[36] Rather than the displacement of the Westphalian model, what we are seeing is more like its modification and reconfiguration to suit the conditions of the new order. 'After the inequality in law which opposes nationals against foreigners,' observes René Gallissot, 'we now have, with the closure of the frontiers of the European economic community, the distinction in nature between those of "European stock" and those who are non-Europeans.' 'It isn't a question of a return', he argues 'but of an enlargement or transposition of the xenophobic and racist discrimination that was previously – and still remains, of course – national in its form.'[37]

What is at issue is the question of community in the new context of

34. David Held, 'By the People, For the People', *Times Higher Education Supplement*, 22 January 1993, p17.

35. Peter G. Brown and Henry Shue (eds), *Boundaries: National Autonomy and its Limits*, Rowman and Littlefield: Totowa, New Jersey, 1981.

36. Pierre Hassner, 'L'Europe et le Spectre des Nationalismes', *Esprit*, October 1991, p20.

37. René Gallissot, 'Dépasser le

globalisation, a new world order, and all the anxieties provoked by such a challenge to old certainties. In such circumstances, there are dilemmas about which kind of community can provide greatest stability and security. Can national communities be sustained? Is it the case that local communities might be more viable in the new global context? Or is more to be gained through the creation of a European-wide community? What is not called into doubt, however, is the value of community and of communitarian belonging. For Iris Young, the ideal of community 'expresses a desire for social wholeness, symmetry, a security and solid identity which is objectified because affirmed by others unambiguously ... The impulse to community often coincides with a desire to preserve identity and in practice excludes others who threaten that sense of identity.'[38] This being the case, there will always be a certain intolerance towards the outsider. By their very existence, outsiders threaten to expose the imaginary basis of our identity: strangers do not have the same inclination to suspend their disbelief about the imaginary contract by which we claim membership of our community.[39] In Europe now, the struggle to sustain the principles of community involves the struggle to adapt the principles of national community – which have most fulfilled the desire for wholeness and security – to the new order. It is a struggle that is being waged in the context of a world in which it is increasingly impossible to avoid strangers; a world in which the fiction of 'our' community is therefore always going to be exposed and vulnerable.

III COMMUNITY AND INHIBITION

The principle, or the aspiration, at work in the formation of national communities has been that of homogeneity – ethnic, religious, linguistic, cultural, territorial. Monolithic and inward-looking, the unitary nation-state has seemed to be the realisation of a desire for coherence and integrity (though we might suspect that, rather than being the realisation of this desire, it was the *realpolitik* of nation-building that created the conditions of possibility for such a desire, or such a kind of desire, to be imagined). And, in so far as it has sought to eliminate difference and complexity, the formation of a national community and culture has involved the extrusion or the marginalisation of elements that have seemed to compromise the clarity of national being. As Zygmunt Bauman argues, the 'promotion of homogeneity had to be complemented by the effort to brand, segregate and evict the "aliens".' As such, this kind of nationalist identity 'is perpetually under conditions of a besieged fortress ... Identity stands and falls by the security of its borders, and the borders are ineffective unless guarded.'[40] Whatever coherence and integrity is achieved, it is at the cost of a perpetual vigilance in maintaining the boundary between natives and strangers. It is this identitarian logic, with its anxious, self-enclosed way of being and of belonging that has come to seem the natural and unavoidable mode of identification in modern times.

It is this kind of identity-thinking that, at a higher order, is now shaping the

Nationalisme sinon les Nationalismes nous Dépassent', *L'Homme et la Société*, no.103, 1993, p12.

38. Iris Marion Young, *Justice and the Politics of Difference*, Princeton University Press: Princeton, 1990, pp232, 12.

39. Dominique Lecourt, 'De la Nation Comme Fiction Efficace et Redoubtable', *Raison Présente*, no.103, 1992.

40. Zygmunt Bauman, 'Soil, Blood and Identity', *Sociological Review*, vol.40, no.4, 1992, p683, 678-9.

present attempts to construct a sense of European community. It is the promotion of homogeneity at this higher level that seems to fulfil our expectations of community, culture and identity. What is being created, then, through the transference or the aggregation of nationalist sentiments, is the unity of a unitary continent. The language of official Euro-culture is significant: it is the language of cohesion, integration, unity, community, security. The new European order is being constructed in terms of an idealised wholeness and plentitude, and European identity is conceived in terms of boundedness and containment. At this higher level, what still seems to be needed is the clear distinction between natives and aliens. Imagined in this sense, of course, it is likely to be as precarious and fearful as the national communities described by Bauman. Its desired coherence and integrity will always have to be sustained and defended against the forces of disintegration and dissolution at work in the world.

In the new European Community, the matter of territorial coherence and integrity is paramount. As economic frontiers have been lifted within the Community to create the single market, the security of Europe's external borders has become, all the more, a fundamental issue. If, for most of this century, the 'communist bloc' defined a 'natural' boundary to the east, the end of the Cold War has brought this convenient state of affairs to an end. Once again the Eastern Question is on the agenda; along its eastern and south-eastern edges, Europe is now seeking to re-negotiate its territorial limits as an economic and political entity. As J.G.A. Pocock argues, 'Europe is again an empire concerned for the security of its *limites*.' It finds itself in a position where 'it must decide whether to extend or refuse its political power over violent and unstable cultures along its borders but not yet within its system: Serbs and Croats, if one chances to be an Austrian, Kurds and Iraqis if Turkey is admitted to be part of "Europe".'[41] Who can be assimilated? And who is destined to be excluded, and thereby to become the 'new barbarians'?

41. J.G.A. Pocock, *op.cit.*, p10.

It is not simply a matter of economic or even political criteria for inclusion and exclusion. What is at issue along these eastern and southern margins is also very much about the culture and identity of Europe. What is at stake can be inferred from Lord Owen's observation in a recent interview with *Newsweek*: 'You have to have clarity about where the boundaries of Europe are and the boundaries of Europe are not on the Turkish–Iran border.'[42] This desire for clarity, this need to be sure about where Europe ends, is about the construction of a symbolic geography that will separate the insiders from the outsiders, those who belong to the Community from the strangers that threaten to disturb its unity and coherence. Through the same process by which it is creating itself, then, this small white and western European community is also creating the aliens that will always seem to haunt its hopes and ideals. Already we see how fears are turning to resentment against immigrants, refugees, terrorists, drug-dealers, asylum-seekers – all those who symbolise disrespect for Europe's frontiers. And we see, too, how machinations of defence are increasingly being mobilised against these intruders and marginal figures. As Jonathan Eyal

42. 'A Europe of Sixteen', *Newsweek*, 6 August 1990, p54.

argues, Western Europe is building up 'a set of defence, often imperceptible but much more efficient than the Berlin Wall. From an airline clerk to a Hungarian border guard, everyone is working to prevent people coming to the West.'[43]

The nature and scale of transformation across the continent is such, however, that those who are considered to be aliens and strangers – the 'new barbarians' – will be increasingly in the midst of the European Community. Europeans will not be able to avoid them. The fundamental question, then, is whether they have the resources to live with them. As Alain Touraine argues, the great issue for society now is 'to teach people to live together, to respect their differences whilst searching for elements of unity.'[44] If Europeans are to address this issue, then they will have to struggle towards some better accommodation between their own needs and desires to belong and the obligation they surely have to be open to the needs of others. They will have to find some way of bridging national and cosmopolitan values.

In the 1990s, in the context of the emerging new world order, whatever it may be, Europe is faced with enormous and daunting problems. It would be foolish to deny the scale of the difficulties presented to Europe by the collapse of the Soviet Union or by the wave of migration from East and South. What I am arguing is that those difficulties, which have to be faced in one way or another, are exacerbated by the mentality of the European Community itself. It is with Europe as an imaginary institution that we shall have to come to terms. It is a certain idea and ideal of Europe that now stands in the way of the broader geopolitical and geocultural changes that are called for.

We hear a great deal about the idea and ideals of European community, about the transcendence of frontiers, about a diversity and plurality of cultures which still has a fundamental unity. Günter Grass makes an ironic observation on these lofty ideals when he writes about the gypsy population of Europe:

> They could teach us how meaningless frontiers are: careless of boundaries, Romanies and Sinti are at home all over Europe. They are what we claim to be: born Europeans![45]

And yet it seems that Europe is afraid of them. There is no place for them in the European Community: 'Because they are different. Because they steal, are restless, roam, have the evil eye and that stunning beauty that makes us ugly to ourselves. Because their mere existence puts our values into question.'[46] What they expose is what is lacking in us and in our project for European unity. This should give us great cause for concern. How are we to comprehend this disparity between the ideals for European Community and what the real Europe is turning out to be? And how are we to explain our seeming incapacity – our refusal or resistance – to deal with this disparity and all its unthinkable consequences?

We need to come to terms with the nature of our identity desires. Julia Kristeva has described the 'psychic violence' at work in contemporary modes of

43. Jonathan Eyal, 'All Subterfuge, No Refuge', *The Guardian*, 15 February 1993.

44. 'Républicains ou Démocrates?', *op.cit.*, p32.

45. Günter Grass, 'Losses', *Granta*, no.42, 1992, p108.

46. *Ibid.*, p107.

identification. 'We are attracted to this violence,' she argues, 'so the great moral work which grapples with the problem of identity also grapples with this contemporary experience of death, violence and hate.'[47] This violence is rooted in the fears and anxieties that are being provoked by the enormous upheaval and change that is shaking the European continent. Fears are associated with – that is to say projected onto – the other, and the perceived threat from that other then mobilises feelings of hatred and violence. Jacques Rancière has argued that the fundamental issue we must confront is 'the question of the other as a figure of identification for the object of fear ... I would say that identity is first about fear: the fear of the other, the fear of nothing, which finds on the body of the other its object.'[48] It is this fear that stands in the way of the European ideal. What concerns Rancière is whether Europe has the means, and the will, to 'civilise' that fear.

Fear and anxiety are always present, and are always likely to give rise to violent and aggressive forms of behaviour. What is needed is some mechanism that will contain and defuse these feelings. As Paul Hoggett argues, this must 'constitute some kind of bounded space within which both meaning and anxiety can be held and therefore worked upon.' Such a space, he suggests, is crucial for 'the development of a subject which can face its own fear without visiting this upon the Other.'[49] Forms of collective association and community can constitute precisely such containing spaces. And in so far as in much of Europe, and for most of the time, overt violence at least is managed and contained, we might assume that appropriate mechanisms are in place to deal with our fears and anxieties.

What I want to argue, however, is that this is not the case. If it were, we might expect to see some release of our tensions, some modification of our behaviour, some greater acceptance of the other. What we see, however, is a condition in which violence is held in check but in which our fears are never worked through and civilised. Communities can function to partially contain our fears but to inhibit our ability to properly deal with them. Isabel Menzies has described how communities of a different order function as a means of social defence against anxiety:

> The characteristic feature of the social defence system ... is its orientation to helping the individual avoid the experience of anxiety, guilt, doubt, and uncertainty. As far as possible, this is done by eliminating situations, events, tasks, activities and relationships that cause anxiety or, more correctly, evoke anxieties connected with primitive psychological remnants in the personality.[50]

In so far as it fulfils this expectation, the institution tends to become idealised. At the same time, however, there is always the fear that its function as a container of anxieties will break down and there is always a sense of impending crisis. 'The social defence system represents,' according to Menzies, 'the institutionalisation of very primitive psychic defence mechanisms, a main

---

47. Julia Kristeva, 'Strangers to Ourselves: The Hope of the Singular', in Richard Kearney (ed), *Visions of Europe*, Wolfhound Press: Dublin, 1992, p106.

48. Jacques Rancière, 'Politics, Identification, and Subjectivization', *October*, no.62, Summer 1992, pp63-64.

49. Paul Hoggett, 'A Place for Experience: A Psychoanalytic Perspective on Boundary, Identity and Culture', *Environment and Planning D: Society and Space*, vol.10, no.3, 1992, p349. We might see Julia Kristeva's discussion of the nation as a transitional object as an example of how such a space might be constructed in contemporary Europe. See Julia Kristeva, *Nations Without Nationalism*, Columbia University Press: New York, 1993.

50. Isabel E.P. Menzies, 'A Case-Study in the Functioning of Social Systems as a Defence against Anxiety', *Human Relations*, vol.13, no.2, May 1960, p109.

characteristic of which is that they facilitate the evasion of anxiety, but contribute little to its true modification.'[51] There is, it seems to me, a striking resemblance between this strategy of coping and that which is mobilised by the organisation of community at both a national and a European level.

We organise ourselves into communities in such a way as to accommodate fears and anxieties without having to come to terms with, and therefore modify, them. Community then becomes resistant to change and development. There is fear of change, a fear of being changed, a fear of being incapable of changing. Community becomes organised around the mechanisms of inhibition. In order to preserve certain features of their way of 'existence', writes Daniel Sibony, 'people are sometimes obliged literally to sacrifice certain avenues of thought. They do it because they fear breakdown, which they think they do not have the means to deal with. And as time passes, it becomes true that they do not have the means. And then they brandish their impotence as an *objective* fact, a given reality, that was not caused by anybody.'[52] The capacity to think and act is inhibited. The community that is organised to evade anxiety is also organised to avoid thinking and learning.

51. *Ibid.*, p117.

52. Daniel Sibony, *op.cit.*

IV THE SILENCE OF POLITICS

> The silence of the masses is also in a sense obscene. For the masses are also made of this useless hyper information which claims to enlighten them, when all it does is clutter up the space of the representable and annul itself in a silent equivalent.[53]

I want now to raise some final questions about the media in the light of this broader discussion of community and identity in Europe. There are many issues that could be covered, for example the way in which the media relate to fear, anxiety and violent emotions.[54] Here I want to consider particularly how the media are implicated in the mechanisms of defence and evasion of anxiety that I have just been discussing. The question of media and community, which has been the central concern of this essay, is usually discussed in terms of the positive sense of community, those evoked by the Yeos: imagined community is about feelings of shared culture and identity in common. But there is another aspect to community, that in which it is held together not by what it avows as its collective values, but by what it collectively disavows. I have argued that community can function as a social defence system, serving to partially contain or to avoid fear and anxiety, but also to inhibit the real working through or modification of those feelings. The institution of community then functions as a mechanism of closure, driven by the compulsion to avoid the painful experience of change and development. What are crucial are the processes of inhibition that militate against thinking and against acting in the light of clear thought.

53. Jean Baudrillard, 'The Masses: The Implosion of the Social in the Media', *New Literary History*, vol.16, no.3, 1985, p850.

54. Kevin Robins, 'View to a Kill', *Marxism Today*, July 1991.

As I pointed out at the beginning of this essay, the media are now being seen, at least by the politicians and the bureaucrats, as fundamental to the creation of European union and an imagined community of Europe. Through the media, it is anticipated, it will be possible to construct a European cultural and political public sphere. I have already referred to Stig Hjarvard's observation that, as yet, there is no meaningful public or public sphere at the European level. Hjarvard believes that this is because the process of Europeanisation is still at an early stage. He does, however, acknowledge some of the difficulties that must be confronted. For one thing, there is the 'unclarified legitimacy' of European political institutions. And there is also the problem of the enormous scale of the European political space, and the question of the sheer number of interests that will seek representation at the European level. To these difficulties can be added the problem of demarcation caused by the changing size and character of the European Community. What is clear is that 'a European political sphere cannot have the same character as its national counterpart.'[55] There is the need for a new kind of media system, and to create such a system will require both effort and imagination.

55. Stig Hjarvard, *op.cit.*, pp89-90.

We must all surely hope that the media can be made to support the development of a European public sphere and political culture. The media could clearly play a significant part in the development of a trans-national civil society, and also in mediating between that civil society and the supra-national institutions of the European Community. But if this is to be the case, I think that we must take account of other difficulties than those raised by Hjarvard; difficulties of a different order, associated not with questions of implementation, but with the nature of contemporary media and media culture. Here I will make just two points. First, I want to draw attention to the fact that the media can actually lend themselves to the processes of evasion and inhibition that I described above; there is the possibility that the media may function to support the mechanisms of collusive interaction and agreement associated with social defensiveness and closure. And, second, I want to argue that there have been recent developments in media systems and practices that work against the creation of a mature and critical political culture, and may even work in favour of depoliticisation and privatism.

The assumption in most discussions about the public sphere is that media audiences have a desire for knowledge and information, which then becomes the basis for political reflection and debate. But what if there are also other processes at work? The psychoanalyst, Wilfred Bion, paid great attention to the desire to not know. Thinking, he argued, is discomforting and disturbing. In thinking 'you have to take the risk of finding out something you don't want to know,' and consequently 'most people want to closure off what they don't want to see or hear.'[56] There is a fear of knowing the truth which can make people desire to limit their freedom of thought and thinking.

56. W.R. Bion, *Four Discussions With W.R. Bion*, Clunie Press: Strath Tay, Perthshire, 1978, pp8-9.

Jean Baudrillard has made a strangely similar observation in the context precisely of media and political culture, and I think that what he says should be taken very seriously. 'The deepest desire', Baudrillard suggests, 'is perhaps to give the responsibility for one's desire to someone else ... Nothing is more seductive to the other consciousness (the unconscious?) ... than not to know what it wants, to be relieved of choice and diverted from its own objective will.'

And now, he argues, the masses have come to recognise 'that they do not have to make a decision about themselves and the world, that they do not have to wish, that they do not have to know, that they do not have to desire.'[57] In this case, though it is not how Baudrillard himself interprets it, we can see the inhibition on knowledge and action manifesting itself in a collective form as a social pathology.

Even if one is reluctant to go along with Baudrillard in seeing this as some kind of challenge by the masses, one must surely acknowledge that he has identified a significant shift in political communication and culture. What he identifies is 'the disappearance from the public space, from the scene of politics, of public opinion in a form at once theatrical and representative as it was enacted in earlier epochs.'[58]

Others have also drawn attention to this degradation of political life and to the functioning of the media as public sphere. There is sometimes the feeling that politics has now just become just a television spectacle, but we should realise that politics has always functioned as a spectacle. The point, as Paolo Carpignano and his colleagues stress, 'is not so much that politics has become a spectacle, but that *the spectacle form itself is in crisis*. Put in a different way, the crisis of representational politics could be read as the crisis of a communicative model based on the principle of propaganda and persuasion.'[59] What has been undermined is the very ideal of public opinion, the belief that public knowledge can, and should, inform and shape political life.

This demise of the age of public opinion is associated with significant transformations in the functioning of mass media systems and practices. Carpignano *et al* describe this in terms of 'a crisis of legitimacy of the news as a social institution in its role of dissemination and interpretation of events', and of the development of new social relationships of communication which, they argue, have made the talk show the pre-eminent expression of the 'public mind' in the new age of television.[60] Ignacio Ramonet has also drawn attention to the undermining of the media as a source of authoritative knowledge. He, too, sees the decline of news coverage as central to understanding the changes in process, arguing that, as the role of journalists and presenters has been undermined, 'it is the force of the image that now prevails': 'the objective is not to make us understand a situation, but to make us take part in an event.'[61] For Ramonet, this abandonment to the immediacy of the image has an enormous social cost. 'Becoming informed is tiring,' he argues, 'but this is the price of democracy.'[62] The mode of information now works against the principles of informed understanding and political action.

What is at issue in this decline of civic and political culture? How are we to understand how changes in the media system are implicated in this development? Without claiming to give a full answer to these questions, I would suggest that what must be taken into account are the mechanisms of social defence systems. One factor, at least, in the 'crisis of politics'[63] may well be the desire to not know, to not act. And it may be that television, particularly, functions to support the processes of inhibition and evasion of anxiety. New

57. Jean Baudrillard, *op.cit.*, p585.

58. *Ibid.*, p579.

59. Paolo Carpignano, Robin Andersen, Stanley Aronowitz, William Difazio, 'Chatter in the Age of Electronic Reproduction: Talk Television and the "Public Mind",' *Social Text*, no.25/26, 1990, p35.

60. *Ibid.*

61. Ignacio Ramonet, 'L'Ére du Soupçon', *Le Monde Diplomatique*, May 1991, p12.

62. *Ibid.* See also, Henri Madelin, 'Les Médias à l'Assaut de la Société, *Le Monde Diplomatique*, June 1993.

63. Martin Jacques, 'The End of Politics', *Sunday Times*, 18 July 1993.

media systems claim to bring us more information and more direct access to events, and yet, at the same time, it would seem that they also ensure detachment and screening from the reality of what is seen; the screen can help us to organise reality in the cause of our own psychic defences.[64] It may be that the rise of the talk show in fact represents a response to the tensions and stresses of contemporary individuals (and individualism); that talk shows and 'reality shows' are the 'therapy' of those who feel socially excluded.[65] Through this form of television the excluded and the powerless are compensated by the sense that they are at least living this experience collectively.

Perhaps this will suffice in a culture where public life seems increasingly inhibited. In this culture as Baudrillard says, 'people are at the same time told to constitute themselves as autonomous subjects, responsible, free, and conscious, and to constitute themselves as submissive subjects, inert, obedient and conformist.' They are caught in a double bind, 'exactly that of children in their relationship to the demands of the adult world.'[66] In the viewers and consumers within this culture, what is created is a schizophrenic feeling. 'You cannot,' comments François Brune, 'at the same time, be treated as a marketing target and be respected as an active political subject.'[67] What happens is that the child withdraws into a kind of autism; the child develops and 'inner silence', what Brune calls 'the silence of the target'.

*

> And I'm neither left or right
> I'm just staying home tonight,
> getting lost in that hopeless little screen.
>
> Leonard Cohen, 'Democracy'

Historically the media have played a central part in the imagination of national communities; it is probably the case that the creation of a culture and identity in common would have been impossible without the contribution of print and subsequently broadcast media. As Stuart Hall puts it in the case of the BBC and the British nation: 'Far from the BBC merely "reflecting" the complex make-up of a nation which pre-existed it, it was an instrument, an apparatus, a "machine" through which the nation was constituted. It *produced* the nation which it addressed: it constructed its audience by the ways in which it represented them.'[68] The expectation in many quarters is that the construction of a European media system will now make it possible to construct a Europe-wide imagined community out of the different and often conflicting cultures in the continent. The objective of the politicians and the bureaucrats appears to be 'to project public service broadcasting onto a European level, by allowing it to act as an integrative, homogenising force, producing an informed community, conscious of its shared history and traditions.'[69] The media industries are expected to be catalyst for the construction of a European Community.

---

64. Kevin Robins, 'The War, the Screen, the Crazy Dog, and Poor Mankind', *Media Culture and Society*, vol.15, no.2, 1993; David Morley and Kevin Robins, 'Cultural Imperialism and the Mediation of Otherness', in Akbar Ahmed and Chris Shore (eds), *The Future of Anthropology: Its Relevance to the Contemporary World*, Athlone Press: London, forthcoming.

65. Alain Ehrenberg, 'La Vie en Direct ou les shows de L'Authenticité,' *Esprit*, January 1993, p17.

66. Jean Baudrillard, *op.cit.*, p588.

67. François Brune, '*Les Médias Pensent Comme Moi!*' *Fragments du Discours Anonyme*, L'Harmattan, Paris, 1993, p157.

68. Stuart Hall, 'Which Public, Whose Service?', in Wilf Stevenson (ed), *All our Futures: The Changing Role and Purpose of the BBC*, British Film Institute, London, 1993, p32.

There must be considerable scepticism about such a possibility. If there was a moment when it seemed possible that the media might contribute to the reimagination of community,[70] recent developments in Europe have served to make clear the profound difficulties that stand in the way of such a project. What have become increasingly clear are the contradictions that beset the project of the European Community. If there has been considerable success in creating the economic space of the enlarged market, the development of political institutions and a public sphere at a continental level remains problematical. If the idea of pan-Europeanism has made some advances, it is also the case that we have seen the resurgence of particularistic attachments which may threaten disintegration and fragmentation. It is difficult to see how any communications or cultural policy can really come to terms with these complex and contradictory logics. Philip Schlesinger is right to argue that the case of European media policy is likely to reveal the limitations of a rationalist approach to cultural management on a transnational basis. The question of political culture and of a European public sphere seems particularly fraught with difficulties, and the belief that the old public service model can be aggregated to a European level seems wishful at best.

The contribution of the media to the declared ideals of the European Community is questionable, then. But what must also be taken into account is their involvement in the more unconscious processes of community. I have described a certain kind of closure that is characteristic of both national and European ways of belonging, seeking to understand this in terms of psycho-geography. Community, at whatever level, may function as a mechanism for social defence and the evasion of anxieties and fears. This is the aspect of its coherence and cohesion about which a group conspires to remain silent. Community is then likely to function to inhibit the processes of knowing, understanding and modification of behaviour. I am suggesting that the media, which we assume to be working in the cause of public knowledge and understanding, may come to function in accordance with these mechanisms of inhibition, and recent developments in media systems and practices would seem to confirm this. Fears attached to knowing may be something we have to take into account in considering the depoliticisation of media culture. What, then, is at issue is the geography of anxiety and fear in the new Europe, and the implication of the media in this psycho-geography.

69. Howard Davis and Carl Levy, 'The Regulation and Deregulation of Television: A British/West European Comparison', *Economy and Society*, vol.21, no.4, November 1992, p476.

70. Kevin Robins, 'Reimagined Communities? European Image Spaces, Beyond Fordism,' *Cultural Studies*, vol.3, no.2, May 1989.

TIME-SPACE COMPRESSION AND THE CONTINENTAL DIVIDE IN GERMAN SUBJECTIVITY

John Borneman

I: OPENED WALL, QUICKENED TIME, COLLAPSED SPACE

Concepts of time and space orientate the way we perceive and understand the world around us and are fundamental to a sense of self. They also differ across cultures and over time. Thus a shift in either category is always experienced as alternately challenging and unnerving, exhilarating and stressful, disorienting and reorienting, in any case, as deeply troubling. The opening of the Berlin Wall in November 1989 precipitated a fundamental shift in the categories of time and space, for Berliners specifically, for Germans more generally, and even, one might say, for the world. What follows is an analysis of the way in which the occasion of the opening as well as events in the year following it – primarily the currency reform and elections – affected a reordering of temporal and spatial categories in both East and West Berlin.

Life in Berlin since November 1989 has been characterized by what David Harvey calls 'time-space compression'. By this he means processes – revolutions are perhaps the paradigmatic example – that simultaneously quicken time and collapse spatial distinctions. 'Space,' he writes, 'appears to shrink to a global village of telecommunications and a "spaceship earth" of economic and ecological interdependencies [...]. Time horizons shorten to the point where the present is all there is.' Harvey argues that time-space compression is peculiar to capitalism, in that both everyday tempo is speeded up and spatial barriers are overcome so that 'the world sometimes seems to collapse inward upon us.' He dates this phenomenon back to the Renaissance, identifying it with the historical transformations accompanying Modernity. But, more generally, 'compression' is a process that can occur at any historical moment or in any place. It should not be conceptualized in an evolutionary sense but merely in terms 'relative to any preceding state of affairs.'[1] The most immediate consequence of the opening of the Berlin Wall, and of the economic and political events staged to unite the two German states, was a time-space compression, involving a basic disorienting and reordering of the spatial and temporal universe. This compression, I will argue, was experienced quite differently by East and West Berliners, 'Ossis' and 'Wessis', and has been fundamental up to the present in accentuating the already existing asymmetry between East and West. The expression, repeated especially by East Berliners in 1990 and 1991, which best captures this experience is 'Alles auf einmal' (all at once).

1. David Harvey, *The Condition of Postmodernity*, Oxford University Press, 1989, p240. Harvey has a tendency to reduce conditions like 'time-space compression' to a function of political-economic factors, specifically, to phases of capitalism. I am trying to account for the differential

II: COLD WAR CATEGORIES OF TIME AND SPACE IN BERLIN

Prior to November 1989, East and West Berliners had come to experience time and space through cognitive categories framed by, if not often directly derived from, Cold War order. These categories were constructed from 1945 to 1989 in an intense process of mirror-imaging and misrecognition whereby East and West Berliners were thought of, and often thought of themselves, as prototypes of specific East and West German, if not more generalized East and West, patterns.[2] However, East and West states and societies were never as autonomous as they often represented themselves to be, but rather symbiotic constructs, perhaps best expressed by the adage: when one side sneezed, the other caught a cold, while denying both the cold and its relation to the sneeze on the other side. Though characterized by mutual interdependencies and antagonisms predicated on an assumption of formal equality, East and West Germans were in an unequal relationship that increased in asymmetry over time. The grotesque examples of this asymmetry include exchange of (East) people for (West) money, private gift-giving from West to East, sale of (West) garbage to (East) dumps, West state loans to maintain political and economic stability in the East. In short, the self-conceptions of the two states and their citizens corresponded to the Hegelian dialectic of one-sided recognition: to be recognized without in turn having to recognize the other. Yet, I will be arguing that while the West and East created the effect of being outside and external to each other, they were in fact inside and internal: the other was always already there. Schematically, then, what were the differences in the fundamental orienting categories or ways of knowing in East and West that enabled the two sides to misrecognize each other?

In the East, after the end of the *Aufbau*, the early stage of (re)construction of the economy lasting to approximately the mid-1960s, time was experienced as petrified or artificially slowed down. Both the state and the citizen had good reason to reject the modernist vision of industrial time, the vision that presupposed an unstoppable race toward a progressive future. On the one hand, the regime had exhausted its economic base in a policy that favoured the building of heavy industry over investment in domestic infrastructure or consumption. No longer able to maintain the ideological mirage that it could compete economically with the West, it increasingly sacrificed 'production' goals in order to slow down time so that it could record and monitor people's behaviours, tastes, and appetites. It feared the overstimulation of its citizens, the appearance of desires or wishes that it had not already anticipated and thus potentially would be outside its control. Two examples may suffice. The *Stasi* (state security) continually expanded its reach during the 1970s, eventually accumulating reports on a third of all citizens. We now know that most of these reports concerned mundane activities that might index potential critical thought or political dissatisfaction: stray comments at a meeting in a youth club, passing remarks made on the telephone, the kinds and numbers of friends one kept, or even daily rhythms such as the time it took one to empty

'experiencing' of time-space compression and its consequences. These experiences cannot be accounted for solely, or even primarily, in terms of the dynamics of political economy or capitalist process.

2. I examine the development of mirror-imaging processes in *Belonging in the Two Berlins: Kin, State, Nation*, Cambridge University Press, 1992. Also see the superbly concise essays in the catalogue accompanying the 1992 museum exhibit of German ideology during the Cold War, edited by the Deutsches Historisches Museum, *Deutschland im Kalten Krieg, 1945 bis 1963*, Argon Verlag: Berlin 1992.

one's garbage in the dump. A second means by which the state monitored citizen desire was the *Eingabe*, a legally sanctioned petition to a person with authority over the request. These petitions expressed directly the perceived needs and wishes of the citizen, ranging from complaints about service in a restaurant to requests for a pair of ski pants or an apartment, or to travel to the West. The regime read these wishes with great interest, sometimes responding like a Santa Claus, sometimes responding by referring the person to the state security for further, more intimate monitoring. Both of these examples indicate the state's enthusiasm for the oft-repeated Lenin maxim: Trust is good, but control is better.

On the other hand, citizens in the German Democratic Republic (GDR) also wanted to slow down time, partly because they had no incentive to speed it up. Accelerated productivity on the job, and thus faster work, was not the principle by which people were rewarded in everyday life in the East. Instead loyalty, stability, political acquiescence, and team-work formed the bases for rewards on the job, to the extent there were any. Punitive sanctions for slowing down time were nearly non-existent, since people were rarely fired. Nor were citizens part of an orthodox class system, of the sort Pierre Bourdieu has outlined for France, where constant distinction-making is the principle that generates and reproduces the system of class hierarchy.[3] Hierarchies in the GDR were based on principles other than social-climbing and productivity. Opportunities for status through conspicuous consumption were simply not readily available, much less pandered to and advertised as in the West. Commodities were in one way or another either available without much ado, or unavailable even with concentrated effort. As János Kornai has argued, Eastern European socialist economies distinguished themselves from capitalist ones in that they were supply-constrained (seeking to control the allocation of goods), whereas capitalist economies are demand-constrained (based on control of resources and manipulation of demand).[4] A demand-constrained economy depends on a constant displacement of consumer desire and thus tends to accelerate the activity of exchange. A supply-constrained economy could best achieve its goal, distribution control, by retarding the pace of exchange. Thus, since the mid-1960s, time in the GDR was experienced as petrified.

With the building of the Wall in August 1961, space in the East was shaped by a sense of confinement and closure. The East German state then developed into the paradigmatic example, the mirror-image, of the American policy called 'containment of Communism'. It encircled West Berliners with the Wall and contained most of its people in its own unambiguous and heavily guarded borders. Additionally, the GDR gradually increased the size of its state security to watch over citizens within those borders. When wanting to go abroad, most East Germans could travel only within socialist bloc countries. Unrestricted travel was possible only in Czechoslovakia, Hungary, and Romania. One could travel to the other socialist countries only with official permission, most often within a group. Much of the Soviet Union was always off-limits; and with the rise of *Solidarity* in Poland, travel there was also severely

3. Pierre Bourdieu, *Distinction*, Harvard University Press: Cambridge, Massachusetts 1984.

4. János Kornai, *Economics of Shortage*, North-Holland Publishing Company: Amsterdam 1980. Katherine Verdery, *National Ideology under Socialism: Identity and Cultural Politics in Ceausescu's Romania*, University of California Press: Berkeley 1991, pp74-83.

curtailed. Cuba was open, but quite expensive. Although the regime modified this pattern of containment in 1987 and 1988, allowing more than a million visits of its citizens to West Berlin and the FRG, it still denied this right to the majority. Among those granted the privilege of travel to the West, the majority were pensioners, and, when those of working age were allowed to travel, they rarely could take with them a spouse, relative, or friend.

Furthermore, the GDR adhered to the socialist principles regarding property: one could possess (*besitzen*) buildings but not land. The ability to occupy space (*besetzen*) was extremely restricted. This limitation in the possibilities for private valuation, through occupying or making one's own of public space in the GDR, created a peculiar relationship to what Freud called *Besetzung* and in English is translated as 'cathexis'. The libidinal attachment and investment in an object, specifically property, was truncated. This truncated 'cathexis', in comparison with the West, resulted in a projection of 'real' value onto two other spaces: valuable space was either totally private (a Western automobile or a country house, for example), or it existed outside the confines of the GDR, such as (and especially) in West Germany.

In the West, time was not experienced as petrified but as quickened. Capitalism as a process accelerates the pace of life, with all things and spaces being continually recommodified, made different from and exchangeable with one another in an impersonal, abstract market. Driven relentlessly to desire and occupy, or cathect with, new objects for personal consumption, to shift and replace old desires with new ones based on market principles of replaceability and endless supply, West Germans have, during the Cold War, been integrated into a hierarchical class society with a very large and affluent middle class. Rather than being confined and slowed down, they were encouraged to open up and speed up. Two of the most distinctive postwar symbols of this were the preferred vacations abroad (as the opening-up to the outside) and freeways without speed limits.[5]

Moreover, space for the *Bundesbürger* was not closed inside fixed boundaries as in the GDR, but open, ambiguous, and imperial. The Federal Republic (FRG), along with some of its citizens acting as members of refugee organizations, contested the land in Poland and Czechoslovakia lost in World War II when Germans in those *Ostgebiete* were driven from their homes. (The fact that some of this land had been initially gained by driving Poles and Czechs from their homes was rarely mentioned.) Contested space was the basic issue in the West German refusal to sign a peace treaty with Poland up until 1990. In fact, the Federal Republic went so far as to claim the entire territory of the GDR along with its people as a rightful part of itself. Hence, during the Cold War neither the FRG nor its citizens made open reference to fixed boundaries, for this territorial ambiguity was a source of potential power for the state, especially in its relations with Poland and Czechoslovakia. (For example, no reparations had to be paid to the nearly one million Poles for their forced labour or for war damages. By disputing the postwar land settlements agreed upon by the Allies at Yalta, many West Germans could claim that they, like the

5. Borneman 1992, *Belonging in the Two Berlins, op.cit.*, pp231-235. See also Borneman, 'State Territory, and Identity Formation in the Postwar Berlins, 1945-1989,' *Cultural Anthropology* 7(1), 1992, pp44-61.

Poles, had been victimized by the war.) In conceptualizing space, West German citizens oscillated between two extremes, those of the cosmopolitan and the provincial. Those who identified as cosmopolitan denied the necessity of place, desiring instead to transcend space altogether, to feel at home either nowhere or everywhere. Those who identified as provincials remained loyal to the local place of either birth or residence, meaning that up to one-fourth of all West German citizens had a right to some type of future settlement over disputed space that lay outside the territorial boundaries of their state. Uniting the cosmopolitan and the provincial was an imperial attitude toward space: West Germans were not to be confined within the borders of the Federal Republic. Thus they were also united to a large extent in pushing strenuously for European unification, even on the issue of refugee policy. This attitude, in turn, demarcated them from the East Germans, for whom space was closed and confining.

III: THE CLOSE-UP OF THE WALL, SHORTENED TIME HORIZONS AND THE IMAGINARY

With these category differences in mind, let us go back to the sequence of events on the evening of 9 November 1989. Already since August 1989, the time horizon between initiatives of the East German politburo and citizen response had been shortening, so that who was initiating and who responding became irrelevant. In fact, both citizen and state were responding to the close-ups on TV: from August to September to the unmanageable and, for many, embarrassing flight of young citizens into the East European embassies, and again on 9 November, to the chaos at the Berlin border-crossings. The opening itself was an accident – a misunderstood response by reporters in the evening news to a poorly formulated politburo ordinance concerning changed visa regulations.[6]

6. Borneman, *After the Wall: East Meets West in the New Berlin*, Basic Books: New York 1991, pp1-4, 20-37.

In this respect, the opening of the Wall was similar to opening events culminating in the other 'revolutions' of 1989 (which, we might note, began with the Philippines' ousting of Ferdinand Marcos in 1988): it was mediated by television, by the cinematic form possible with filmed images. Stationing itself on the border-crossing Bornholmer Straße, West German television enlarged and magnified through close-ups every move on the other side. These filmed revelations initiated a process of re-imaging the Wall and the perceptions of those on the other side. For most East Germans, who had foregrounded an image of the West as Other to whom you do not have access but who has access to you, this event radically questioned their subjectivity as mirror image of the West. The opening disrupted the stable binary of the Cold War, the fantasies of protagonists and antagonists in complementary opposition. East and West were suddenly brought into a new relation with one another, or, in Lacanian terms, the Imaginary was destabilized by confrontation with a self other than that which had been imaged.

In its twenty-seven years of history before the TV portrayal on that evening, the Wall was imagined in terms of its stolidity and concreteness, its impenetrability, its clean and scrubbed whiteness on the East side – with an opposite set of associations on the West side: of a penetrable, graffiti-covered, illegality. In other words, the Wall was part of the Imaginary register, a perfect authoritative closure, secure, contained, orderly, stable. This register of images, both conscious and unconscious, had been reinforced in actual experiences with the Wall, for very few East Germans had been allowed to pass to its other side (though people from the Western side would suddenly appear out of a chaotic Nowhere, and within a day, disappear behind the Wall again). Hundreds of East Germans died, and hundreds of other were imprisoned, in escape attempts while challenging this image of the Wall. On 9 November, television cameras confronted this Wall in the Imaginary with a cinematic portrayal that revealed its fragility and human scale through repeated showing of movements, previously hidden, of guards and people at the border. People's own signifiers and linguistic conventions used to perceive this Wall and the Cold War and themselves in a divided Germany, in short, their entire Imaginary proved inadequate to comprehend this new event, this sudden chaos at the very site of Order itself.

East and West Berliners, specifically, most clearly expressed this confusion by claiming that with the opening they were *sprachlos*, speechless, and that this was an experience of *Wahnsinn*, madness, or literally, delusional sense. The images projected on the TV screen initially functioned as a 'third' dimension, interrupting the stability of the mirror-imaging process; they became the standard of reality for citizens and leaders alike. Thus the citizens, thrown out of the closed and complementary order of the Cold War, had to find a language and reformulate their relation to 'knowledge' of the world and of their selves.

Within days of the opening, the joke I heard was that foreign policy was being made not by the politburo at the centre of power but by the border guards on the periphery. Although it seemed as if periphery had replaced centre as the seat of power, this was not in fact the case. The guards had initiated nothing: they merely responded to the people who were responding to their own images on television. Indeed, as the time horizon between initiative and response shortened, East German leaders were required to react more quickly; they acted in a new tempo in which they were constantly forced to acknowledge events already displayed on the screen. In an age of mechanical and electronic reproduction, the question of the *origin* of the image becomes secondary, if not irrelevant, to the issue of the image as simulacrum, to the image's *reproducibility* and *audience*.

The TV close-ups did not simply render more precise a reality that people could see by going to the Wall and viewing it for themselves. That they had done many times before. Rather, the close-ups revealed possibilities for, to cite Walter Benjamin, 'entirely new structural formations of the subject.'[7] That subject, the East German, was a person in time and space who prior to these events could cross that border, if at all, only with a visa, for which one had to

7. Walter Benjamin, *Reflections*, Peter Demetz (ed), Harcourt Brace Jovanovich: New York 1978, p237.

apply months, even years ahead. Now one could cross that border without preparation twice, or three, or four times, within a single day. The East German became a new subject with a changed relationship to time, to space and to power. Instead of being overwhelmed by the Wall with its Cold War aura of cleanliness, fixity, and closure, the masses penetrated the Wall, climbed on it, chopped at it, poured champagne on it. They opened it up, moving it from the Imaginary to the Symbolic order, revealing the binary to be unstable, forcing it to justify its asymmetry.

For West Berliners, as I argued above, openness and ambiguity were already shared spatial categories, as was quickened time. Therefore they experienced this moment of time-space compression as reaffirmation of what they already were. The opening of the Wall may have involved some disorienting for them, but it provoked no fundamental reordering, at least not initially. Rather, they soon acted on the third spatial category held in common, that of imperial space. The FRG had consistently maintained not only that it was the only legitimate Germany, thus whole and complete in itself, but also that the GDR had always belonged to it, thus a necessary addition in order to complete itself. Hence West Germans did not initially get very excited about unity. The Federal Republic was just enlarging, completing itself, and Chancellor of Unity Helmut Kohl had promised them that unity would be costless.

IV: CREATING NATIONAL SPACE THROUGH ECONOMIC AND POLITICAL UNION

Two subsequent events have been integral to the restructuring of temporal and spatial categories since the opening: the unification of the economies and the governments – perhaps the only two domains where East and West Germans are unified. On July 1, 1990, eight months after the opening, a currency union took place. Three months later, on 3 October 1990, political union was completed. During these initial eight months, anyone living in or travelling through the East could use both currencies. This 'territorial unity' at the monetary level severely weakened the already inferior East German currency, as it eliminated the state's ability to control the value on its internal markets. This happened through a compression of space. Three examples may be cited: the incorporation of East German people and things into West German markets; the (ongoing) breakdown and pulverization of coherent space within the GDR by privatizing former East German holdings (after October 1990, through the actions of the Treuhandanstalt, a para-public trustee); and the huge population transfer of skilled labour from East to West.

The creation of a single market and single national space enabled many West Germans to exploit their superior position by buying labour, real estate, and other East German goods in the increasingly fragmented and unprotected spaces of the GDR. But, significantly, East Germans could not do the same in West Germany. They were still paid in East German marks. At most they could flee to West Germany to secure a D-Mark return for their increasingly devalued labour. The result of economic unity was not an 'imagined community' in the sense explicated by Benedict Anderson, but a territorial and fiscal community in a homogeneous space with quickened time.[8] No matter how much people imagined and experienced a national unity by reading a tabloid *Bild Zeitung* together in the morning, they were divided by their differential orientation and access to the new temporal and spatial world in the afternoon. Moreover, though Anderson may be right that print capitalism made people into nationals in the eighteenth Century, its function in the late twentieth Century German unification process was to exploit, not to overcome, a set of pre-existing distinctions for the purposes of expanding market shares. Creating the united nation – or at least its image – was a task more suited to those in control of visual technologies, a union of media consultants and politicians.

8. Benedict Anderson, *Imagined Communities: Reflections on the Origin and Spread of Nationalism*, Verso: London 1983.

Nonetheless, initially East Germans seemed pleased that finally they could buy goods in the West, outside of the state-controlled Intershops. Paradoxically, though, East Germans actually weakened their own position within Germany by eliminating the need for their own labour, for purchases in the West reduced demand for the goods that they themselves were producing. The introduction of a single currency in July 1990 inflated the price of East German goods for the East Germans, but made these same goods cheaper for the West Germans. As the goods they produced lost their value, East German labour was also further devalued, which promoted a flight of young skilled labour to the West. This entire process both quickened the collapse of what was spatially the East and enlarged the space in which West Germans could manoeuvre.

While the territory of the Federal Republic actually enlarged with unity, the sense of space contracted and time horizons shortened. With the opening of the Wall, people could suddenly move back and forth without long waits before state authorities. This ease of movement effaced the distances between West and East, prompting immediate demands for improvements in telecommunications. It also facilitated the creation of a single labour market that increased labour mobility in both directions. A trip from East to West or vice versa that had previously taken six months or even several years to plan (and without guaranteed success) was suddenly possible overnight. Whereas the initial experience of most West Germans in the East was of an imperial space, formerly withheld from them but now open for use and development, the initial experience of East Germans in the West was coloured by *Begrüßungsgeld*, – the 100 D-Marks of 'greeting money' (more for families) each East German was to receive yearly from the FRG to help finance travel in the West. This fund had been created when less than one percent of all East Germans could travel in the West. Suddenly all seventeen million East Germans were free to travel. The gift had lost its purpose. Yet West German politicians and bureaucrats, who were not prepared for the opening, did not immediately rescind the law. This 'greeting money' set the tone for future relations between East and West: the West German government giving money, East German citizens receiving.

The other major event leading to unity was the election of March 18, 1990, when the majority of East Germans voted to eliminate the GDR and swiftly become part of the Federal Republic. In the previous five months, the authoritarian political structures had been crumbling. East Germans responded with a groundswell of democratic will-formation, expressed, for example, in the creation of the interim roundtable, the registration of 800 'civic' organizations, the development of a critical and diverse press and electronic media, and the formation of twenty-four political parties. Beyond the winners and losers of this March election, it was decisive in replacing two semi-sovereign spaces with a single national space. Unification was thereafter understood no longer as a question about ends or goals, but as one about means and procedures toward the unquestioned goal of national unity. Moreover, these procedures could be handled as administrative problems to be solved by German bureaucrats and politicians. Thus, by the final election of 1990, a pan-German election on 2 December, the twenty-four East German parties that competed in the first bout were reduced to five. The media reporting on these elections also assumed more uniformity in the East: one of the two television stations was closed, the sole film conglomerate was put up for sale, and nearly all of the major newspapers, journals, and presses were either bought up by West German (and British) concerns or simply closed. Primarily responsible for shrinking this spectrum of representable interest and molding political will into West German form were West German political professionals and an intellectual elite. At stake in the election rituals was legitimation for the political and economic steps – primarily with respect to shifting ownership and regulatory authority – already being taken to dissolve the GDR. The process of assessing value, restructuring, selling, and closing corporations, factories, academies, day care centres, and the like came to be known as *die Abwicklung* (a carrying to completion or unwinding – both temporal metaphors).[9]

9. For different perspectives on *Die Abwicklung*, see the collection of essays edited by Heinz Ludwig Arnold and Fauke Meyer-Gosau, *Die Abwicklung der DDR*, Göttinger Sudelblätter: Göttingen 1992. For two analyses of the work of the Treuhand, see Peter Christ and Ralf Neubauer, *Kolonie im eigenmen Land*, Rowohlt: Berlin 1991, and Christa Luft, *Treuhandreport*, Aufbau: Berlin 1992.

V: UNITY IMAGINED

If observed abstractly or 'objectively' – in other words, from the perspective of no one in particular – the creation of a single national space and economic market opened up many new opportunities for 'Germany'. Some Germans in the new 'Germany' have undoubtedly capitalized on these opportunities, as have some non-Germans. Nonetheless, I would argue that for most East and West Germans, unity has been experienced as a loss – though for different reasons by those on each side of the Wall. One of the major losses for West Germans has been that of their East German Other, which has now reconstituted itself in altered form with respect to the West. If West Germans during the Cold War had always thought of themselves as central, they were only so with respect to their inferior, supplementary mirror-image in the East. And though this East had its own state and form of social organization, constituted as the antithesis of the state and society in the West, the Federal

Republic insisted that it was the only territorial state that represented German nationals. Thus the West in the Cold War maintained a double fiction: of the East as a lost part of the West, rightfully belonging inside the West and needed for completion of self. Unity has meant that the East – land, people, machinery, debt – has been fully absorbed inside the Federal body. East Germans may have initially felt that they were coming in from the cold, but West Germans are being asked, or forced, to provide the heat. The insider joke repeated by both sides goes: An East German says to a West German, 'Wir sind ein Volk' (We are a/one people), and the West German replies, 'We are too!'

With respect to time, the accelerated tempo of unity with the East was soon paralleled by a slowing down of the pace of unification within Western Europe. Furthermore, the impatience and *rush* to unity with both East Germany and the other European community countries was due less to popular pressure than to strategic manipulation of both national feeling and superior economic and cultural capital by West German elites.[10] As a result, this unity was realized only with respect to East Germany, whose citizens, unlike the Danes, for example, were not only disorientated but divided among themselves and thus incapable of articulating a credible opposition. Moreover, West Germans were immediately confronted with real costs in their unity with the East: the FRG was forced finally to cede the territory it had lost during and after World War II, pay money to Poland and the former USSR, and thus acknowledge fixed boundaries. Hence for West Germans, although their state had gained territory and enlarged in size, space was no longer open and ambiguous. They, of course, experienced this territorial circumscription as a loss. Slowly this loss was compounded for many by an anticipated decline in the standard of living or threat to prosperity. West German postwar identity, which had been based in part on the ability of the political system to deliver economic goods, to protect Germans as consumers, and to integrate them into the West, has now been threatened. Furthermore, incorporation of part of the East into the old Federal Republic has meant a territorial movement East instead of West, thus reluctantly reorienting the attention of the affluent and complacent West Germans from Western Europe to the East. In short, while formal unity with the East (Germans) has gone ahead, formal unity with the West (Europeans), as prescribed by the Maastricht Accords, has stalled.

10. Claus Offe, 'Vom taktischen Gebrauchswert nationaler Gefühle,' *Die Zeit* 51/14, 1990, p42.

West Germans to some degree have been compensated for their ego-anxiety, for the loss of coherence and direction, by a successful projection of the East Germans as *inferior* in space and *behind* in time.[11] Most East Germans have remained speechless and internalized these projections.[12] Having already signalled a desire for and a prioritizing of the material wealth enjoyed in the West, most East Germans are hardly positioned to engage in a critique of Western consumer culture. With West Germany now the desired End, East Germans are conceptualized and have conceptualized themselves as merely needing to recapitulate steps already taken since the fifties in the FRG. Critical to this positioning of the East Germans as inferior and behind has been the notion, also applied to the other (former) East Europeans and Soviets, that

11. For a critique of this form of temporalizing the Other, see Johannes Fabian, *Time and the Other: How Anthropology Makes its Object*, Columbia University Press: New York, 1983.

12. Hans-Michael Diestel, former Christian Democratic Minister of the Interior under the de Maizière regime, referred in public to himself and his compatriots as 'aus den Früheren,' (out of the former/earlier). Perhaps the most widely read published works that portray an internalization of these representations are those by Hans Joachim Maaz, dealt with later in this essay.

13. Jürgen Habermas, 'What Does Socialism Mean Today? The Rectifying Revolution and the Need for New Thinking on the Left,' *New Left Review* 183 1990, pp3-23.

14. Norbert Elias, *The Civilizing Process: The History of Manners*, Urizen Books: New York 1978.

15. Michael Weck, 'Der ironische Westen und der tragische Osten,' *Kursbuch* 190, September 1992, pp76-89.

their revolutions were *nachholende* or catching-up revolutions, aimed at recovering freedoms enjoyed by Western Europeans since 1945. An article by Jürgen Habermas published shortly after the events in the fall of 1989 seemed to capture this new positioning of peoples. These revolutions, he claimed, were driven by a desire to make up for lost time. Of primary importance in this recovery, he wrote, are the political and economic freedoms guaranteed in civil society by Western capitalist, liberal democracies.[13] Whether this was the initial motivation behind the revolutions is debatable, but I do think that within months after the overthrow of the regimes, most East Europeans began expressing their motivation in these terms. They sought to recover lost time and regain what was denied to them by the Russian occupation and the pseudo-socialist systems they had lived under.

This placement of the recovering East versus the advanced West, employed in all domains, is reminiscent of the structure Norbert Elias posits for the development of the Western world in *The Civilizing Process*.[14] All of the former socialist states and their citizens, including the East Germans, are now expected to undergo a similar process of changing etiquette, work habits, and individual psychology, marked above all by an internalization of forms of authority that previously had been exercised by coercive means from an external source. Much like Elias' presumptions about civilizing the West, however, assumptions about the new civilizing process with regard to the former socialist societies involve a fundamental misunderstanding of the direction of psychological change. Elias assumes that, with civilization, tighter controls over affect are accompanied by an increase in shame and a postponement of gratification, and that this results in a processual strengthening of the superego. In fact it is not superego but ego controls that are strengthened under capitalism and the civilizing process that accompanies it. To the extent that the East Germans are being 'civilized', they are encouraged to drop any inhibitions or ties to tradition which they already have, and instead to abandon themselves to an external authority (capitalist managers, political and educational policy experts, primarily from the West) and submit their egos to a general reformation. Indeed, East Berlin is witnessing a wave of newly opened beauty parlours, aerobic and nautilus centres, and 'finishing schools' for adults to aid in this process.

As Michael Weck has shown in a recent illuminating analysis, this reformation entails an 'orientalizing' of the East Germans.[15] They are constructed as the *wild* and *ungezähmt* (wild and undomesticated) in contrast to the model civil society of West Germany. East 'authoritarian' or 'autocratic' (more Prussian and more *Urdeutsch* [original German]) habits are to be eliminated and replaced by the democratic principles of enlightened and tolerant citizens and by the 'free market' that characterize the Federal Republic. Moreover, politically, East Germans are assumed to be unable to speak for or represent themselves. Thus, since formal political unification in October 1990, four of the five elected Minister-Presidents from the East have been replaced by West German cronies. And legally, the *Unrechtsstaat* (illegal state) of the Nazi period is constantly equated with the *Unrechtsstaat* called the GDR, both of which are then compared to the *Rechtsstaat* (legal state) called the Federal Republic.[16]

From an economic perspective, the Deutsche Bank has conceptualized the former East Germany as undergoing 'a time of transition and stabilization ... before the onset of a growth phase.'[17] Immediately after the opening, East Germany was envisaged as an area for new markets for West German goods, a land of virgin consumers eager to buy from the West. With 'open markets' and West German leadership, it was generally assumed that the 'five new states', as they are called, would undergo an economic miracle much like the West did in the 1950s. Though we might think of the chaos, imbalances, and 'considerable risks' in this transition as lurking tragedies, where the protagonist is engaged in a morally significant struggle that might end in ruin and personal disaster, liberal economics is at base not a tragedy but a comedy. The plot always leads through the 'time of transition' to a positive 'growth phase'. Such obstacles as declining GNP, growing unemployment, environmental pollution, and cultural displacement are unintended costs attributable to past (ergo Communist) inefficiency. They can and will be overcome, however, as economic laws – the scientific 'laws' of the market or, alternately, the 'laws' of prosperity theology – predict a reassertion of liberal order. East Germans are, on the one hand, expected to initiate personal changes like characters in a *Bildungsroman*, but on the other hand, the specific rites of passage are elements of enlightened stages of development already predetermined by economic laws. Yet, the logic of its plot is engaged in a double paradox, for, to paraphrase Jonathan Culler, the story's ending, or the result of the 'free market', is both the effect and the justification of the plot.[18] In other words, the ending (freedom of choice and national economic wealth) is supposed to be the result of the workings of a free market, but the free market is also supposed to be the cumulative result of free choices. Thus cause and effect are obscured – both presuppose one another; and the relative efficacy of economic policy during 'the transition' becomes impossible to ascertain.

Finally, this process of unity, wherein the East is positioned as spatially inferior to and temporally behind the West, has another level, a psychoanalytic one. This psychoanalytic level has nothing to do with the essentialist pathologies posited for East and West by Hans-Joachim Maaz, an East German psychologist who became a pan-German media darling after the opening. Appearing on an endless number of TV talkshows, Maaz has repeated the conclusions he drew in his books: East Germans are 'psychologically defective, infected by a "virus" of a pathological social deformation.' West Germans, he claims, are engaged in a merciless striving for domination. The revolution itself he characterizes as an 'uprising in neurosis'.[19]

Where Maaz finds the most public resonance, I suspect, is in his use of familiar clichés and kinship metaphors to describe the process of unification. He assumes, as do a majority of German pundits across the political spectrum, that East and West are like siblings separated or a divorced couple, in any case

16. Political unity was expedited by using Article 23 of the Basic Law instead of Article 146, for Article 23 enabled an immediate transplanation of (superior) West Germans structures onto the (inferior) East and avoided any extended negotiation of the terms of unity. I explore these negotiations in more detail in 'Uniting the German Nation: Law, Narrative, and Historicity,' *American Ethnologist*, May 1993, pp1-24.

17. Deutsche Bank, *Unification Issue No. 51*, Deutsche Bank: Frankfurt am Main 1991, p1.

18. Jonathan Culler, 'Story and Discourse in the Analysis of Narrative,' *The Pursuit of Signs*, Routledge and Kegan Paul: London 1981, pp169-187. I owe this suggestion to Irmela Krüger-Fürhoff.

19. Hans Joachim Maaz, *Der Gefühlsstau: Ein Psychogramm der DDR*. Rowohlt: Berlin, 1990, pp104, 137-169. Also see his *Das*

gestürzte Volk, Rowholt: Berlin 1991, and a book he co-authored with Michael Moeller, *Die Einheit beginnt zu zweit*, Rowohlt: Berlin 1992. Maaz and Moeller, in this most recent book, take an explicit family therapy model and project it onto East and West relations. He and Moeller argue that 'Ossis' play the traditional role of the woman (depressive, hesitant, and dependent) while the 'Wessis' play the role of the dynamic, dominant, and aggressive male.

20. Spätere Liebe nicht ausgeschlossen: Die Deutschen in Ost und West müssen einander erst kennenlernen' *Die Zeit* 51, 21 December 1990, p5. When unity is thought of as a wedding, the bride always becomes the GDR. In this vein, the Frankfurt sociologist Karl Otto Hondrich recently wrote that the GDR's *Mitgift* (dowry), which it has brought into the unification process, was a revival of the identification of Germans as one *Volk*. The German word *Gift* means both poison and gift (Hondrich, 'Das Volk, die Wirt, die Gewalt,' *Der Spiegel* 1/47, 4 January 1993, pp29-30).

21. Roland Barthes, *Mythologies*, Hill and Wang: New York 1972, pp84-87.

male and female, preparing to reunite. The new union involves bringing together or founding a family, half of whose members have been deformed, argues Maaz, by premature separation of the child from the mother and by authoritarian education. A West German Social Democratic Party politician recently put it this way: 'We Germans from the East and from the West have contracted a marriage – and not without a certain liking for each other – which is indissoluble. Even genuine love, at some later point, can't be ruled out altogether. It was a nice wedding, really, but now we have to get to know each other.'[20] Nothing could be more misleading than uncritically replicating this cultural metaphor at the analytical level. East and West Germans are not kin reuniting, but two separate peoples, each with its own set of dispositions, who are suddenly, in one of those accidental moments in history, thrown together in a national whole.

VI: EROTICIZATION, STRIPTEASE, DEATH/BURIAL

The cultural encounter between East and West Germans made possible by the opening of the Wall has followed a sequence that in many ways is reminiscent of other first contacts between two differently imagined communities. Before unity, East and West were partly hidden from each other, full of private secrets, each part hiding behind the Wall. Secrecy and hiding, partial covering, as we well know, infuses an object with desire, makes it more desirable than it would have been had it been uncovered and revealed. Thus during the Cold War, East and West always exhibited some curiosity for and erotic interest in each other. Moreover, with the massive migration of people from East to West throughout the Cold War, many kin who were initially separated by the 'Iron Curtain' would reunite in West Berlin or the Federal Republic. Among the West Berliners I met during fieldwork from 1986 to 1989, it is my impression that approximately two-thirds had relatives in the East in the 1950s, but this dropped to less than one-third by the time of my research. Thus the simultaneous excitement and repugnance of incest became less of a factor over time in the eroticization of the Other. For several weeks – even months for some – after the opening, the erotic differences were explored in a series of both spontaneous and organized private encounters, parties, and ceremonial gatherings. Within six months, however, the two sides stood naked before a disassembled border, and with this uncovering, the erotic investment in the other was gone.

Pre-contact erotics were quickly replaced by a process that might be likened to an East German striptease – again, with each side perceiving the event differently. 'Ossis' see their strip as a narrative process, much as Roland Barthes described narrative as striptease.[21] They are not really interested in the end but in all the moves along the way, in the shedding of props acquired since the end of World War II. Obsession with their own history, constant exposés about the *Stasi*, rehabilitation commissions, and re-examination of individual relations are not seen as end-products but as a process of reflection whereby they discover their own significations. It is a coming-to-consciousness of the semiotic properties of the body, a body inscribed over 45 years by Russian occupation and the GDR. Time is a crucial medium of desire in this strip, for without time there is no eroticization; the performance will be flat and meaningless. For 'Wessis', however, the East must engage in a quick ritual shedding of its props: law, politicians, industries, research institutes, daycare centres – all must go. Thereafter East Germany can be envisioned as a newly discovered pristine body, an unmapped and chaste body, a blank space waiting to be signified, ready to be remade by them. 'Privatization', primarily by the Treuhand, is the process they have initiated to disassemble this body, to remove the 'deformed culture' and reduce the body to a state of raw materials. West Germans, moreover, tend to view the repeated East German exposés along the way, all the *Stasi* stories and whining about injustice suffered in the GDR, as deflections from the course of history. They are not interested in the strip as a narrative that unfolds. The whole thing should be sped up so the show can go on. They are interested only in the end result, the goal of producing a replica, a mirror-image of the body and ego in the West.

Yet, it is 'only the *time taken* (sic) in shedding clothes', as Barthes notes, that 'makes voyeurs of the public'. Nearly everyone agrees that the striptease will soon end, and East Germany will stand unveiled before Western eyes – to cite Barthes again, 'desexualized at the very moment when [s/he] is stripped naked.' Part of this disassembling has included, for example, making East German markets some of the most open and unprotected in the world, eliminating twenty percent of all jobs in the service and public sectors, fifty percent in state-owned industrial enterprises, seventy percent in agriculture.[22] Its automobile industry is dead, and its ship-building industry has been destroyed – justified largely in terms of eliminating subsidies for inefficient businesses. Furthermore, this paring and 'bringing to completion' is accompanied by a metaphorical shift in representation. Three years after the opening, East Germany has ceased to be a wild or virgin territory waiting for development. Unification increasingly resembles more a funeral than striptease, and this funeral metaphor, always latent in representations of the East, has come into common usage. In fact, recently East German author Werner Heiduczek offered the following picture: The East is a corpse that the West expected to bury. Instead, the West is not only carrying that cadaver on its back, but the corpse keeps showing signs of life.[23]

Anthropologists have often stressed that when 'death and rebirth' become dominant tropes – in this case, replacing 'development and growth' as metaphors for 'the transition' – then women and gender symbolism tends to be pronounced. In many different cultures, the putrescence of the dead body is associated with women, who in funerary rites must literally carry the corpse in order to transform the death into life.[24] This holds true across a wide geographic range of cultures, among others, the Merina and Bara in Madagascar, the Zulu in South Africa, the Gimi and Melpa in New Guinea, Greeks and Andalusians in Western Europe. In many of the ex-'actually

22. GIC (German Information Centre), *The Week in Germany* – 16 October 1992, German Information Center: New York, p4.

23. Werner Heiduczek, 'Germany: NOT a "Winter's Tale", Rather the "Outsider".' Symposium on *Restructuring our Lives*, organized by Robin Ostow, sponsored by the Goethe Institute-Toronto, Canada, 26-27 September 1992.

existing' East European socialist countries, including Hungary, Poland, Bulgaria, and Romania, a similar association is often made of women with Communism and its legacy.[25] In contemporary Germany, however, the deficits of communism in the ex-GDR are not linked specifically with women, but with a generic, geopolitically placed person, the 'Ossi'. Another frequent cross-cultural distinction, noted by Maurice Bloch and Jonathan Parry in their seminal essay on death symbolism, is that between 'bad death' and 'good death'.[26] A bad death tends to occur when a social death precedes its physical or biological counterpart. Likewise, the GDR is a 'bad death' in that its death sentence at the social and rhetorical level has not completely killed it, as mentioned above, but instead seems to have transformed it into a Schwarzenegger–Terminator figure that keeps resurrecting itself.

In most of the cultures mentioned above, after women take on and embody the death symbolism, the funeral comes to a completion with the transformation of the death into a life-giving process. In these cultures, women's reproductive abilities are so central to the reproduction of the society that in the process of transforming the death into life, women are also 'reclaimed' for the social. In Germany, however, most East Germans – both men and women – carry the stigma of being the agents and the dross of a failed system. They are considered not only prior and behind, but also untrainable and costly. It is not their reintegration that is imagined after the not-yet-completed burial of the GDR, but their expulsion. Indeed, more 'Ossi' labour is not needed in the new Germany, and 'Ossis-as-workers', who since the opening have continued to migrate West as the rate of approximately 2,000 a week, threaten to crowd an already tight labour market in the West, thus undermining the postwar corporatist agreement reached between West German labour and management.

This crisis in representing and integrating the East has even wider implications, however, for the East is no longer conceived as outside of and supplementary to the Federal Republic, but as on top of or inside the formerly healthy (West) German body. Thus we might understand the necessity of the 'death of the GDR' and its burial to West Germans, for how else will unity with the East be transformed into a more general life-giving process? This particular vision reinforces the salience of economistic metaphors, like those of Dr Hans Tietmeyer, head of the Deutsche Bank, and other mainstream economists, who insist that only after the destruction and death of the old GDR, seen as an undifferentiated whole, will rebirth and growth be possible.[27] The hitch in this picture, as Heiduczek notes, is that 'Ossis' are not properly dead; they are still kicking. If we take the metaphors of the psychologist Maaz and the banker Tietmeyer and other public figures at their face value, then West Germany is the male life-giver and East Germany a female body that refuses to submit to death and burial. By refusing to accept its role in this process, East Germany becomes a hermaphroditic parasite, a part male-part female, part dead-part alive thing – a species in-between that eats on the living. Such ambiguous creatures, like amphibians are neither fit for eating nor good

---

24. See Maurice Bloch and Jonathan Perry, 'Introduction: death and the regeneration of life,' in *Death and the Regeneration of Life*, M. Bloch and J. Parry, (eds) Cambridge University Press, 1982 pp1-45.

25. Gail Kligman, 'When abortion is banned: the politics of reproduction in Ceausescu's Romania,' Report prepared for the National Council for Soviet and East European Research, 1992. For a more detailed analysis of East German women, see Dorothy Rosenberg, 'Shock therapy: GDR women in transition from a socialist welfare state to a social market economy,' *Signs* 17 1991, pp129-151.

26. Maurice Bloch and Jonathan Perry, *op.cit.*, pp1-45.

27. Hans Tietmeyer, 'The Economic Unity of Germany: An assessment one year after the monetary union,' paper delivered at, and published in, the *First Stanford Berlin Symposium on Transitions in Europe: Economic Transformation in Germany – Social, Political, and Psychological Dimensions*, Berlin, July 4-6 1991, pp16-22.

as domestic pets. Rather, they are zombies who signal danger and elicit fear.

VI: A CIVIL TRANSITION TO UNITY

I have merely taken us through the effects of time-space compression and the sequence of events during the first several years of the so-called transition. Other processes having to do with property disputes and status reallocations are not placed in the centre of this analysis, though they are probably equally significant in their long-term effects on the restructuring of everyday life in Berlin and in Germany at large. I hope to have shown that East and West Germans had moved into unity with very different categories of time and space. And although these old categories have indeed been transformed since November 1989, they still do not comprise a consensual set of classificatory devices by which 'Ossis' and 'Wessis' perceive the same reality. Rather, new differences have replaced the old ones.

For 'Wessis', space is no longer open and ambiguous, though still imperial. Furthermore, they fear that their material progress is being endangered by the integration into the FRG of the 'Ossis', whose petrified time is likely to bring growth to a halt. For 'Ossis', space is no longer confined, and valuable space is no longer projected onto the West or maintained in their own private. Rather, their own spaces, including private ones, have been penetrated and pulverized, bought-up, reclaimed, resignified, and reterritorialized, quite often by 'Wessis' who were better situated to take advantage of the quickened tempo and rapidly changing conditions produced under time-space compression.

I am tempted to go further and argue that East German assimilation into the West German state, its entrance into the world of late capitalist liberal democracies, is an extreme case of the 'civil transition' being made to some extent in all the formerly socialist countries. Whether the specific features and effects of time-space compression outlined here are generally true of other 'first-contact' situations, or of other contexts analogous to a colonial situation where a smaller social Other is absorbed by a more powerful social unit, is, however, a matter for further research. Likewise, the particular plot sequence in this encounter – 'pre-contact' eroticization, striptease, funeral/burial – may well hold true for similar encounters of this type. In any case, the East German transition is less accurately characterized as a movement from an undeveloped stage to a civilized one than a union of unequals in a Dadaesque pastiche, assembling different elements of the past in a present collage that produces entirely new subjects. This new German subject is still a plural one, as it was in the Cold War, with East and West counterparts. Though Germans are formally united, they are far from being unified.

Perhaps the major obstacle to unification lies in the refusal in both East and West to recognize how the Hegelian dialectic of lordship and bondage continues to construct interactions. East and West Germans had no independent consciousness during the Cold War, but in fact constituted themselves as self and other in a relationship marked by domination. The dissolution of the East has done two things: first, denied the West an object capable of reflecting back to it its conception of itself as a free self, and second, strengthened the dependence of the East on the West by undermining the East's sense of self-worth. If, as Hegel argues, selfhood or self-worth involves the desire for self-certainty, and if this self-certainty requires recognition by the other, then the one-sided recognition that characterized the Cold War and that now characterizes actions of the dominant West cannot succeed.[28] The West can maintain its self-certainty only at the cost of the self-certainty of the East, in other words, through domination. Furthermore, West Germans conceal from themselves their dominion over the East by representing the 'Ossis' as formally free and equal to 'Wessis' when this pretence does not in fact structure the relation of the two parts to each other. Indeed, a 'more perfect union' will be possible only when the diverse histories and orientations of East and West as manifested in the present, the continental divide in their subjectivities, are fully acknowledged and respected, with an orientation to understanding the nature of these differences and the conditions of their production rather than clinging to the illusion of national unification.

28. G.W.F. Hegel, *Phenomenology of Spirit*, transl. A.V. Miller, Oxford University Press: 1977, pp111-119.

WOMEN AND 'ADVENTURE TRAVEL' TOURISM

Anne Beezer

Stephen Greenblatt closes the Introduction to *Marvelous Possessions* with what he admits is a utopian invocation: 'This is the utopian moment of travel: when you realize that what seems most unattainably marvelous, most desirable, is what you almost already have – if you could only strip away the banality and corruption – at home'.[1] In this article I shall use the connections Greenblatt makes between what we see and register 'at home' (relocating that dense concept within a different set of adjectives to those used by Greenblatt) and what we are able to see and understand 'abroad', as a means of thinking through the issues raised for feminism by the 'reinvention of adventure' in 'real' or 'adventure travel' tourism.

1. Stephen Greenblatt, *Marvelous Possessions*, Clarendon Press: Oxford 1991, p25.

'Adventure travel' is that segment of the tourist industry which organises trekking or camp-based expeditions to what are described as 'the remotest areas of the globe'. Typically, expeditions are organised in Africa, India, South-East Asia, the Himalayas, China, Tibet, Pakistan, Afghanistan, by tourist companies such as *Exodus, Hann Overland, Guerba Expeditions, Discoverers, Explore, Sherpa Expeditions, Himalayan Kingdoms, Encounter Overland,* and the most recently established, *Society Expeditions.* The promise of these holidays is, as the brochure for *Encounter Overland* emblazons on its front cover, the opportunity 'to see the world from a different point of view'. *Hann Overland* asserts that their expeditions will furnish the tourist with 'experience of other lands, peoples and situations', while *Explore* gestures towards a postmodernist sensibility when it claims that 'the intention is not only to see and enjoy great and famous sights, but also to get to know the 'other' side so rarely seen.'

These 'adventure travel' companies distinguish the experience they offer from that typically sought by the mass tourist. For example, *Encounter Overland* uses a form of personalised address to position the potential traveller as a non-tourist:

> The wide-bodied jet, the air-conditioned high-rise hotel, the tourist cliché and the contrived folk show are providing for the package tourist in most corners of the globe ... (an) ... infrastructure, created to appeal to the tourist and to smooth his path, that will insulate him from the very things he has travelled half way around the world to see.[2]

2. *Encounter Overland*, Asia, Africa, South America, 1990/91.

The 'adventure traveller', by contrast, is someone who 'travails', 'the custodian of the ancient relationship between traveller and native which throughout the world has been the historic basis for peaceful contact'. Today's adventure

© Encounter Overland 1990/1

traveller will visit distant places in order 'to feel [their] social and political pulse and sense the price paid for progress', and will 'dwell on a region's ecology, beliefs, values and taboos' in order to gain 'a perspective on a culture and its context'.

My intention in selecting these very typical quotations from 'adventure travel' brochures is not to reinscribe the opposition between 'inauthentic tourism' and the 'authenticity' of travel since it is precisely that opposition I wish to examine, particularly as it connects to issues of gender. Jonathan Culler is surely right when he claims that 'travel' and 'tourism' are purely relational terms, a sign relation whose central topos is the distinction between the 'authentic' and the 'inauthentic'. As he notes, such a distinction rests on the dilemma 'that to be experienced as authentic (travel) must be marked as authentic, but when it is marked as authentic it is mediated, a sign of itself and hence (is not) untouched by mediating cultural codes'.[3] However, Culler's use of the impersonal pronoun effaces the mediations of class and gender which, historically, have produced travel as the privileged term within a predominantly, although by no means exclusively, Western, upper-middle class, male discourse.

According to Mary Louise Pratt, the travel narratives of nineteenth century colonial explorers, such as Richard Burton, James Grant and John Speke, were characterised by a 'rhetoric of presence' which constructed them as 'monarchs of all they surveyed'.[4] Landscapes were aestheticised, given a density of meaning, and were laid out before the surveying male who became the masterful possessor of 'the newly unveiled landscape-woman'.[5] This same sense of travel as the exclusive provenance of upper middle-class men continues into the twentieth century in Paul Fussell's account of inter-war travel writing.[6] For Fussell, the art of travelling and travel writing together comprise the recording of a kind of Leavisian response to encounters and experiences by men of independent means whose travelling is characterised by a kind of 'purposive aimlessness', a disposition from which he explicitly excludes women. Fussell sees this (male) heroic age of travel as irretrievably lost, superseded by tourism, which amounts to no more than a feminised consumerism in which tourist sights are purchased in a globalised shopping spree.

Fussell's politically unruffled arrogance is increasingly being called into question. Women's travel writing has been 'rescued' from the margins of a literary orthodoxy imposed by such as Fussell, and feminist scholarship has re-examined the difference that gender makes to the conventions and rhetorics of travel writing.[7] In addition, the modernist confidence and certainty about what counts as a movement from the centre to the margins has been replaced by a postmodernist awareness that the right to gaze, and the discursive regimes that produce some sights/sites as centres and others as peripheral, is the product of an uncritical and unreflexive imposition of Western metanarratives on to the multiple and local stories of other places and peoples. It is these two critical positions – feminism and postmodernism – that I wish to bring into

3. Jonathan Culler, *Framing the Sign*, Blackwell: Oxford 1991, p25.

4. Mary Louise Pratt, *Imperial Eyes, Travel Writing and Transculturation*, Routledge: London 1992, pp201-213.

5. *Ibid.*, p213.

6. Paul Fussel, *Abroad, British Literary Traveling Between the Wars*, O.U.P. 1980.

7. For a useful bibliography, see Sara Wheeler, *To Lake Tanganyika in a Bath Chair: the eccentricities of women travel writers*, British Book News, February 1992.

'abrasive contact' as a means of exploring the possibilities for the grounds of a feminist critique of the 'reinvention of adventure' that is occurring within the late-twentieth century tourist industry.

Mary Louise Pratt and Sara Mills have both drawn attention to the difference in discursive positions occupied by nineteenth-century women travel writers.[8] Mills points to Mary Kingsley's use of ironising rhetoric as one of the devices women used to negotiate the contradictions arising from a women's occupation of a predominantly male (heroic) field of activity and discourse. And Mary Louis Pratt, similarly, argues that women's accounts [of travel] follow a different 'descriptive agenda' to that of men.[9] While women travellers were still enmeshed in hierarchies of race and class, Pratt notes how the South American 'exploratrices', Flora Tristran and Martha Graham, deployed an 'interactive' rather than an 'objectivist' rhetoric, producing 'centripetal' accounts of their journeys, which moved outwards from a personal, domestic space and back again, in contrast to the linear, goal-directed journeys described in male conquest narratives. But as Mills recognises, nineteenth-century travel writing by women displays a 'discursive instability': drawing upon available 'feminine' discourses of philanthropy, the personal, etiquettes of behaviour and dress, they are nevertheless transgressive in their production of 'female heroics' which cuts across and subverts typical masculinist versions of colonial discourse.[10]

Yet this 'female heroics', transgressive as it was of the dominant discourse which confined women to the domestic sphere, could complement rather than contest colonially established racial hierarchies. Kingsley supported the imperialist project of expansion and, despite the personalised nature of her account of her relations with 'her natives', subscribed to evolutionary theories of racial difference.[11] Kingsley appears to be an 'escapee' from the confinements, within marriage and the domestic sphere, which circumscribed the lives of Victorian women; and she construes Africa as a playground wherein she can deflate her own and others' pretensions and follies and ironically subvert the heroics of male travellers. But as Christine Bridgwood has noted, 'irony, while declaring itself as an analytical, "deconstructive" mode, is also classically conservative in its operations. It implies that if a long enough view is taken, all current events and individual dramas are insignificant in the face of the "immensity of life".'[12] It may be that Kingsley is an escapee from a history that enmeshes her at home, travelling through the 'natural playground' she finds, and wishes to preserve, in Africa. Colonialism may be the production of, rather than a discursive instability in, Kingsley's female heroics.

There is a quite different relationship constructed between 'home' and 'away' in the writings of the South American 'exploratrices' that Pratt examines. In these, the political concerns of 'home' are not left behind but brought into dialogue with individuals and issues encountered 'away'. Flora Tristran, for example, deploys a language of rights to criticise the exploitation of slave labour; and the inequities of 'marriages' between plantation owners and black slave women are judged by criteria informed by a sense of the injustice of all

8. Sara Mills, *Discourses of Difference, An Analysis of Women's Travel Writing and Colonialism*, Routledge: London 1991.

9. Pratt, *op.cit.*, pp147-158.

10. Mills, *op.cit.*, pp157-198.

11. *Ibid.*, p160.

12. Christine Bridgwood, 'Family Romances: the contemporary popular family saga', in Jean Radford (ed.), *The Progress of Romance*, Routledge and Kegan Paul: London 1986, p177.

forms of forced female dependency on men. Tristran learns from this dialogue as much as she contributes to it. She admires the dress of the women of Lima, seeing it not as some inert form of tradition, but as a strategy to preserve the freedom of public anonymity.[13] This is a dialogue with difference which is used not to impose a coercive identity on all women, but to reflect on the construction of difference itself as this is experienced at 'home' as well as 'away'.

13. Pratt, *op.cit.*, p167.

We find this same 'dialogue with difference', according to Greenblatt, in Montaigne's essays on the New World. Greenblatt argues that what distinguishes Montaigne's exploration of the New World from those who would, like Columbus and Cortes, approach it as a 'marvellous possession', was the recognition that domestic differences (between peasant and gentleman) mirrored the cultural otherness that was encountered in the New World.[14] In an anti-heroic gesture, difference is neither asserted nor denied but interrogated, in a movement that connects the strangeness of that which is most familiar to more distant disruptions of familiarity.

14. Greenblatt, *op.cit.*, p167.

Clearly, the ways in which twentieth-century adventurers are constructed in 'adventure travel' publicity differs from these earlier travel discourses. They are, for example, now invited to escape from the modern Western world and to 'explore' or 'encounter' other cultures, dwelling on their difference. The traveller is described as nomadic, moving through countries and acquiring 'experience' on the way. The 1991/2 *Hann Overland* brochure describes the 'exploratory tours or experiences' it offers – to places such as Iran – as embodying 'the intention to look at local life and perhaps obtain another viewpoint on religion, history, people, even politics (but not too much of that)'. But to be able to experience other localities and other cultures, the traveller must be prepared 'to get down to basics', a process which is not merely learning to 'rough it' but also involves a willingness to break out from constraining Western perspectives. Adventure travelling, therefore, strips Western 'selfhood' of its supports, which are constructed as an over-dependence on consumerism and the bureaucratic apparatus of fixed schedules and routines. *Explore* (1993/4 edition) insists that 'on the road or trail, there can be no place for rigid attitudes, personal prejudices or false expectations'. Adventurers explore and discover this 'stripped-down' self as they move nomadically through cultures.

'Real travel' publicity insists that it is this willingness to learn from others, to accept difference, and to dismantle prior conceptions and prejudices which distinguishes the late-twentieth century adventure traveller from his or her nineteenth century counterpart, and from the tourist of today who is only interested in 'buckets of cheap wine and a suntan'. This emphasis on the dissolution of self resonates with certain postmodernist perspectives on identity. As Douglas Kellner notes, 'recent discourses of postmodernity problematize the very notion of identity, claiming it is a myth and illusion'.[15] For Croker and Cook, for example, the self is not merely fragmentary but, in an electronic age, 'a galaxy of hyperfibrillated moods'.[16] Although it is precisely the electronic age that the traveller apparently leaves behind, the dissolution of

15. Douglas Kellner, 'Popular culture and the construction of postmodern identities' in Scott Lash and

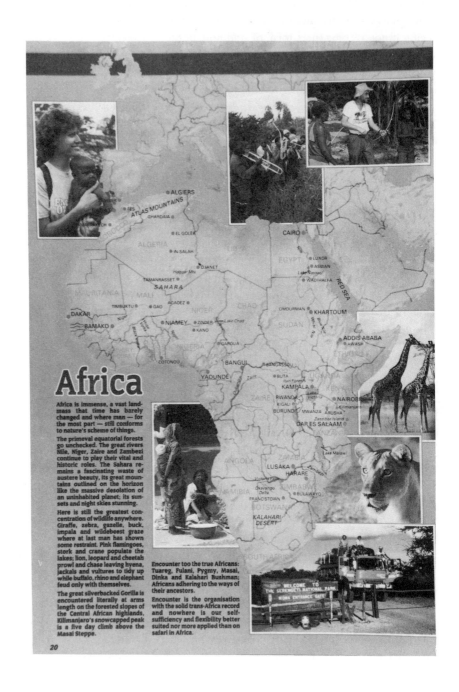

© Encounter Overland 1990/1

the self that Croker and Cook find to be characteristic of the 'postmodern scene' is similar to the state of 'stripped-down selfhood' the adventure traveller must achieve if s/he is to experience 'cultures, lifestyles and conditions that are often totally different ... (and) outside normal experience'. While it is clear that 'normal experience' is registered in adventure travel publicity in a way that certain forms of postmodernism deny, it is far from being validated. It is this normal self that is left behind as the adventurer escapes from the over-comfortable constraints of modernity, in a journey towards a new selfless self which is responsive to cultural otherness.

However, this postmodern dissolution of the self that is advocated by adventure tour publicity, has as its necessary counterpart the construction of 'other cultures' as pre-modern, as fixed in a timeless traditionalism. Thus, Africa can be described as an 'immense landmass that time has barely changed and where man – for the most part – still conforms to nature's scheme of things'.[17] This way of ascribing to the Third World the role of preserving for the West a cultural truth to discover persists despite the muted admission that 'unfortunate political turmoil afflicts these remote areas of the globe from time to time'.[18]

Adventure travel publicity draws on a discourse which John Tomlinson suggests is shared by some Western critics of cultural imperialism. He points to 'the constant temptation for the Western cultural critic to displace their own cultural dilemmas on to concern for other cultures'.[19] Adventure travel, as constructed by these brochures, amounts to the 'exportation of the sense of loss' that is attributed to consumption-satiated Western travellers. Dean McCannell argues that this search for authenticity in the supposedly simpler lifestyles of other cultures is not some harmless nostalgia that afflicts the West, but is in fact a component of 'the conquering spirit of modernity – the grounds of its unifying spirit'.[20] As Tomlinson argues, one of the political consequences of the 'exportation of loss' in the contemplation of other cultures, is that it allows us the sense of escape from the contradictions inherent in the condition of modernity.[21]

The world that escapees are invited to, through adventure travel, is one that is characterised by cultural difference conceived in spatial terms, as a kind of cultural diversity the traveller moves 'through'. It is a patchwork quilt of cultures, in Homi Bhabha's terms a *musée imaginaire*, where cultures are stitched together as forms of fixed asymmetries.[22] The 1993/94 edition of *Explore* is typical in the way that it invites readers to engage with Otherness. Alongside 'wildlife and natural history', 'raft and river journeys', 'culture and adventure' and 'ethnic encounters' are offered as reasons for participating in adventure travel. Ethnicities are then ranged before the traveller: travel 'affords the opportunity' to meet tribal peoples such as the Tuaregs of Algeria's Central Sahara, the Maya of Yucatan, or the 'colourful Huli of Papua New Guinea'.

These 'ethnic' peoples and the worlds they inhabit are offered as a kind of cure for the spiritual malaise which afflicts the Western traveller. The 'friendly

Jonathan Friedman eds., *Modernity and Identity*, Blackwell: Oxford 1992.

16. As quoted by Kellner, *op.cit.*, p144.

17. *Encounter Overland*, Asia, Africa, South America, 1990/91.

18. *Ibid.*

19. John Tomlinson, *Cultural Imperialism*, Pinter Publishers: London 1991, p120.

20. Dean MacCannell, *The Tourist, A New Theory of the Leisure Class*, Macmillan: London 1976.

21. Tomlinson, *op.cit.*, pp122-125.

22. 'The Third Space, Interview with Homi Bhabha', in J. Rutherford (ed.), *Identity, Community, Culture and Difference*, Lawrence & Wishart: London 1990, p208.

© Sherpa Expeditions 1990

© Sherpa Expeditions 1990

villagers' in the Akdaglar mountains of Turkey are described as 'the perfect antidote for world-weary bodies and minds', offering both physical and spiritual nourishment to adventure travellers. Adventure travel, then, is a movement between two 'worlds': the Western world which is the cause of the traveller's malaise, and the world of travel, which is a kind of patchwork, a series of places, an infinite number of locales to be 'discovered'. This reduction of societies to 'cultural space' is evidenced by the frequent use of maps to signify variety and difference. No map, of course, is purely functional, but the maps that are used in adventure travel brochures either consciously refer to previous epochs of discovery, suggesting that then as now there are simply worlds waiting for travellers to encounter; or they contain 'significant absences', so that all reference to political or economic configurations is omitted.

Within this patchwork of cultures, it is often women and nature, condensed into a single figure, which are made into representatives of the 'otherness' the Western traveller seeks. In the brochures there are numerous photographs of 'native' women and children who are emblematically described as 'Zanskar mother and child' or 'village girls, Marysandi Valley'. In such descriptions, people are made to stand for place and individuals are reduced to types, as if that exhausts their meaningfulness. This reduction of people to place is used so often to signify the range of differences to be encountered by the traveller, that the two are often juxtaposed. Ethnicities are spatially distributed across a map, so that culture and place lock together in a timeless communion.

The tourist gaze invited by the brochures bears a strong resemblance to the convention Pratt finds in nineteenth-century male travel writing. Landscapes are aestheticised and given a density of meaning: forests are 'primeval' and to be 'penetrated'; land is 'untamed'; deserts are 'arid' and 'austere'. These landscapes are presented as places where the process of 'stripping down' the Western self can begin. Indeed, adventure holiday brochures make a virtue of the basic amenities they offer since it is through this process of losing the Western 'consumer self' that travellers can acquire a 'closer sense of reality and a better feeling for the locale'.

There is, however, a difference between the late-twentieth century brochures and nineteenth-century travel narratives. The central topos of the heroic male adventurer, the 'monarch-of-all-he-surveys', has been turned 'inside out'. It is a loss rather than certainty that impels the journey, a dissolution rather than a vindication of self that is sought. The adventure traveller is invited to escape from Western consumerism and from those selves that are enmeshed in it.

The brochures' address to this 'escaping self' is direct and personal; it assumes that traveller and adventure tour operator alike are concerned about the issues that arise from the despoliation of 'our world'. Thus, most brochures include photographs as well as brief personal profiles of the tour operators. *Explore* (1993/4 brochure), for example, provides 'location shots' of its tour leaders, and describes itself as offering 'a special kind of travel for a special kind of person'. Photographs from previous 'expeditions' show 'explorers', men and women, on 'remote mountain sides', in 'arid deserts', or canoeing down 'swollen rivers'. Landscape and peoples become a 'playground' for these adventures of the self.

Here, too, some elements of postmodern critical consciousness can be found in adventure travel publicity. Both, I think, are based on a discourse which marginalises feminist criticism. One example of this postmodernist male anti-heroics will illustrate this marginalisation. The author, consciously adopting (in postmodern pastiche?) the persona of the wandering male figure of the romantic traveller 'driven by loss and journeying towards what cannot be recovered', constructs the difference between the West as 'home' and Bogotà, Columbia as a movement between the phallic Mother, for whom he feels 'disturbed tremblings of love, repulsion and pity', and the sights and experiences of Bogotà. These sights and experiences, including begging children described as 'sooty spawn', are condensed on to the beautiful face, haloed by the pool of light given by a kerosene lamp, of an Indian woman, the object of the male gaze. The romantic western male traveller buys chocolate from this silent (silenced) woman to give to the begging children of Bogotà.[23]

Dana Polan suggests that 'every postmodern discourse on difference – and we might see the male journey to Bogotà as self-consciously deploying postmodern tropes – involves a discourse on sexual difference, no matter how allegorical, no matter how much the discourse remains below the surface as part of the discourse's "political unconscious".' Polan argues that 'postmodern hierarchies of difference versus reference are mapped onto hierarchies of an adventurous masculine privilege as against a dangerously debasing, earthy world of a feminine in-itself'.[24] While adventure travel brochures may be differently situated to writings of cultural critics in the academic journals, belonging to what E. Ann Kaplan describes as a commercial, 'coopted' postmodernism, there are, I think, sufficient similarities to raise doubts about the value of postmodernist conceptions of the self for a feminist critical practice.[25] There is in both an opposition constructed between 'home' and 'away'. The individual bloated by consumerist excess but driven to relinquish the excessive self that inhabits home, uses adventurous travel to explore other selves as well as other landscapes. I have referred to Polan's argument that, either explicitly or implicitly, the opposition between the place to be explored and the exploring self takes on connotations of gender which privilege a male (anti)heroics. I have also noted how, in adventure travel brochures, 'away' is constructed as a timeless place cut off from the problems of modernity. What also connects the 'coopted postmodernism' of the adventure travel brochures and some forms of academic postmodern discourse is the conceptualisation of 'home' as a fixed place. Doreen Massey argues that 'the "identity of place" is much more open and provisional than most discussions allow (and) ... what is specific about a place, its identity, is always formed by the juxtaposition and co-presence there of particular sets of social interrelationships, and by the effects which that juxtaposition and co-presence produce.'[26] If this is the case, then it

23. Peter D. Osborne, 'Milton Friedman's Smile: travel culture and the poetics of a city', *New Formations*, Summer 1990.

24. Dana Polan, 'Postmodernism and Cultural Analysis Today', in E. Ann Kaplan, *Postmodernism and its Discontents*, Verso: London 1988, p50-51.

25. E. Ann Kaplan, 'Feminism/Oedipus/Postmodernism', in *Postmodernism and its Discontents*.

26. Doreen Massey, 'A Place Called Home?', *New Formations*, Summer 1992.

may well be that adventures, including adventures of the self, can be had at home, since it, too, is a place of difference.

An apparent difference between the kind of cultural criticism I have cited and adventure travel publicity is that, whereas the adventure traveller is invited to escape the modern world of consumerist excess in order to rediscover uncorrupted cultural difference, the cultural critic refuses this essentialising gesture. His journey provides the space to revel in epistemological uncertainty and to express doubts about the value of a universalising vision of progress. Although the loss may be differently conceptualised, what seems to connect the cultural critic and the 'coopted postmodernism' of adventure travel publicity is that both export their loss, a form of Western epistemic privilege that, despite the substitution of loss for confidence, still retains the unidirectionality of this act of conceptual exportation.

A feminist critique of 'adventure travel' tourism will need to consider the strategic use of the modernist emphasis on historical time and 'development' as a way of combatting the nostalgic conservatism that imbues discourses which essentialise place. This critique will also need to question the premise underpinning adventure travel, namely that a generalised and corrupting consumerism characterises the West, of which 'mass tourism' is one of its most visible and despoiling forms. It is ironic that adventure travel holidays offer a semblance of hardship and 'roughing it' at highly inflated prices. To sleep under canvas and to 'muck in' may be getting back to basics for those who can afford the prices it requires to do this in 'Third World' destinations. The point needs to be made that while for the privileged in the West consumerism may bring with it a sense of loss, for the less privileged in the West and for millions in the Third World, consumerism, in the sense of the provision of the material supports of life, is an aspiration.

Implicit in the idea of adventure travel as an escape from the corruptions of consumerism into the self-dissolving otherness of other countries, is a twin refusal: to engage with the inequities within the 'consumerist West', and the possible political/cultural inadequacies of consumerism; and to recognise that, in marginalising 'political turmoil', there is an avoidance of the face that modernity is now a global rather than a solely 'Western' phenomenon. The postmodernist gesture to emphasise the 'local', and to posit cultural difference as inscribed within a kaleidoscopic arrangement of infinitely extending local sites, tends to overlook the contradictory relations between local sites that the globalisation of modernity brings in its wake. Feminists have to be particularly wary of a postmodernist celebration of difference that fails to recognise these connections. We have to work towards establishing a dialogue with difference, a dialogue that will recognise that the 'sooty spawn of Bogotà' are the 'homeless children' in our Western cities, and that the kerosene-lit Indian woman's face can be found in Birmingham as well as Bogotà. In a reverse movement, the unequal and inequitable impact of 'modernisation' means there may be a familiar 'Western' affluence for privileged groups in even the most distant of places. This is not to 'universalise the local', as Gayatri Spivak has rightly

27. See 'Subaltern Studies: Deconstructing Historiography' in Gayatri Chakravorty Spivak, *In Other Worlds, Essays in Cultural Politics*, Methuen: London 1987.

28. Sabina Lovibond, 'Feminism and Postmodernism', in Roy Boyne and Ali Rattansi (eds.), *Postmodernism and Society*, Macmillan: London 1990.

29. For a re-evaluation of Adorno's theorisation of subjectivity, see Peter Dews, 'Adorno, Post-Structuralism, and the Critique of Identity', in Andrew Benjamin (ed.), *The Problems of Modernity, Adorno & Benjamin*, Routledge: London 1989.

warned against;[27] nor need it involve 'some central [feminist] authority keeping all other feminist strategies in check', a danger Sabina Lovibond recognises to be a possible consequence of positing feminism as 'a component or offshoot of Enlightenment modernism'.[28]

It is perhaps Flora Tristran's account of her travels in South America that can provide us with a model of a strategic feminist critical practice that can avoid the twin dangers of an authoritarian denial of difference and a postmodernist dissolution of self, which depends on maintaining the 'otherness' of others. Tristan recognised the Mayan women as her own 'non-identical moment',[29] in that their distinctive form of dress was a strategic practice of independence, a recognition that was enabled by her own differently constituted lack of independence within bourgeois marriage. 'Woman' is not here an 'identity' but a possible future position, based on the recognition of identity-in-difference. A feminist critique of adventure travel might begin by re-examining its Western 'other': the 'feminised mass tourist'.

'A LATTER-DAY SIEGFRIED':
IAN BOTHAM AT THE NATIONAL PORTRAIT GALLERY, 1986[1]

Marcia Pointon

On 28 February 1993, following a series of apparently serious national set-backs ('black Wednesday' when the pound fell through its ERM floor, IRA bombings, inner-city violence and the murder of an infant by two minors) the BBC programme *The World This Weekend* chose not to interview the Home Office, the Exchequer, the Police Force but instead took its microphones and tape-recorders to rural Wiltshire. Here reporters questioned members of the village cricket-team and their wives on the state of Britain. Subsequently, on 22 April 1993, John Major made a speech invoking county cricket grounds and warm beer as a reassuring image of the survival of essential England. Cartoonists were, however, quick to exploit the gap between the nostalgic ideal and the persona of the Prime Minister as an implausible (failed) captain of the local cricket team (pl.1).

In this essay I shall examine a paradigmatic episode in which the national sport is mediated through a particular aspect of organised State populism, the operation of the National Portrait Gallery. I shall examine how the unveiling of a commissioned portrait of a celebrated cricketer, Ian Botham, (pl.2) creates a mythicizing space in which multi-national commercial interests can appear to be contained by traditional national strengths. Through the contemporary portrait, commissioned by and shown within the national museum, an heroic masculinity is constructed. Simultaneously, however, (through a ceremonial unveiling and a train of press events) the trauma of national and individual unsexing is confronted in a discursively staged sequence of potential threats to that masculinity. The manly game of cricket – struggling for retention of its powerfully symbolic role as an image of national survival – is threatened by the very state strategies designed to preserve it. To look at it another way, one might say that the state is itself open to disruptive critiques at the points where it is ideologically manifest in traditional cultural forms such as sport. Ian Botham, a rabid populist, has been both necessary to the sport and a threat to its stability. Through the exigencies of high culture (portraiture in paint on a large scale) it might have seemed possible that he would be brought under control, thus preserving the traditional values of cricket and widening the influence of a state institution. The process of representation and display, however, achieves precisely the reverse, opening up a terrain of desire and repudiation that unsettles both the idea of sport and the notion of nationalism by its exposure of the problem of masculinity. Annexation of a cultural myth

1. An earlier version of this essay was delivered at the Association of Art Historians' conference in London in 1993. I am grateful to Andrew Stephenson for inviting me to contribute to his session 'Visualizing Masculinities', and to Mark Crinson and John Hayes (not to be confused with the Director of the NPG) for reading the paper and making helpful suggestions.

THE INDEPENDENT
ON SUNDAY
40 CITY ROAD, LONDON EC1Y 2DB (telephone 071 253 1222, telex 9419611 indpnt)

Unfit to compete

IT HAD to come eventually. Fall down a very deep hole and you will eventually reach the bottom. So, as the signs of recovery pile up, John Major at last carries what newspapers report as "a buoyant manner". "Britain is on the up," the Prime Minister asserts.

But, if we are on the up, it is only in the sense that a drowning man is on the up before he sinks for the third time. The truth is that Britain cannot afford another consumer boom. It could not afford the last one. Because we were not earning enough money ourselves, we paid for the boom by importing. We paid for the imports with IOUs. We still have to redeem the IOUs. We must do so by exporting more than we import. The Government has implicitly recognised this by introducing deferred tax measures that will restrain home consumption from next year. Thus, we have the first recovery in history where action to damp it down was taken before it had officially started.

This ought to surprise nobody. For most of the century, the economy has been chronically incapable of supporting the living standards to which people aspire. Hence, each boom must be followed by a roughly corresponding bust. An outsize boom, such as that of the late 1980s, must be followed by an outsize bust, such as that of the past three years. But the late 1980s boom was so disproportionate that, this time, we cannot really be allowed the next one. Ministers promise no more boom-bust cycles. They have reason: the prospect is of bust-bust cycles, with insignificant intervening recoveries.

Why should Britain be in this bind? Low manufacturing investment, bad industrial relations and lack of coherent government intervention have all, at times, played their part. But the most consistent reason is the most uncomfortable one: the mass of the workforce is not clever enough. It is not clever enough because it has not been properly educated or trained. So we have to use less sophisticated machinery than our foreign competitors. When production encounters some minor problem, it has to stop while a specialist is fetched because the average worker is incapable of fixing it. When we introduce some new production process, it takes longer for our workers to get to grips with it. This is not armchair speculation: it has been exhaustively demonstrated in a series of reports from the National Institute of Economic and Social Research, comparing factories producing the same goods in Germany, France, Japan, the US and Britain.

A typical British firm cannot compete on quality of goods; it must therefore compete on price. This is why the Government's strategy is to reduce wages and other overheads – by, for example, abolishing statutory councils that set minimum wages and by allowing employers to shed labour more easily. It is also why ministers remain so determined to resist the social chapter to which other EC countries agreed at Maastricht. But this strategy entails competing with the emergent economies of South-east Asia. These countries are gradually adopting the higher skill levels that Britain neglects; but they will be succeeded by other developing nations. The logic is that British wages and working conditions decline to those of the Third World.

The alternative strategy is to raise the skill levels of the British workforce. (One set of figures here: 27 per cent of British workers have technical qualifications, against 63 per cent in Germany, 57 per cent in the Netherlands, 40 per cent in France.) Remarkably, ministers show no sign of grasping this necessity. The Government's only approach to the manifest inadequacy of vocational training is to keep changing the names of the various schemes. "The tragic reality," said a report from the Centre for Economic Performance at the London School of Economics last year, "is that, despite all the rhetoric about new initiatives, real expenditure on off-the-job vocational education and training has if anything fallen over the last five years." Further, the Government provides free tuition, and a combination of loans and grants, for students on degree courses but charges fees for the vast majority on vocational training.

Britain on the up? Until ministers remove the low-skill shackles from the workforce, Britain will be almost continuously on the down.

What a lot of tosh

THE FUTURE of Britain lay in Europe, John Major said in his speech on Thursday, but the character of Britain would "survive unamendable in all essentials". Fifty years from now, said the Prime Minister, Britain "will still be the country of long shadows on county [cricket] grounds, warm beer, invincible green suburbs, dog lovers and pools fillers". As Mr Major made an otherwise good speech, let's be generous and overlook his confusing of Britain with certain parts of England. The fact is that the Prime Minister speaks tosh. Like many people before him, he has succumbed to the disease of eternalism. Nothing in this world is "unamendable" these days; never mind the warm beer, think about the ozone layer.

So where does Mr Major derive his lyrical certainties? The answer is George Orwell, who supplied the quote in Mr Major's speech about "old maids bicycling to Holy Communion through the morning mist" as another unamendable emblem of Britishness. Orwell depicted these old maids in his long essay, *The Lion and the Unicorn: Socialism and the English Genius*, which was published in 1941, post-Dunkirk and pre-Pearl Harbour, when Britain stood alone against Germany. Orwell pondered the unique attributes of "English civilisation" and concluded that it was "somehow bound up with solid breakfasts and gloomy Sundays, smoky towns and winding roads, green fields and red pillar-boxes". Ah yes: that solid breakfast known as muesli, that winding road called the M25, that gloomy Sunday spent in Tesco, that bright-yellow field of rapeseed, that old mill town where the only smoke is on bonfire night, that pillar-box which may be privatised. Our case rests.

Plate 1 *Independent on Sunday*, 25 April 1993.

for propaganda – whether by Prime Ministers or the National Portrait Gallery – produces unforeseen consequences. Representation of the heroic allows free play to what may be considered unheroic.

First, a few words about the sense in which I am using the word 'masculinity'. In her most recent book, Kaja Silverman uses the terms 'normative masculinity', 'conventional masculinity', and 'classic male subjectivity' to indicate the forms of masculinity that constitute the dominant ideological fiction which, she argues, lost conviction in the historical trauma post World War II.[2] Classic male subjectivity – as many have argued over the past twenty years – rests upon the denial of castration. I want to argue that outside the fantasmic world of Hollywood film, the dominant fiction – that of the wholeness, plenitude and mastery of the phallic subject – is sustained by collective forms of representation fostered by State mechanisms, since, politically, it is in the final count the Nation State that has the most powerful investment in disavowing its own castration. Masculinity in my account denotes, therefore, dominance and mastery both in the very specifically English cultural paradigm of manliness that the late twentieth-century has reviewed as a part of the 'Victorian Values' syndrome, and in relation to the critical vulnerability of the phallus as symbolic term in the struggle of sexual difference.

The mythic power of cricket as ideology is separate from the game as played. Yet, of course, that ideology offers ways of comprehending what is understood as real life. Thus cricket is 'the national summer pastime of the English race' as the *Encyclopaedia Britannica* tells us. Moreover, 'cricket has never flourished vigorously in Scotland, Ireland or Wales, a fact that may be partly accounted for by the comparative difficulty of obtaining good grounds in those parts of the kingdom, and by the inferiority, for the purpose of cricket, of their climate.'[3] As an arena in which ideology is made visible, it is particularly interesting as, through test matches, it provides constant reminders of England's colonial conquests. Though England may be trounced by the Pakistani or the West Indian teams, the very fact that cricket is what is played is ample compensation for the loss of any particular game, a perpetual and visible reminder of England's power to subordinate foreign nations and other races.[4]

Cricket, like football and rugby, as a live spectator sport is virtually exclusively male. Not only are all the players male but so are 90 per cent of audiences. Unlike football and rugby, cricket is both popular and genteel and it is perhaps for this reason that it has attracted relatively little attention from the sociologists of sport whose interest has centred on cultural and class analyses around football, its representations and audiences.[5] The language of cricket has, however, permeated national rhetoric in a most notable way; cricketing metaphors are commonplace in all the dominant arenas of public male discourse: the conference chamber, the House of Commons, the formal after-dinner speech. Forms of language in which boys are educated from earliest childhood are bounced back and forth from individual to individual, producing a collective rhetoric that works to exclude non-participants. Someone will deliver a 'googly', a second will declare it is his 'innings', a third

2. Kaja Silverman, *Male Subjectivity at the Margins*, London: Routledge 1992.

3. *Encyclopaedia Britannica*, 11th edn., Cambridge: University Press 1910-11.

4. The idea that sport is outside politics has been rigorously challenged by sociological analysis and the connection between sport and nationalism is widely acknowledged (see for example, H. Whannel, *Fields in Vision*, London and New York: Routledge 1992, p121).

5. See, for example, G. Whannel, *op.cit.*; J. Hargreaves, *Sport, Power and Culture*,

Plate 2 *Ian Botham* by John Bellany. By courtesy of National Portrait Gallery.

will be 'stonewalled', while a fourth will declare something 'not cricket'.

Sport in general, and cricket in particular, for all these reasons, forms a place of refuge in the late twentieth century that is powerfully politically invested. Margaret Thatcher's notorious philistinism towards the arts has been consolidated under Prime Minister John Major through forms of state populism with their rhetorics of the 'classless society', family values, and moral rectitude. The portfolio of the Minister for Sport has expanded to accommodate also the arts suggesting an equation whereby heterogeneous potentially subversive forms of representation can be subsumed into a State-controlled and populist monolithic category. The establishment of these institutions and the apparatus that backs them up in turn cements a notion of a team spirit in government and invites us to understand ministers as also 'men in the street' whose allegiance to a particular team or club may, in the tabloid press, be given more prominence than their political record. Since these sports are predominantly (if not exclusively) male this discourse also serves to assert the vigour and masculinity of a government whose power to determine events nationally and internationally is constantly revealed as enfeebled.

The history of cricket as a manly sport, an intrinsic part of male public school culture, goes back to the early nineteenth century[6] though it had been known as a game, often disparaged on account of its interfering with archery, since the Middle Ages. The MCC (Marylebone Cricket Club) which controls the rules and practice of the game dates from 1787 and is, of course, a male club, members of which (recognizable to each other by the club tie) are like masons and other well-established male groupings, powerful in promoting their interests in diverse ways that serve to exclude those who do not belong. While a man might conceivably borrow an MCC tie for a job interview, it is no more conceivable that a woman would sport such a thing than that she would wear an artificial penis. Such is the importance of symbolic forms of representation to the phallic power that is defined by its exclusions. The relationship of sport to the deployment and management of power in English life cannot be underestimated. It was a French sociologist who noted that what French designates with one word ('jeu') English separates into two concepts, that of 'game' and that of 'play'.[7]

When John Bellany's portrait of Ian Botham, commissioned by the National Portrait Gallery, London, was 'unveiled' on 22 January 1986, it received coverage that was unusually widespread for an arts event (pl.2).[8] Newspapers from Worcester and Exeter to Liverpool and Darlington reported the occasion. Portraiture, the national art, was united with cricket, the national sport in the production and dissemination of what the National Portrait Gallery press release described as 'unlike the conventional notion of a commissioned portrait' and 'very much a personal statement by the artist.' Botham, the press release went on, is presented 'in a large-scale popular icon as a folk hero of our times with a mirror-like panel emblazoned with the legends of the sitter's own allegiances, both public (to England, Somerset and the Hollywood XI) and to

Cambridge: Polity 1986; F. Inglis, *The Name of the Game*, London: Heinemann 1977; E. Cashmore, *Making Sense of Sport*, London and New York: Routledge 1990.

6. For an account of the relationship between sport and colonialist power structures, see J.A. Mangan, *The Games Ethic and Imperialism*, Harmondsworth: Penguin 1986.

7. J. Duvignaud, *Le Jeu du Jeu* Editions Balland (no location) 1980, p14.

8. John Bellany, *Ian Botham*, 1985, (addition of Becky's name Jan. 1986), oil on canvas, 171.9 x 152.4, National Portrait Gallery, London, no. 5835.

9. National Portrait Gallery press statement, 22 January 1986.

10. R. Gibson in *John Bellany: New Portraits. The Maxi/Hudson Collection*, National Portrait Gallery 21 February to 18 May 1986, p31.

11. *Standard*, 30 January 1986.

12. M. Brown, 'How Botham faced up to the artist's bodyline blitz'. *Sunday Times*, 26 January 1986.

13. *Guardian*, 20 April 1993.

14. See R. Gibson, *John Bellany: New Portraits*, pp27-8 and *John Bellany: A Renaissance*, Scottish National Gallery of Modern Art, 24 March–30 April 1989.

15. R. Seddon, 'Filling a gap', the *Yorkshire Post*, April 1986.

16. J. Fowler, 'A breath of sea air as the new John Bellany celebrates life', *Glasgow Herald*, 26 June 1986.

private (his wife and children).[9] This is repeated in the catalogue accompanying the exhibition of the work of John Bellany which opened the following month, in which Robin Gibson further describes Botham as 'like some latter-day Siegfried, the golden boy of British cricket, emerging proud and unassailable, unbowed after sundry skirmishes with sporting opponents and the media alike.'[10]

The National Portrait Gallery gained a huge amount of publicity and some kudos from the commission. In 1985 it had already achieved record admission figures with over three million visitors. This – in an age when counting numbers through turnstiles is synonymous with achievement – was considered remarkable. Brian Sewell, the *Evening Standard* art critic and a man who prides himself on his populist no-nonsense mediation of old-fashioned values in the arts, remarked that 'when you consider that the portrait is a bore nine times out of 10, and that the Gallery is a reference library of faces in which the historical likeness is important but the quality of the picture is not, it is little short of a miracle that sleep does not immediately overwhelm the visitor.'[11]

Ian Botham is a cricketer and around the year 1986 was much in the public eye as a controversial figure renowned not only for his outstanding performance on the pitch but also, for 'bar-room brawling, … drug conviction, ungentlemanly conduct on the field of play, streaking his hair and lending his name to the most tasteless line in "casual wear" imaginable'.[12] Recently Ian Botham has been described as 'the most dominant and enthralling player of his age'.[13] In 1986 he represented the kind of loved and hated *enfant terrible* the British enjoy celebrating. John Bellany, also in his way an *enfant terrible*, a Scottish artist who had recovered from a near-fatal liver disease consequent upon alcohol addiction, is one of Britain's neo-Romantics. His biographers and critics describe him as a visionary who has, in his portrait interests, much in common with Beckmann and Bacon.[14] The desire of the National Portrait Gallery to fulfil a role appropriate to a post-modern society, that is, to incorporate into the public collection an icon of a knight-errant fresh from skirmishes with the media, reflects the preoccupation of political and cultural organisations in Britain in the 1980s with media and communication matters. The Botham portrait by this account would seem to be a bold bid by the state (through its Gallery's Trustees, appointed by Downing Street) to upstage television and the tabloids. At the same time it was able to stage a media event which would receive maximum publicity by claiming a transgressive popular hero for the Pantheon.

The portrait attracted a great deal of publicity, most of it critical of the painting – and some of it accusing the Gallery of promoting a particular, 'unprepossessing style' in art[15] – but on the principle of all publicity being good publicity, the Gallery appeared in the guise of a national (if misguided) benefactor. Bellany presents a slightly different account of events, claiming that Botham was *his* choice, not the National Portrait Gallery's. The Trustees provided him, he alleges, with a list of notables, few of whom he recognised, and he chose Ian Botham.[16] So the artist's narrative of the portrait's origins

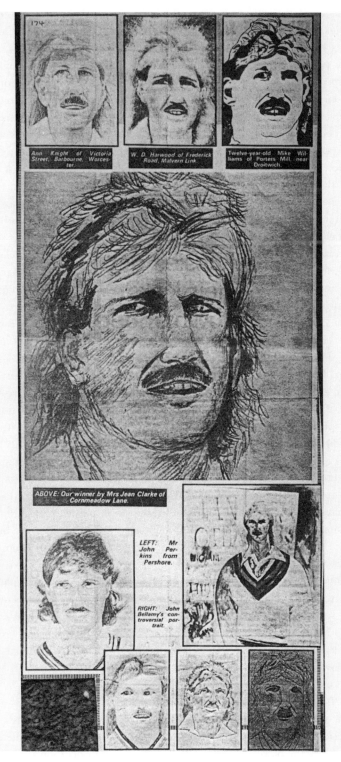

Plate 3 *Worcester Evening News*, 1 February 1986.

situates the artist with, as it were, 'the common man' ignorant of the sort of notables that the trustees of a National Gallery might name and thus forging an alliance between artist and sitter.

The portrait is larger than life – as befits such a hero – and confounded attempts to place it clearly within a visual tradition. Critics in the national press were largely amused if not outraged; most criticism being directed at the likeness.[17] The *Worcester Evening News* ran a competition for its readers to see if they could do better and published a selection of the results (pl.3); a correspondent in the *Liverpool Daily Post* meanwhile claimed that one of his children thought the Botham portrait was an image of Jesus Christ and the other thought it was an 'identikit' police construction.[18] The theme of 'any child could do it' was widespread with cartoonists taking advantage of the elision between what was perceived to be a child-like painting and a subject who was the proverbial small boy's hero (pl.4)[19]. But the non-naturalistic mode of portrayal was in sharp contrast to the action portraits of Botham exhibited at the New English Art Club by William Bowyer in 1986 and at the Royal Academy in 1987 and also differs substantially from the photographs of Botham that appear in popular books on cricket where vigorous exertion is underscored by captions. Thus one, from B. Green, *A History of Cricket* published by Barrie and Jenkins in 1988, reads 'Botham crashes Lillee to the boundary at Headingly in 1981. There has not been such a ferociously clean hitter of the ball since Jessop'. But the Director of the Gallery, wishing to place Bellany's portrait in an artistic rather than a sporting genealogical train, expressed pleasure with the result of the commission and was reminded of an 'early Renaissance portrait'.[20] It also pleased the sitter who was reported to have thought 'he might be painted like a Sir Joshua Reynolds.'[21]

The commission for Ian Botham's portrait was both a patrician gesture and an intensely media-conscious ploy. The portrait (refusing the action-packed stadium-type sports image) worked with notions of 'knowing' the 'inmost man' that have been most energetically fostered by 'kiss-and-tell journalism and by television documentary. The ideal of the lonely hero – transgressive but noble – is part of the masculinist cult of the twentieth century with prototypes as various as Jimmy Dean and the 'Lone Ranger'. To display the cricketer-hero as a solitary and contemplative man is to endorse all the ideals of masculinity that attach to those models. The fact that they contradict the actualities of a team game suggests just how forceful the cult has been. At the same time, the inscription of his allegiances on the panel behind his body tell, as we shall see, of a different kind of hero. The National Portrait Gallery's patrician gesture was, however, itself upstaged when the indissoluble triumvirate of sport, media and money, stole much of the limelight on 22 January 1986.

Ian Botham being unavoidably absent at the 'unveiling' (he was detained with a virus in Hong Kong), his manager Tim Hudson, a swashbuckling Californian erstwhile hippy wearing a cricket pullover, cowboy hat and earring, represented the player. He took the opportunity of the occasion at the National Portrait Gallery to announce that Botham had just signed a deal with the

---

17. See, for example, *Northern Echo*, Darlington, 23 January 1986; *Hastings Evening Argus*, 22 January 1986; *Coventry Evening Telegraph*, 22 January 1986; *Daily Telegraph*, 24 January 1986; *Yorkshire Evening Press*, 29 January 1986; *Evening Post*, 24 January 1986; *Punch*, 5 February 1986.

18. *Worcester Evening News*, 1 February 1986; *Liverpool Daily Post*, 29 January 1986.

19. See, for example, Griffin in *Daily Mirror*, 24 January 1986.

20. Reported in *Stoke on Trent Evening Sentinel*, 22 January 1986: Dr Hayes said 'It is a powerful image, larger than life, like an *sic* early Renaissance portrait. I like its colours and resonance and the way it takes you back in art history.'

21. Botham's manager, Tim Hudson, quoted in *Birmingham Post*, 23 January 1986.

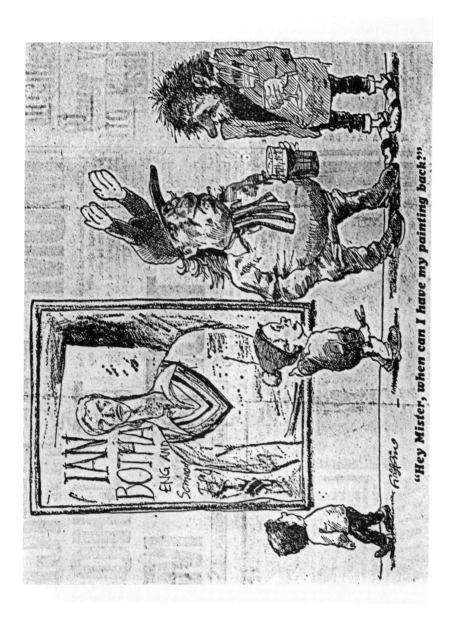

Plate 4 Griffin in *Daily Mirror* 24 January 1986.

22. *Birmingham Post*, 23 January 1986 and many other papers.

23. *Sheffield Morning Telegraph*, 23 January 1986.1

24. *Glasgow Herald*, 4 February 1986.

25. *John Bellany: New Portraits*.

sportswear firm Nike, and was all set to become the highest-paid British sportsman.[22] Set against this coup, the portrait is just 'another first'.[23] Tim Hudson, excited by his encounter with the world of art, had, it transpired, bought up John Bellany's entire available output.[24] This collection (the Maxi-Hudson collection – Maxi being Tim Hudson's wife and reportedly the source of his wealth), was accorded the honour of an exhibition at the Portrait Gallery from February to May 1986 accompanied by a catalogue with illustrations and an evaluation of Bellany's work.[25]

John Bellany's portrait of Botham works differently from contemporary portraits commissioned by the National Portrait Gallery from artists like Tom Phillips and Maggie Hambling who have depicted subjects like the writer Iris Murdoch and the Queen Mother. The 'legends' of Botham's 'allegiances' inscribed on the 'mirror-like panel' are less part of the iconic apparatus of early Renaissance portraiture than implicated in a popular tradition of graffitti and working-class memorabilia with which sport, at the popular level, has long been associated through autographs, caps, scarves, fragments of narratives religiously gathered and preserved. The portrait also acts as a site for the celebration of the traditional notion of the extended 'working class' family with its 'Coronation Street' loyalties.[26] The fact that the name of Botham's new baby, Becky, was added to the portrait in January 1986 evinces this relationship between the portrait and the family drama at a material level.

26. These kinds of ideals have been consistently stressed both by Botham and by his wife, Kathryn, in interviews.

Along with the team, the family is the permissible arena of masculine sentiment in popular 'working class' narrative. Male tears, the expression of intense personal feeling on the part of the masculine subject, are legitimate in the sports arena when they would be proscribed on the shop floor. The frozen-moment of the television screen, the sporting climax, is now a visual commonplace. What was once the epitome of avant-garde modernist endeavour (the attempt to capture the moment) is now the orthodoxy. The non-representational elements in Bellany's portrait of Botham (the smallness of the head, the cursory depiction of features, the symbolic background) constituted for the tabloid-reading cricket enthusiast a moment of transgression in the representation (yet another representation) of a model whose photographed and televised features were (and are) thoroughly familiar. There is a high degree of commitment to realist conventions in television and media representation of sport.[27] Bellany's portrait disrupts that regime of realism. In so doing, it introduces a post-impressionist style which stands – through handling of paint and individuality of vision – for an intimacy with the psychic concerns of the painting's maker, something which becomes important when we consider the homosocial spaces of the painter's studio. At another level transgression from the assumed rules of representation served to endorse the heroic character of Botham with his transgression from dignified sportsmanlike behaviour. Equally the 'naughtiness' of the National Portrait Gallery in commissioning a portrait of someone known to everyone which no-one would recognise worked to enhance the status and attraction of the Gallery.

27. For a discussion of modes of representing sport, see G. Whannel, *op.cit.*, p92 *passim*.

Plate 5 Ben Shailo in *Daily Telegraph*, January 1994.
By courtesy of National Portrait Gallery

The question posed by the little boy in Ben Shailo's *Daily Telegraph* cartoon: 'Do you still want to be like Ian Botham when you grow up?' (pl.5) might have been addressed, with appropriate adjustment, by an adult to any child in the Roman forum in the age of Augustus or in the court of Charles I. The gap between the question and the possible – but never delivered – answer is the gap within which portraiture fulfils its particular social and political function, creating bridges between real and ideal worlds. It is also an area of particular resonance in the oedipal drama; what is in doubt – and what has provoked the question – is the issue of masculine identity.

Brian Pronger has pointed out that 'because sport is an apprenticeship in orthodox masculinity, it is ironic to some and fearful to others that that world is also an arena for the paradox of homoerotic experience'.[28] This paradox, in Pronger's account, relates to the notion that the erotic confirmation of gender lies in the attraction that superiors have for their subordinates. The erotic desire that men have for other men is thus understood to undermine their culturally determined position of mythic superiority.[29] Silverman's argument about male subjectivities would appear to undercut this simple proposition but what does remain clear and useful for my account is that sport is a major site of both the construction of classic (heterosexual) masculinity *and* of homoerotic fantasy and pleasure.

Cricket, as the national sport, symbolizes orthodox masculinity and, through its participation in a mythology of nationhood (which recent Tory rhetoric has reinforced), stands for the essence of Englishness. But the attempt to annexe Botham as an ideal of masculinity by the National Portrait Gallery fails. The official insertion into the public domain of the representation of the hero as intact male subject produces a crisis. What should have stood for the authority both of cricket and of the institution generated only discourses of repudiation and discontent. And the moment of unveiling, the moment of exposure, is a positively Freudian moment of discovery in which the hero is recognised as inadequate, as castrated. The small head surmounting the long muscular neck emerging from the prominently striped cricket sweater, a truncated view that refuses the viewer the lower part of the body (inviting, at some level, a reading of the upper half as male body in totality), the vast but curvaceous shoulders, appeared to viewers to be an insufficient symbolic substitute for the rumbustious man. Disavowal, refusal, misrecognition follow in a collective shoring up of a pre-castration fantasy. Realist conventions of representation that regulate sports entertainment are suddenly exposed for what they are – forms of masquerade.

But there is, I suggest, a more specific reason for the 'failure' of the painting (and it seems implausible that its huge dimensions are the *only* reason for its having been kept more or less permanently in store). Bellany's *Botham* foregrounds the ways in which the portrait commission enacts not only the permissible – and state endorsed traditions of homosocial exchange – but also the illegitimate arena of homosocial desire. Symptoms of ambivalence manifest in a search for a secure frame of reference characterise both the presentation

28. B. Pronger, *The Arena of Masculinity: Sports, Homosexuality and the Meaning of Sex*, London: GMP 1990, p10. Many writers on sport address questions of sexuality but only in relation to difference of gender. They generally agree, however, that sport is closely related to the nurturing of orthodox masculinity eg. G. Whannel, *op.cit.*, p126: 'There is a close fit between sport and masculinity; each is a part of the other, so that prowess in sports seems to be, and is seen as, the completion of a young boy's masculinity.'

29. *Ibid.*, p141.

of the portrait and its reception. There is what some described as 'a pea-sized head on top of an odd-shaped body'[30] but what others saw as a 'Greek god-like head with fair curls'.[31] There are the reservations about a portrait which made the cricketer, it was claimed, look like 'a thin, weedy aesthete'[32] or a 'perfect specimen of a malformed wimp',[33] all articulated in language influenced by a dominant view of classic heterosexual masculinity. Greek gods, aesthetes, wimps are not the stuff of which the English sportsman is popularly thought to be made. The discourse of homoerotic desire, as well as the fearful spectre of castration, are countered in the NPG official publicity material. To describe Botham as a latter-day Siegfried is perhaps to invoke Nordic models of masculinity that have been powerfully associated with Aryan polemic. Even leaving aside any Wagnerian overtones, by identifying Botham with Siegfried the National Portrait Gallery constructs the cricketer as a violent and impetuous dragon-slayer and as a hero who is unequivocally heterosexual, a perfect match for the spirited young wife, Kriemhild/Kathy.[34] The cue is taken up by many of the reviewers; a chartered surveyor from Havant testifies to Botham's phallic credibility by remarking to a journalist that he had always thought Botham 'a randy bugger' and complaining that the portrait 'hasn't caught his sensuousness at all'.[35] As if to secure this remark, as well as to defend the sport, we are told that the accountant is himself a cricketing man.

The commission and exhibition of Bellany's portrait of Ian Botham is characterised by forms of overdetermination calculated to counteract the potentially homoerotic content. The *Yorkshire Post* juxtaposed a photo of the Botham portrait with a photo of Annigoni's portrait of Dame Margot Fonteyn, 'her gracefulness and charm ... effectively captured in the national costume of Panama, the country of her husband, in front of a wooded background reminiscent of a stage setting'.[36] The *Financial Times* conducted damage limitation by providing an anonymous portrait of the bearded W.G. Grace dating from the late 1880s. Bellany's portrait is likened to that of Grace: Botham 'is also presented half-length and full face, a massive, imposing and, in its own way, hairy figure.'[37]

The most powerful denial of the homoerotic is that which is provided by Bellany and Botham in the collusive act of portraiture. A scene of male bonding between Botham and Bellany, recorded in the intimate relationship of studio sittings, constitutes a camaraderie which is commemorated in a 1985 self-portrait (drawn and then etched) by Bellany (pl.6). Here the artist stands behind and to the right of his portrait subject, brushes erect and at the ready.[38] The convention (that of a double portrait featuring artist and sitter) that might seem to shore up an orthodoxy precisely serves here to unsettle it. A similar form of subversion is offered in the representation of a graffitti-covered wall, a cultural site with specifically homosexual connotations. Thus the medium through which the family is named disrupts the effectiveness of the message. This is not a family portrait – such an image could not fulfil the paradoxical needs to which Brian Pronger alludes, could not offer an object of homoerotic desire *and* an exemplum of orthodox masculinity – but the family is

30. *Daily Mirror*, 29 January 1986.

31. *Glasgow Herald*, 28 January 1986.

32. *Yorkshire Evening Press*, 29 January 1986.

33. *Northern Echo, Darlington*, 23 January 1986.

34. See *The Nibelungenlied*, transl. A.T. Hatto, Harmondsworth: Penguin (1965), 1979.

35. *Sunday Times*, 26 January 1986.

36. *Yorkshire Post*, 14 April 1986.

37. *Financial Times*, 25 January 1986.

38. A comparable scenario of masculine intimacy is recorded in Bellany's portrait of himself and his surgeon, see *John Bellany: A Renaissance*, Scottish National Gallery of Modern Art, 24March–30 April 1989.

Plate 6 © John Bellany. By courtesy of National Portrait Gallery.

nonetheless present. It is, moreover, not the extended family of brother, sister, mum and dad but very specifically wife and children. In recording not only legitimate issue already born at the commencement of the portrait but also the child born shortly after its completion, the portrait stands to affirm and vouchsafe for heterosexuality; its claim is that classic masculinity is safe in the sponsorship of the national institution, that whatever else he may get up to, Botham is husband and father. The image's premeditated strategies of disavowal were compromised strategies, and they failed at the moment of public display. Cricket-lovers, faced with Bellany's *Botham*, confronted an other which challenged a regime of representation (a regime which guaranteed the very existence of sport as an ordered and ordering system) and which threatened the authority vested nationally in an orthodox heterosexual masculinity.

A LITTLE INNER MYTHOLOGY: KRISTEVA AS NOVELIST

Vassiliki Kolocotroni

With the publication of her first novel in 1990, Julia Kristeva exposed herself to yet another type of critical scrutiny, added to criticisms of the direction which her theoretical work has taken in recent years. While the novel attracted the inevitable media attention already surrounding intellectuals in France, it was largely ignored by the academic community in Britain, considered perhaps as a slightly embarrassing, if not simply irrelevant, phenomenon. For Kristeva the linguist, semiotician, feminist, psychoanalyst, cultural critic, however, the writing of novels seems to be a new but not incompatible aspect of intellectual production. It will be argued in what follows that for Kristeva the novel provides an alternative space for the working through of theoretical and personal concerns, as well as for the expression of a desire for continuity and transmission.

In *The Weary Sons of Freud*, a critique of psychoanalysis as an institutionalised and conformist practice, Catherine Clément, a feminist psychoanalyst and novelist, speaks of the problematic configuration of language, gender and psychoanalysis:

> Inside, then, means going inward to find out where what I write comes from, in order to know where it's heading. Stripping oneself of one's secret, nice little inner mythology, keeping only what can shed light, what can be transmitted. ... Activism means, still more, a desire to transmit fast, fast, in a state of urgency constantly overtaken by reality. Anything that does not aim at being transmitted is of no interest to me. But transmission, for a woman, cannot mean the same thing as for a man, since no child will ever in my lifetime bear my name – which I got from a man. This desire for transmission is blind, like any kind of desire, blind to its symbolic roots. What came to me first was what had been transmitted to me: precisely, it was what had been programmed – I was destined to be an intellectual.[1]

1. Catherine Clément, *The Weary Sons of Freud*, Verso: London 1987, p27.

The paradox of 'transmission' as both an active and passive principle, linked at the same time with activism and the awareness of 'descent' or 'legacy' is a pertinent aspect of the role of women intellectuals. When psychoanalysis enters this configuration, the 'desire to transmit' becomes even more problematic in that the analytical discourse (and practice) presupposes a relationship of complicity with the structures against which this 'activism' is directed. In Clément's terms, however, the 'blindness' to this desire's symbolic roots can be equally a burden and a challenge: the confirmation (and celebration) of one's position in a symbolic order, handed down, as it were, in the perpetuation of the name of the Father, but also the interference with and questioning of its power. Thus daughters speak and write a discourse which they claim as their own. For those psychoanalyst-daughters, or daughters of psychoanalysis, the burden and challenge of the urge for transmission may result in the articulation of a critique. This is for Clément the hopeful message and effect of a female psychoanalytical project:

> But strangely enough, I have a feeling I'm not alone. Still more strangely, the people who advocate this kind of criticism and keep it alive are female psychoanalysts rather than male psychoanalysts. ... Whom I saw, more often than others, being sensitive to the political role they might possibly be playing, caught in the same movement that politicizes women and crosses the path of psychoanalysts over their dead (social) bodies. Women psychoanalysts who (as I do) have a secret laugh over the narcissistic, professorial peacock struts of their peers and spouses. Who won't listen to any tall tales any more, except on their couch. Here too, the modest feminine mechanism is at work, subverting – not destroying, just working in a different way, the only possible meaning of the word *subversion* – everything that comes its way, ready to make changes.[2]

2. *Ibid.*, p30.

Kristeva would subscribe to this view, in the sense of both a personal and a political concern. From the concept of semanalysis, developed in her earlier work as the conflation of semiotic and analytical projects to her more recent work on themes such as the abject, melancholy, foreignness and love, Kristeva has been exploring psychoanalytical discourse. Despite this apparent continuity, however, it could be argued that her interests as a theorist have gradually shifted towards an almost exclusive focus on individual experience. In what concerns women in particular, Kristeva has argued for the abandonment of a collectivity of difference, which places women in a generalised context of a common cause thus promoting social and natural dichotomies between male and female choices, strategies, languages. For Kristeva, the challenge for women in Western societies should be articulated and worked through in terms of individual action, expression, creativity:

> I think that the time has come when we must no longer speak of 'all women'. ... There is a community of women, but what seem[s] to me important is that this community should be made up of particularities and that it not be a uniform mass. ... There have to be 'I's' and women have to become authors, actors, not to hypostasize or overvalue those particular kinds of work, but I say this so that this perspective will push each one of us to find her own individual language.[3]

This is a shift that has caused considerable discomfort and disillusionment to those readers/followers who saw in her work the potential for an articulation of

3. Kristeva interviewed by Elaine Hoffman Baruch and Lucienne J. Serrano, in *Women Analyze*

Women in France, England, and the United States, Harvester Wheatsheaf: New York 1988, p135.

4. Feminist critics of Kristeva's work have questioned the applicability of her notion of the *subject in process* and of the *semiotic* for feminist theory and, more importantly, for the connection with a concrete notion of feminist struggle and social change.

a radical and collective project: for feminists worldwide, Kristeva's increasing reluctance to align herself with the collectivity of feminist experience has been considered suspect.[4] Indeed, from various perspectives (not only feminist), it is becoming increasingly hard to defend Kristeva's position within the context of a possible politics of change. It should be pointed out, however, that the majority of Kristeva's critics choose to dismiss her project on the basis of a few familiar notions which tend to dominate the debate about the efficacy of her work. Very few feminist critics, in particular, seem to be aware of the third part of her *La Révolution du langage poétique* (1974) which deals extensively with the role of the subject within social and economic formations. This is mainly due to the fact that only the first part of her thesis has been translated into English – although limited access should not prevent a critic from ensuring that an opinion is reached after thorough research. While one has to acknowledge Kristeva's contribution to theories of ideology and the subject, it is nevertheless the case that these are past concerns. Similarly, her involvement in the post-structuralist circle of *Tel Quel* – as the forum for the exploration and promotion of revolutionary social and artistic practice – is now a thing of the past, with most of the original contributors following separate paths. It seems that collectivity is now, literally, *passée*, and intellectual projects can only at best be sustained in the expression of individual brilliance, of this or that theorist.

Kristeva's own development could be considered as a representative case of this demise. It has certainly been seen in this light, especially by those occasional readers of her work who approach her as a media phenomenon. In this Sunday-supplement-view-of-the-world context, Kristeva confirms every disinterested observer's worst fear, or desire. Lucy Hughes-Hallett's piece in the *Independent on Sunday* (9 February, 1992) typically summarises this view; the title 'Egghead out of Her Shell' is used to introduce the writer and her current concerns: 'Julia Kristeva, once the darling of the Paris *avant-garde*, explains why she now thinks individuals are more interesting than isms.' With no more than a passing reference to Kristeva's inclusion as one of the speakers invited to deliver the Oxford Amnesty Lectures later in the month, the piece puts forward a trivialising view with an inevitable focus on the anecdotal.

5. The term 'mediatic' is used by Kristeva in order to identify (and castigate) a pervasive aspect of contemporary Western societies.

Equally mediatic,[5] though more openly dismissive, is John Weightman's account of Kristeva in the *European*, Weekend 1-3 June 1990. Clearly impatient with what he presents as French (or Parisian) intellectual pretension, Weightman reminisces about 'those days' in the 1970s, when, presumably, he also followed those Left Bank trends: I once heard her [Kristeva] lecture in those early days, but all I remember of the occasion is the heretical thought: 'Why is a pretty girl like you talking this abstract nonsense? Why not leave it to the sillier men?'

What brought back these memories was the publication of Kristeva's first novel, *Les Samouraïs* (1990), which Weightman proceeds to review. Not surprisingly, he finds it flawed by 'Parisianism', its tone '*mondain*, even gushing, without any trace of humour or distancing to give it depth.' The novel's heroine, whom Weightman unambiguously identifies as Kristeva herself, is accordingly, 'not a person of genuine feeling and thought, but a compendium of fashionable attitudes, an intellectual chameleon.' It seems that Kristeva can't win either as a theorist (talking 'abstract nonsense'), or as a novelist (writing pretentious gossip). For Weightman, Kristeva's pretentiousness is clearly confirmed by her choice of title for the novel which, as he correctly points out, refers to Simone de Beauvoir's *Les Mandarins* (1954). He thus accuses Kristeva of comparing Sartre, de Beauvoir's companion, to Philippe Sollers, Kristeva's husband: an outrageous comparison, since, according to Weightman, the former was a 'heavyweight' while the latter 'an intellectual playboy'. Weightman then marvels at what is obvious to him but not to Kristeva: '[she] treats ... the Sollers-figure, kindly, even admiringly, and she doesn't seem to realise, even when recounting his antics, what a minor personage he is.' The problem here is not so much Weightman's judgement of Sollers's intellectual weight, a judgement which he may very well be qualified to make in another context, but the implicit assumption that *Les Mandarins* is about Sartre and *Les Samouraïs* about Sollers. The literal quality of this accusation is one that neither de Beauvoir's, nor Kristeva's novel can escape. For the purpose of this particular review, however, Kristeva is more severely criticised: her novel lacks the irony granted to de Beauvoir's treatment of the analogous milieu, despite the deliberate echoing.

Weightman's comments may pose no great challenge to the academic reception of Kristeva's work, written as they are in the inevitable journalistic style; nevertheless, it is exactly that arena which Kristeva enters with the publication of her novels, inviting both the trivial and the thoughtful response. Attempting the latter, I wonder: is Kristeva's recent role/performance as a novelist a further re-enactment of a self-celebratory intellectual exercise or an attempt at an exploration/critique of self, sensitised by the intimate experience of analysis? Even in terms of the latter possibility, to what extent is a personal discourse a transmissible one? Does the urge to transmit necessarily imply that there exists an equal desire to receive? These are questions which echo Sartre's famous 'Why Does One Write?', 'For Whom Does One Write?'[6] Interestingly, the same questions resonate throughout de Beauvoir's *Les Mandarins*, the prototype, in a sense, for Kristeva's novel. Ironically, the character who does get to ask these questions openly in the novel, is not 'the Sartre figure' (Robert), but the American writer with whom 'the de Beauvoir figure' (Anne) is in love:

> Lewis's face grew darker and darker. He hated theories, systems, generalizations. I knew why: for him, an idea wasn't merely a collection of words; it was a living thing. ... Often, he withdrew completely. It was obvious that he was withdrawing now. And, then, suddenly, he exploded. 'Why does one write? For whom does one write? If you begin asking that, you stop writing! You write, that's all. And people read you. You write for the people who read you. It's writers nobody reads who ask themselves questions like that!'[7]

6. Jean-Paul Sartre, *What is Literature?* Trans. Bernard Frechtman, Methuen, London, 1967.

7. Simone de Beauvoir, *The Mandarins* Trans. Leonard M. Friedman, Fontana: London 1989, p497.

For Anne, the female 'I' in the novel, writing is a crucial act but one which the men in her circle are destined to do – Robert Dubreuilh, her famous husband; Lewis, the American lover: Henri, her daughter's lover are some of these men. The broken figure of Paula, wife of Henri, becomes a poet only briefly in a desperate struggle with madness, brought on by her refusal to accept that Henri does not love her any more. Anne herself is faced with the question:

> 'Why don't you write?' Scriassine asked.
> 'There are enough books in the world.'
> 'That's not the only reason,' he said, staring at me through small, prying eyes. 'The truth is you don't want to expose yourself.'
> 'Expose myself to what?'
> 'On the surface, you seem very sure of yourself, but basically you're extremely timid. You're one of those people who pride themselves on not doing things.'
> I interrupted him. 'Don't try analysing me; I know every dark recess of myself. I'm a psychiatrist, you know.'[8]

8. *Ibid.*, p48.

In fact, Anne does write and *Les Mandarins* is her story as well as Robert's and Henri's. De Beauvoir's novel then is the *roman à clef* which may also hold the initial 'key' to Kristeva's own, *Les Samouraïs*. I would argue that the novel, more than occasional pseudo-literary gossip, is Kristeva's attempt at an exposure of self, a looking inward, a reassessment and the expression of a desire for continuity. As a novelist, Kristeva explores the possibility of speaking in more than one voice; she allows herself the distance from the self as already constructed in her other writing. In *Les Samouraïs*, she looks critically and ironically at an earlier self (or selves), at those surrounding her and creates a space for the insertion of other voices which may represent her, though never totally so.

Kristeva's story is told through the configuration of three parallel, and occasionally intersecting lives: the life of Olga, a foreigner arriving in Paris from 'over there' ('*là-bas*'), the other side of Europe; the life of Carole, anthropologist, member of the intellectual milieu, follower of trends and friend of Olga; finally, the life of Joëlle, psychoanalyst and the only first-person voice in the book. Olga, the central persona, is the 'literary scientist' who immediately joins the writers and theorists of the day in discussions about the use of art, its revolutionary potential, but also the impossibility of changing the world without transforming the individual. She is welcomed and assimilated in this world of sophisticated, heated debates, yet remains a foreigner and occasionally observes as if from a distance:

> She was struck, actually disorientated, by the immediate proximity that they showed her. More than an acceptance, a sort of spontaneous familiarity. As if they had lived together since childhood. Maybe, after all? She was ready to

think that. Since they had read the same books. ... At the same time, she envied their free access to all memories, to all libraries, to all countries, all sexes, all consciences: an exorbitant advantage with a value which they seemed to be miles from appreciating.⁹

9. Julia Kristeva, *Les Samouraïs*, Fayard: Paris 1990, pp29-30. All translations from the original are my own.

Olga experiences the cruel yet self-imposed detachment from her past:

> ... as if by a caesarian, she was separated from them (from her parents). She had of it no conscience nor sensation (of being brutal or avid). Available. Empty. The detachment of astronauts. Of orphans. Of strangers ['*étrangères*']. Of licentious men and licentious women who permit themselves all games because they find themselves detached, outside the world, hard and ascetic, blank pages offered to all experiences (until the day their memory is extinguished). Her memory was being toned down. She was ready to betray it. To betray. Agility of body and soul in space.¹⁰

10. *Ibid.*, pp17-8.

The strange world she makes her own holds the promise of a new life, of success and unlimited possibilities, of the exploration of other worlds, of revisions and new beginnings. Here, Kristeva elaborates on a favourite theme, that of the foreigner's double status as cosmopolitan and exile: the paradoxical condition of melancholy freedom attainable only through betrayal. In *Strangers to Ourselves*, she exposes the foreigner's 'aloofness' as 'the resistance with which he succeeds in fighting his matricidal anguish.'¹¹ This necessary hardness becomes more than a protective shield:

11. Kristeva, *Strangers to Ourselves*, Trans. Leon S. Rondiez, Harvester Wheatsheaf: New York 1991, p9.

> Without a home, [the foreigner] disseminates ... the actor's paradox: multiplying masks and 'false selves' he is never completely true nor completely false, as he is able to tune in to loves and aversions the superficial antennae of a basaltic heart.¹²

12. *Ibid.*, p8.

Thus self-confidence and deprivation coincide in the new and exhilarating experience of free-floating in a strange world. Like Olga, in *Les Samouraïs*,

> Free of ties with his own people, the foreigner feels 'completely free'. Nevertheless, the consummate name of such a freedom is solitude. Useless or limitless, it amounts to boredom or supreme availability. Deprived of others, free solitude, like the astronauts' weightless state, dilapidates muscles, bones, and blood.¹³

13. *Ibid.*, p12.

Olga, the foreigner, is one of the selves/masks which Kristeva (equally and in the same terms a foreigner) creates in the process of writing her individual language, a language of memory and exploration of self. If Carole is the persona who accompanies Olga through her journey of assimilation, establishing a female friendship based on intellectual and emotional support, Joëlle's is the voice of contemplation. Her story, told in the first person, counteracts Olga's in that it conveys a different experience – that of the analyst. It is here that Kristeva's writing becomes more intense, attempting, as elsewhere in her work, to speak a discourse which is both personal and faithful to what she considers the truly transformative experience of analysis. This is Joëlle from her diary:

> That is the miracle of analysis, of which no one ever speaks. You learn to inhabit your past so intensely that it is no longer separated from your present body, and every particle of memory is transformed into a real hallucination, into a crude perception, here and now. The astounding thing is that this quasi-mystical metamorphosis is prolonged through the patients, uniquely, of course, in those analytical moments of grace, when I am so close to them that I reconstitute them, by my speech, by my own memory, that is, my own body, they discover as their own. For years, I have lived with a multiple body which is not truly my own, but which survives and is even transformed into the rhythm of others. Joëlle the multi-tentacled, proteiform medusa ...[14]

14. *Les Samouraïs*, pp171-2.

Joëlle speaks of transference as a formative experience, a true discourse of love. Here Kristeva seems to fuse the psychoanalytical with the religious, in an uneasy configuration which she has explored elsewhere. Again, the novel becomes an alternative space for the elaboration or enactment of theoretical positions. The proximity of terms does not necessarily imply that Kristeva argues for a new religious experience. A committed secularist, she fights any such notion of religion, as the discourse which will replace all others and save. Still, she engages with it and in the name of 'tolerance' and 'understanding' she considers its various manifestations and its hold on the imagination, even on one as rigorous and analytical as hers.

In *Les Samouraïs*, Kristeva exposes her own 'little inner mythology': the wisdom and fascination that psychoanalysis holds for her is certainly foregrounded in the novel through Joëlle's discourse, and the resulting solemnity of tone can at times sound tired or repetitive. Equally, one could argue that it is a fascination with the self with which this novel more convincingly deals. If so, Kristeva would probably own up to such a narcissistic pleasure: as a novelist, Kristeva seems to be both on the couch and at its side, as it were. In this sense, she seems to disagree with Clément's assertion that 'the fact that one is a psychoanalyst is by no means a guarantee that artistic writing will come of it. ... Nothing in analytic practice prepares you to be a writer';[15] on the contrary, Kristeva stresses that

15. Clément, *op.cit.*, p36.

> ... there is a kind of permanent connection between the work of the analyst and that of the writer. ... it is the analytical listening that allows me to look at the world in a specific way; less naïvely, perhaps, than the way a writer unexposed to that listening would regard it, with less illusions, maybe in a less refined manner, less beautiful, more serious, but linked, anyhow, with the Freudian vision.[16]

16. 'Julia Kristeva Interviewed by Vassiliki Kolocotroni', *Textual Practice*, Summer 1991, p164.

In this sense, the inner mythology remains as both a confirmation and a celebration of self. At the same time, it is the only device which ensures continuity, a sense of 'time regained'. At the end of the novel, the publication of Olga's book is announced, a book for children, called (self-referentially) *Les Samouraïs*. The idea apparently came to her as she was watching her husband and son miming a war game. Future belongs to the children. The guarantee of continuity. Before this circle closes, however, Joëlle learns of her father's death. She writes: 'The "nevermore" is incompatible with the thought which is devoted to linking up, to walking along. ... Never more ... Maybe one day I will write a story for my father to reassemble the drops of my memory in ruins.'[17] The death of the father here adds to the sense of loss explored in the novel through the theme of deracination and the reported deaths of other, intellectual 'fatherly' figures. The latter is linked in the novel with the sense of the passing of an intellectual era, as well as with the (personal) mourning for the loss of friends and companions. In 'A Paragon and her Position', her review of *Les Samouraïs* for the *Times Literary Supplement* (September28–October 4, 1990, p1038), Elaine Showalter sees no evidence of a serious engagement with the connotations of such losses: 'Despite Olga's tears, the death of the father awakens no sense of her own intellectual mortality, no questioning of her own positions, no fear that another woman, even more brilliant and with even higher cheekbones, may be getting off a plane from *lá-bas* to take her place.' Showalter's lack of sympathy with Kristeva's handling of this theme in the novel springs from an implicit suspicion of Kristeva's overall tone and intention: ultimately, she concludes, the novel lacks 'humility and self-doubt'. Indeed no female voice in *Les Samouraïs* is humble, but there is no clear reason for assuming that this should be the case. However, while on the one hand Showalter introduces the novel as 'an interesting and daring fictional début by an adventurous thinker who is always breaking new ground', on the other she accuses Kristeva of frivolity, pretentiousness and pomposity.

17. *Les Samouraïs*, pp460-1.

The attempt to work through the feeling of loss is thus seen as false, the expression of a thinly-disguised desire for self-aggrandisement. That Showalter reaches this conclusion on the basis of Kristeva's arrogance in her treatment of the 'fathers' is ironic, since it is usually for the opposite that Kristeva is criticised. In fact, the theme of the death of the father and its symbolic connotations is the focus of Kristeva's second novel, *Le Vieil homme et les loups*.[18] The point of departure here is the theme of hate, rather than love. The theme of transformation/metamorphosis is used again but this time with a nightmarish, almost dystopian effect. *Le Vieil homme et les loups* is a philosophical fable and a detective story. The Old Man, or Professor, or Septicious Clarus, as he is also called, is at the centre of a society and culture in the process of disintegration, compared to the Roman Empire awaiting its fall. The implicit reference here is to the figure of St Jerome (Eusebius Sophoronius Hieronymus) pondering the sack of Rome by barbarian hordes. He writes to a friend, c.410: 'I shudder when I think of the calamities of our time. ... Indeed, the Roman world is falling; ... The East, indeed, seemed to be free from these

18. Julia Kristeva, *Le Vieil homme et les loups*, Fayard: Paris 1991.

perils; but now, in the year just past, the wolves of the North have been let loose from their remotest fastnesses, and have overrun great provinces.'[19] In an ambiguous analogy, the Old Man of Kristeva's novel sees around him a society of wolves, humans metamorphosed by hate. The novel begins:

> Hunted by the great winds of the North, the wolves crossed the frozen river, rushed into the open, snowy plain and arrived to watch out for their victims at the outskirts of cities. All through the night, the Old Man heard their howls. ... No, he couldn't say that he was scared. Is one scared when one dreams, numb with nothingness? ... This battle with the wolves, however, was daily, permanent, because, fed by the night, it went on all day long. ... There was no doubt: the savage hordes were there, hidden but present. They seized villages and cities, infiltrated men's skins, the entire world became more and more canine, wild and barbaric.[20]

'A dream or a nightmare?' It is unclear, or rather, irrelevant, as the traumatic vision recurs throughout the novel, sustaining the ambiguity of an allegory. Intertextually, one is also reminded here of the Wolfman, one of the most famous cases of infantile neurosis analysed by Freud.[21] What is important in this transposition of theoretical material, however, is not the analogy with the case as such, but the affirmation of a belief in the signifying powers of psychoanalytical discourse. Kristeva here speaks from within that discourse, deploying it as the central and linking device. Interestingly, what Freud learned from the Wolfman was, according to Jacques Lacan, that 'it is in as much as the subjective drama is integrated into *a myth which has an extended, almost universal human value*, that the subject brings himself into being.'[22] The significance which psychoanalysis ascribes to the mythopoeic process is that of an explanatory, transformative and healing link with the lost object of a primary, pre-symbolised scene. For Kristeva, signification and language rely on this original loss and the arbitrariness of signs is a symptom of the continual attempt to recover it. In this sense, one can only 'say other' than the original, can only accept the loss in filling it with meaning. Thus 'allegory', literally 'saying other', could be seen as a manifestation of the imaginary dynamic itself. Its arbitrary power lies with creating meaning out of a reference to a symbolisation which is never totally effected, never a total identification. In the novel, the wolves, as allegory and dream, signify the instinctive power of hatred, the other – and primary – pole of the love instinct. Echoing Freud's assertion that 'The relation of hate to objects is older than that of love',[23] the Old Man voices a melancholy truth:

> ... it has taken us twenty centuries to discover that in the beginning was hate. ... But hate has not just been brought to light, Stéphanie, hate is installed. Imperturbable, insolent, unstoppable. It passes as the truth that speaks and acts with a naked face. I think of the wolves invading us, or within us, in the name of a cause – country, race, family, ego-ego,

---

19. M. Lincoln Schuster ed., *A Treasury of the World's Great Letters*, Simon & Schuster, New York, 1940, p32.

20. *Le Vieil homme et les loups*, pp13-4. All translations from the original are my own.

21. See Sigmund Freud, 'From the History of an Infantile Neurosis ([1914] 1918)', *Case Histories II: The 'Rat Man', Schreber, The 'Wolf Man', A Case of Female Homosexuality* ed. Angela Richards, trans. James Strachey, Penguin: Harmondsworth 1973.

22. Jacques-Alain Miller ed., *The Seminar of Jacques Lacan. Book 1: Freud's Papers on Technique 1953-1954*, Cambridge University Press: Cambridge 1988, pp190-1. Emphasis mine.

23. Sigmund Freud, 'Instincts and their Vicissitudes (1915)', *General Psychological Theory: Papers on Metapsychology* ed. Philip Rieff, Collier Books: New York 1963, p102.

oppressing, oppressed, class, under-class, over-class, group, under-group, regroup ...[24]

The Old Man lives in Santa Barbara, a totalitarian state. Here, we read 'barbarism', but also Santa Barbara, the American city one would associate with the most barbarously banal of soap operas. Solemnity with a touch of (black) humour? Kristeva's use of such signs, evocative but in a clichéd way, points to a tension in the writing which constantly tries to accommodate both the meaningful and the banal. In terms of stylistic transposition, this practice could be seen to partake of a crucial element of allegory which Walter Benjamin has illustrated in his analysis of baroque drama:

> ... allegory is both: convention and expression; and both are inherently contradictory. ... the very same antinomies take plastic form in the conflict between the cold, facile technique and the eruptive expression of allegorical interpretation. Here too the solution is a dialectical one. It lies in the essence of writing itself.[25]

For Kristeva, the 'essence of writing' is equally dialectical but also, and perhaps more importantly, transformative. Allegory and myth are thus reworked as forms of expression which still have the power to reveal albeit in an arbitrary and contradictory way; signification thus retains a redemptive value, a meaning which the world suggested in the novel seems to have lost. In a discussion of allegory in the context of modernist and contemporary art, Craig Owens defines its use in the following terms:

> Allegory first emerged in response to a ... sense of estrangement from tradition; throughout its history it has functioned in the gap between a present and a past which, without allegorical reinterpretation, might have remained foreclosed. A conviction of the remoteness of the past, and a desire to redeem it for the present — these are its two most fundamental impulses.[26]

In this sense, the 'allegorical impulse', as Owens calls it, is present in Kristeva's novel. It is also expressed in the 'diagnosis' of the Old Man as he ponders the present and mourns the past. He speaks to Stéphanie Delacour, the French reporter, another Kristeva-figure:

> We have lost the link, Stéphanie, the meaning of link (which is a tautology, since a signification is always a linking). Don't think that this is a plea for a return to religion, which today is either tired or virulent. Of course, the link that inspired the elegy of Tibullus or Ovid's tales was passionately a sacred link, I mean, *respectful*. Yet, free, doubtful, sceptical, spiritual ... It was the dawn of the link. That is what we need.[27]

24. *Le Vieil homme et les loups*, p138.

25. Walter Benjamin, *The Origin of German Tragic Drama*, trans. John Osborne, Verso: London 1985, p175.

26. Craig Owens, 'The Allegorical Impulse: Towards a Theory of Postmodernism' (1980), reprinted in Charles Harrison and Paul Woods eds., *Art in Theory 1900-1990: An Anthology of Changing Ideas*, Blackwell: Oxford 1992, p1052.

27. *Le Vieil homme et les loups*, pp138-9.

'The link': again, religion looms in the distance while Kristeva tries to re-establish a sense of continuity with her past. The father, the death of the father: the original crime.[28] Kristeva blends memory with nightmare, primal trauma with political commentary. The call for the missing link here, however, is also a sign of the melancholy disposition which seeks to express a deep and complex sadness: the sadness of mourning for the loss of a parent (Kristena's own), but also that which transforms mourning into melancholia, a permanent and impossible desire for the recovery of an always already lost meaning. The imagined plenitude of the union with the maternal body which the melancholiac refuses to surrender. That constitutes a loss of faith in language itself, the inability to live in a symbolic world. Through the Old Man and his encounter with the inquisitive, mystery-solving journalist, Kristeva attempts to speak the language of sadness and loss. The attempt triggers another move inwards, in this case, a journey back to the origins: language. Stéphanie remembers:

28. In a interview with Jonathan Rée, filmed by Channel 4 as part of a series highlighting the work of the five theorists invited to present the Oxford Amnesty Lectures ('Talking Liberties'), Kristeva spoke of her father's death as an 'assassination': the result of the Bulgarian state's negligence and inadequacy of medical care.

> Everybody has a maternal language. Mine comes from father [*papa*]. From his songs, the poems he used to recite to me and which I quickly learned by heart, from his stories, nursery rhymes, summaries of all sorts of books he had read in order to share with us – novels, histories, biographies. A language that he sustained with his big eyes ... persuading me that speech escapes the everyday, that it lives an autonomous existence, luminous or light, vagabond. Free.[29]

29. *Le Vieil homme et les loups*, p241.

In this, the more Freudian of the two novels, Kristeva reaffirms her faith in language, especially that which is sensitised by the analytical experience. She locates there the healing power of 'forgiveness' (*le pardon*), as the 'will, postulate, or scheme' which declares that 'meaning exists'.[30] Moreoever, it is an aesthetic gesture/act which affirms and inscribes meaning by retaining and transforming memory and suffering within a linguistic adventure: '*Forgiveness first manifests itself as the putting into place of a form*. It has the effect of an acting out, of a doing, of a *poiesis*. Putting into form of the relations between humiliated and offended individuals: harmony of the group. Putting into form of signs: harmony of the *oeuvre*, without exegesis, without explanation, without comprehension. Technique and art.'[31] The result is Kristeva's 'individual language'. It is a blend and a working through of multiple concerns, personal and, she would claim, collective. The distillation of voices of suffering (those of her patients) and the transposition of her own memories, masks, mystifications become the material of a 'little inner mythology' to be explored, analysed and transmitted. As Stéphanie observes towards the end of the novel, this is an open-ended process:

30. Kristeva, *Soleil noir*, p216. Translation mine.

31. *Ibid.*, p216.

> I had set out for a political commentary and ended up with a detective novel. On top of that, the Professor's death, reviving that of my father, brought me close to myths once again. Nobody believes in myths nowadays,

I least of all ... I only ask myself whether the Old Man or father have really reconciled me with myths. Or, the opposite: whether, by having found again those myths with which these beloved men of my childhood lived, and which, to my amazement, they have transmitted to me, I haven't been thrown out into empty space. Emptiness of this political turmoil that my diary keeps trotting out. Emptiness of our detective novels where nevertheless crime abounds, feeble and rebellious hatred. Emptiness of the errant form that I am.[32]

32. *Le Vieil homme et les loups*, p259.

As memory redeems and overcomes trauma so does writing effect a reconciliation with past (and lost) certainties. In the writing of novels, Kristeva exposes a self in shock, in motion, in crisis. As an analyst, she may be expected to distil from it an ultimately healing experience; as an intellectual, to transmit its message; as a writer, to explore its multiple forms and meanings. The result of the exercise, however, remains one of private illumination, despite the public exposure. The transformation of crisis into critique is thus a step not taken, an avenue left unexplored in Kristeva's writing. The enactment and resolution of the memory of the father (actual and Freudian one), as testimony of a debt and a legacy, ultimately seems to celebrate the 'little inner mythology' rather than strip it of its power. This reinforcement of the mythological in the allegorisation of private concerns may overlap with a more general practice of catharsis through writing and reading, as indeed Kristeva would hope, but the overall effect remains one of reconciliation rather than subversion. Nevertheless, to dismiss this choice per se, thus accusing Kristeva of regression and retreat, might be too harsh an indictment of what, after all, was partly intended as the expression of a personal need. That the novels expose a Kristeva in a conciliatory rather than activist mode does not signify a betrayal of intellectual positions; if anything, it signals a branching-out and braving-out into a space which, unlike the theoretical and academic, allows for the exploration of multiple and 'errant forms'.

SOVEREIGN SELVES

Andrew Thacker

Sean Burke, *The Death and Return of the Author Criticism and Subjectivity in Barthes, Foucault and Derrida*, Edinburgh University Press, 1992, £35 cloth, £12.95 paperback.
Simon During, *Foucault and Literature: Towards a Genealogy of Writing*, Routledge, 1992, £35 cloth, £10 paperback.
Lois McNay, *Foucault and Feminism: Power, Gender and the Self*, Polity Press, 1992, £39.50 cloth, £10.95 paperback.

In the essay 'The Subject and Power', first published in 1983, Michel Foucault considered the way that his earlier work on the dispersal of power in society had developed into the study of how human beings transform themselves into subjects. The essay is a curious document to read, by turns cryptic yet stimulating, baffling but provocative. It contains in miniature many of the themes that preoccupied Foucault after the publication in 1976 of *The History of Sexuality*: a view of subjectivity in terms of a struggle to be a more freely self-created being; a re-engagement with previously rejected philosophical traditions shown in a fascination with Kant's definition of the Enlightenment; and a call to carry out intellectual work on power and resistance which falls foul neither of the worrisome 'privileges of knowledge', nor of the 'skeptical or relativistic refusal of all verified truth'.[1] In many ways the essay demonstrates how Foucault eludes easy definition as a 'postmodernist' thinker. Foucault ends the first half of the essay by drawing attention to subjectivity and the possible forms of resistance to what he has described as the 'government of individualization'. The object of struggles today, he states, is 'not to discover what we are, but to refuse what we are'. This refusal aims for a form of 'liberation' from the dominant 'type of individualization' articulated by modern western states. The message for political projects, concludes Foucault, is that they should 'promote new forms of subjectivity through the refusal of this kind of individuality which has been imposed on us for several centuries.'[2]

Refusing who you are as a subject is, however, not necessarily linked to the promotion of new forms of subjectivity. One might incessantly challenge the ascription of multifarious subjectivities, in the manner of an anarchistic dance against identity, without ever feeling the need to outline any fresh subject position. For any new form of subjectivity would be prey to the governmental individualising of the state that one had strenuously been occupied in rejecting. Forming oneself as a homosexual dandy may only result in being categorised as a 'homosexual dandy'. In this moment in Foucault's text we glimpse something of the return of the repressed in his own work; that of the human self, which

1. Michel Foucault, 'The Subject and Power', in Hubert L. Dreyfus and Paul Rabinow, *Michel Foucault: Beyond Structuralism and Hermeneutics*, Chicago: University of Chicago Press, p212.

2. Foucault, *ibid.*, p216.

had previously been normalised into the 'docile bodies' of *Discipline and Punish* or, as in the tale told in *The History of Sexuality*, constructed by discourse into a sexual being naively eager to discover both the truth of sex and the way in which sex is the truth of the modern subject. Foucault's advocacy of a refusal of these governmentalities – for the sake of refusal alone since, as many critics have pointed out, he evokes no norms by which to legitimate opposition – was replaced in his later work by a quest for historical instances of the active promotion of new identities. The last two volumes of the history of sexuality – *The Uses of Pleasure* and *The Care of the Self* – and important essays such as 'What is Enlightenment?' show Foucault's search for more positive examples of subjects being in control of the creation of their own individualities. These are unearthed in the 'technologies of the self' or the 'aesthetics of existence' Foucault reveals to be at play in Greek and Greco-Roman texts upon sexual conduct. Treatises to guide the behaviour of relations between men and boys or man and wife yield, for Foucault, a set of practices where individuals self-fashion their identities according to criteria drawn from aesthetics. In a Wildean gesture one must turn one's life into a work of art. But this is a thoroughly moralised aesthetics, strenuously ascetic, and patrolled by an ethical demeanour which is not that of universal Kantian-style rules but rather is judged by standards of beauty and style. As Foucault commented in an interview in 1984:

> From Antiquity to Christianity, we pass from a morality that was essentially the search for a personal ethics to a morality as obedience to a system of rules. And if I was interested in Antiquity it was because, for a whole series of reasons, the idea of morality as obedience to a code of rules is now disappearing, has already disappeared. And to this absence of morality corresponds, must correspond, the search for an aesthetics of existence.[3]

3. Michel Foucault, 'An Aesthetics of Existence', in Lawrence D. Kritzman (ed), *Politics, Philosophy, Culture: Interviews and Other Writings 1977-1984*, New York and London: Routledge 1988, p49.

It is thus by this recourse to aesthetics that Foucault can move from the *refusal* of given subjectivities to the *promotion* of new identities. Creating your subjectivity according to an 'aesthetics of existence' entails that you have 'liberated' this new subjectivity from the normalising force of state institutions. Constant and vigilant refusal of what you are is no longer necessary since identity is forged in that imagined free-space of aesthetic autonomy where moral codes or state institutions no longer hold jurisdiction. One of the many curiosities of this later work by Foucault, aside from the problematic valorization of the aesthetic, is the way in which a critic who made us most suspicious of so many accepted categories of the modern world – knowledge, liberation, sexuality – should embrace the 'aesthetic' in so warm-hearted a fashion. Foucault does not seem to pause to consider the institutional formation of contemporary aesthetics in its post-Kantian mode, or the genealogical distance of this notion from that of the Greeks. All three of the books under review discuss Foucault in broad relation to questions of aesthetics. Burke and During consider the questions of authorship and literary criticism as influenced by Foucault, while McNay directly discusses his later work as a possible framework for contemporary feminist theory. None however quite address the problematic position of aesthetics in Foucault's later work.

Sean Burke's account of Foucault is perhaps the least satisfactory chapter of what is a provocative, well-written and scrupulously argued book. Burke's argument is that post-structuralist negations of authorship, as detailed in Barthes, Foucault and Derrida, undermine themselves, almost in the very instance of their utterance (in this respect Burke unknowingly replicates Maud Ellmann's powerful discussion of the subversive role of personality in modernist theories of the impersonality of the author). Declarations of the 'death of the author' in post-structuralist criticism are covert manoeuvres that re-introduce the authorial subject and thus, 'the concept of the author is never more alive than when pronounced dead' (p7). This is because, as Burke argues, one must 'be deeply *auteurist* to call for the Death of the Author' (p27). Post-structuralist criticism overstates the role of the author, creating a tyrannical sovereign scriptor who must then be cut down to size by the overweening critic. Citing Bakhtin, Burke suggests that we can conceive authors in ways other than as omniscient gods. But a more tempered view of authorship would deny the critic the chance to kill the author, in the name of the liberation of the reader or of returning the text to language, and to then occupy the throne of authorship, allowing the critic to ascend to the role of 'creative writer'. So, at bottom, the call for the death of the author is a ploy to privilege the critic, who returns to 'authorship' after earlier denying its validity.

Burke's argument has more than a grain of truth in it, and it certainly indicates with some panache problems that have surrounded post-structuralist work on authorship. However, in a gesture that replicates the sin he attributes to the post-structuralists, Burke has to overstate his case in order for it to stand up. He often seems to miss some of the rhetorical reasons for the opposition to authorship by Barthes et al, reading their texts as straight-forward philosophical arguments, and ignoring the fact that the most forceful part of their critique was directed at the *institutions* of authorship. Foucault, in 'What is an Author?' (which Burke oddly treats in just a few cursory pages), is clear to state that his discussion is about the 'author-function' as it 'is linked to the juridical and institutional system that encompasses ... the universe of discourses'[4] and that the power of the author is as an 'ideological figure' and as a 'functional principle' by which meaning is limited, excluded and chosen.[5]

Burke is best on Barthes, offering an interesting analysis of *Sade Fourier Loyola*, but even here his range of material is perhaps too narrow. All three of the critics Burke discusses are represented by quite a small selection of texts, so that Foucault's position on authorship is almost entirely represented by *The Order of Things*, and Derrida's work is summed by analysing *Of Grammatology*. Consideration of the later Foucault's work would have been useful, partly because it might have strengthened some of Burke's points about the resurgence of a repressed interest in self and subjectivity in post-structuralism.

4. Michel Foucault, 'What is an Author?', in Paul Rabinow (ed), *The Foucault Reader*, London: Penguin 1984, p113.

5. Foucault, *ibid.*, p119.

It would also have tempered Burke's tendency to view Foucault entirely through the lens of Nietzsche, such that he almost accuses Foucault of a form of hero-worship of the German philosopher in order to draw out the conclusion that Foucault really espouses a form of authorship that he is meant to deny (p86-88). This ignores Foucault's re-discovery of Kant and his admission of the value of certain parts of Critical Theory as derived from the Frankfurt school.[6] An examination of the later volumes on the history of sexuality would also have revealed that Burke's claim towards the end of his book that critics kill authors in order to raise their own discourses to the level of creativity is not quite correct in relation to Foucault, even though it holds more truth in connection with the Barthes of *Roland Barthes par Roland Barthes* or the Derrida of *Glas*. *The Uses of Pleasure* certainly does not elevate its style to that 'pitch of creativity with language' (p160) which distinguishes the traditional literary auteur.

6. Michel Foucault, 'Critical Theory/Intellectual History', in Kritzman, *op.cit.*, p26.

Simon During's book is the first sustained account of the topic of Foucault and literature, although a little of the discussion of the role of transgressive art in Foucault was covered in David Carroll's *Paraesthetics: Foucault, Lyotard, Derrida* (1987), to which During does not refer. *Foucault and Literature* possesses a depth of analysis and a range of coverage not offered in Burke, but this results in some loss of overall focus. During is very astute as a commentator and the book offers some excellent links between Foucault's work and that of other philosophers such as Kant and Heidegger. He is also good at fleshing out Foucault's arguments with more historical detail, as in the discussion of sexuality and bio-politics in nineteenth century Britain (pp167-170). The discussion of Foucault's influences is always judicious, especially in showing Foucault's trajectory out of phenomenology in his early work on madness. But During's wish to write a comprehensive guide to Foucault's intellectual development sometimes jars with the intention to draw out Foucault's relevance and applicability for literary studies. It is as if there are two books here: the first is an excellent advanced guide to Foucault, the second a more speculative analysis of Foucault's position in contemporary literary studies. Often the application of Foucault to literature appears at the end of detailed explicatory chapters, such as those on *The Birth of the Clinic* or *Discipline and Punish*. These sections are too perfunctory to really make a convincing case for a Foucauldian literary criticism, although the sketches of crime and representation in eighteenth and nineteenth century novels, or medicine in *Middlemarch* and *The Wings of the Dove* are very stimulating.

The last two chapters of During's book venture a more coherent Foucauldian criticism, interrogating the New Historicism of Stephen Greenblatt and the role of authorship in *Hamlet* and Dreiser's *An American Tragedy*. This is in order to outline 'what a genealogy of literature might look like' (p186). These chapters are interesting, especially the sympathetic critique of Greenblatt which draws out with subtlety the difficulty of generalising into a critical method a 'cultural poetics' that tracks down the 'social circulation of energy' in the Shakespearean period. It might have been interesting at this point to consider the selective manner in which other critics, such as Francis Barker in

The Tremulous Private Body or Terry Eagleton in *Literary Theory*, have appropriated elements of Foucault in order to bolster forms of Marxist criticism.

During suggests that the key issue for a genealogy of writing would be a critical analysis of the category of representation. This is because the notion of representation 'legitimates and suffuses that of "literature" ' (p193) and thus enables the use of literary texts, as transmitted by humanist critics like Matthew Arnold, for governmental purposes such as schooling and examinations. For During, 'Individuals invisibly embody and represent the culture; the political sphere represents (groups of) individuals. It is in these terms that one can say that the complex system, within which education, culture (including literature) and politics are interlocked, rests on an acceptance of the efficacy and validity of the notion "representation" ' (p194). This critique of representation is, of course, not just derived from Foucault but is, as Sean Burke also notes, one of the central branches of post-structuralist criticism. In some ways it seems odd that During tries to characterise a nascent Foucauldian criticism in terms of representation rather than of institutions and discursive practices. Although he suggests that Foucault does not discuss the 'institution of literature' because of a scepticism towards the implied continuity of such a category (p186), it is revealing that During calls upon Derrida when arguing for the problematic status of representation. A quizzical attitude towards representation might characterise a literary criticism rooted in the early works of Foucault; it seems less likely that any such approach would necessarily inform a Foucauldian criticism based on his later work, which During only briefly discusses. This is because the critique of representation became, for Foucault, a symptom of the political impasse reached by post-structuralism. Rephrasing During a little, we can say that even a 'non-representational politics' will find it 'difficult to abandon representation as a tool for analyzing culture' (p194). Foucault's discussion of Classical sexual ethics relies upon quite conventional modes of representation and does not try to outline a politics that refuses representation. Rather it tries to discuss the practices that subjects employ in order to represent themselves differently. The inevitability of representation is conceded; the important struggles involve refusing certain representations of subjectivity in order to be at liberty to produce other versions of the self.

The difficulty of a postmodern politics, representational or otherwise, is the starting point of Lois McNay's excellent guide to the rapprochement between Foucault and contemporary feminist theory. The book is a model of clarity and will prove useful as a introduction not only to any possible Foucault-derived feminism, but also as a map of contemporary debates about postmodernism and feminist social theory. The novelty of McNay's book is the serious attention she pays to the later Foucault, a feature lacking in the two previous books on feminism and Foucault (see the essays *Feminism and Foucault*, edited by Irene Diamond and Lee Quinby and the book by Jana Sawicki, *Disciplining Foucault*). McNay is concerned to see how far Foucault's aesthetics of existence might be valuable for recent feminist theories that, while ackowledging the force of 'the post-structuralist deconstruction of unified subjectivity into fragmented subject positions', still wish to see 'individuals as active agents capable of intervening in and transforming their social environment' (p1). In other words, McNay wants to know whether Foucault's theory of the self-fashioning of subjectivity can enable feminism to push beyond 'difference', without reverting to a totalising political narrative, but while still upholding a politics of resistance. It is, of course, a tall order, and it would be somewhat surprising if Michel Foucault could provide the answers to a key problem for recent feminist theory. McNay realises this, and is not about to invest all of the aspirations of feminist politics in a couple of books concerning topics such as the right diet one must follow in order to practise good sex in Ancient Athens. However McNay argues that while Foucault's early work had shown how power so soaks into the pores of all modern societies that it reduces the self to a mere 'docile body', his swerve to subjectivity in his later work resembles some key debates in contemporary feminist theory. McNay thus discusses Foucault's 'ethics of the self' in tandem with such feminist theorists as Carole Gilligan on 'feminine ethics', as derived from Chodorow's 'mothering theory', and Nancy Fraser and Linda Nicholson on the possibility of a 'postmodern feminism'. McNay remains sceptical about the viability of a feminist postmodernism (p7) and uses Foucault's later commitment to 'games of truth' and the idea of the self as something more than 'the subject in dispersion' (p133) in order to clear the ground for future feminist theory. Foucault's critical work on the self 'converges with the internal feminist critique of essentialism while, at the same time, it retains a notion of agency upon which a politics of resistance could be articulated' (p193).

This is not to say that McNay ignores problems for a feminism influenced by Foucault, and her critique consists of two points. Firstly, Foucault's final texts display 'an unresolved tension between his commitment to emancipatory social change and his refusal to outline the normative assumptions upon which such change should be based' (p8). Secondly, an ethics of the care of the self, though originating in 'an attempt to block institutional regulation of individuality' (p178), leads ultimately to 'a conception of the individual as an isolated entity' (p10) rather than as a self actively constituted in the context of social dialogue. Both points, argues McNay, cause acute problems for any feminism that would seek to use Foucault. More positively, however, McNay suggests that recognising these problems in Foucault's work might help the resolution of similar difficulties in contemporary feminism, especially around how to transcend certain instances of polarized modern/postmodern thinking. These include resolving 'how basic normative standards need not necessarily threaten the autonomy of the individual' (p197) or discovering how a politics of the self can avoid lapsing into privatized individualism.

McNay's book, then, has an open-ended quality which is refreshing to read, and it is interesting to note that Habermas is not wheeled on simply to resolve Foucault's problems. It is curious, however, that in a book that pays serious attention to Foucault's later work, the question of what he means by 'aesthetics' in his account of an 'aesthetics of existence' does not receive prolonged attention. The differing ways in which the aesthetic operates in postmodern debates is not clearly grasped in the book. For example, McNay suggests at one point that 'the notion of an aesthetics of existence is too rational or intentional a category' to explain certain aspects of sexuality' (p80) and that aesthetics cannot explain how people 'invest in certain discursive positions in a not necessarily conscious or rational way' (p80-1). This is odd, given that one key definition of the aesthetic in post-Romantic thought is that it embodies non-rational, unconscious or affective behaviour. Indeed this kind of definition is used by certain critics to accuse Foucault's 'aesthetics of existence' of introducing a damaging whiff of irrationality into pre-eminently rational realms of debate.[7]

Although of the three books McNay pays most serious attention to the later Foucault, she does not fully draw out what the relationship might be between normativity and the aesthetic. Is it the case that, for Foucault, a notion of the aesthetic as an open-ended, self-justifying set of practices enables him to sidestep questions of normativity? Without normative standards, writes McNay, 'it is not possible for the individual to distinguish between an arbitrary stylization of life and the development of genuinely oppositional subject positions' (p147). Foucault might well reply that even with norms one cannot lay down in advance which formations of the self will turn out to be oppositional in any political sense. Only when the self-fashioning is complete can such a judgement be made. An expanded notion of the aesthetic which somehow includes a normative set of criteria might, however, usefully inform this process of self-production. The problem is that of determining how moral, epistemic and aesthetic categories are to be rearranged, given that so much recent theory has demonstrated the unhappy ways in which modernity has mapped the relative positions of these life-worlds. It appears that McNay's difficulty with this issue is no real fault of her book, but rather a symptom of how hard it is to think through rearrangements in the relations between art, morals and knowledge when one writes out a distinctive disciplinary base that requires concentration upon only one of these spheres. Perhaps this demonstrates that refusing who we are – as social scientists, cultural theorists, feminist critics or whatever – is a more difficult task than even Foucault envisaged.

7. See, for example, Richard Wolin, 'Foucault's Aesthetic Decisionism', *Telos*, no.67 (Spring 1986), pp71-110.

TURNING THE SCREW OF *SENTIMENTAL EDUCATION*

Eva D. Bahovec

James Donald, *Sentimental Education*, London Verso 1992, £32.95 cloth, £10.95 paperback.

In the field of education, the lack of theoretical elaboration seems to present a permanent problem. Pedagogical and psychological discourses on schooling remain largely untouched by the broader debates on society and culture, in spite of some stimulating projects (e.g. the journal *Das Argument* in Germany, *Ideology and Consciousness* and *Screen Education* in Britain) which were directly engaged in crossing the lines between the two. Therefore, the need to situate discourses on schooling in contemporary theoretical debates is even more pressing today.

In a famous quotation from 'Analysis terminable and interminable', Freud designates education as one of the three impossible professions, the other two being government and psychoanalysis. The very act of using this famous quotation as a starting point in asking what sort of institution education is could be understood as indicative of a need, even a necessity, to transgress the usual boundaries of pedagogical and psychological discourses on schooling. In Donald's *Sentimental Education* this transgression is twofold: it is polemical, and it develops a coherent theoretical position throughout.

The book could therefore be regarded as an elaborate argument against the widespread conviction that the theory of education is of little theoretical relevance or nothing to be really concerned with. The reference to an 'eclectic intellectual formation' of Althusserian Marxism, Lacanian psychoanalysis, semiotics and Brechtian aesthetics, Gramsci and Bakhtin in the preface is much more than 'a catalogue of intellectual debts'. Contrary to the arbitrarily unified 'theoretical' position of the academic discourses on education, it could be understood as an indication – not a pedagogical red herring, but a clue for detection – of the fragility and instability of boundaries of concepts related to the question of education and its relation to the 'art of government' (p1).

The dangerous liaison between education and government is developed along two lines. The first one concerns an elaboration of the Althusserian idea about the school apparatus as the site of not only transmission of knowledge produced elsewhere, but a site of the very production of national language, literature, culture. The second one derives from the Foucauldian idea about schools as institutions, largely comparable to hospitals, asylums, prisons etc., of the modern age, which, instead of adopting a psychological notion of development or a sociological notion of socialization, are 'better understood as technologies of government' (p47). Both lines of argument converge in a setting of contours of what might be called a post-Enlightenment interpretation of education in the broadest sense of the word, bringing to the surface its impasses and the sources of its impossibility.

If we proceed along the first line of analysis, the instability of boundaries proves to be one of the reasons why the 'impossible professions' are not only so difficult to perform, but even to define. What constitutes relevant knowledge and ensures its transmission? How is subjectivity shaped in the process of this transmission? The instability of boundaries becomes intelligible through the process of delimitation by which the basic categories are produced as distinct entities. In this process, formation of the outside (the outside of the Negative to Positive, Low to High, Them to Us) becomes constitutive for the formation of 'the inside'. It is created by the expulsion of 'what does not belong to', or, in Edward Said's words, is 'not at home in a place.'

In the chapter on popular literature and national culture, for example, this process comes to light in drawing the 'boundary between what is and what is not Literature' (p49). National literature, national culture, nation-people etc., all these categories are not a pre-given object of analysis (as in pedagogical discourses on schooling). Along the lines of Althusserian perspectives on the formation of national language and national literature as an academic discipline and a school subject, the reverse perspective opens up: cultural apparatuses and technologies (education, publishing, broadcasting, mass media etc.) produce these categories as an *effect* of culture, not its origin. And, to make a further important step in the polemic, 'what is produced is neither an identity nor a single consciousness'; it is a heterogeneity, 'given a certain fixity as "the nation" differentiates it from other cultures by marking its boundaries' (p51).

These two initial steps in defining the 'boundaries' and 'identities' have an important impact on the political meaning of all the diverse effects of culture as a whole. The political dimension is not a fixed one and cannot be determined in advance: 'there is nothing necessarily progressive about the popular, nor inherently reactionary about the national' (p57). It depends on the inner articulation of the elements in open, always unfinished signifying practices. Following the formation of such a *bricolage* of recombination of discourses (in juxtaposing education and popular culture, communities, political concerns, broadcasting), the regulation of the semantic field could be seen 'as one aspect of the policing of a population.' Literacy and literature as the core of the school curriculum form 'the symbolic mode through which the pedagogies and disciplines of schooling ... are enacted' (*Ibid*).

The questioning about what sort of institution education is brings us to the other intellectual source, introduced in the chapter on the state as educator. The analysis of the process of installing compulsory schooling in nineteenth century Britain focuses on several lines of investigation: educational ideologies, apparatuses of knowledge, regimes of surveillance, pastoral technologies of self-monitoring, gathering information about each child etc. What they reveal is 'an emerging conception of popular education as a technique of government close to Foucault's notion of bio-politics or Jacques Donzelot's policing of families' (p29).

Perhaps the most influential 'discipline and punish' Foucauldian perspective on schools displays the subtle mechanisms through which power is exercised: regimes of surveillance, inspection and regulation in the daily routines of the schools. In the nineteenth century English school, the fantasy of transparency was built into the very architecture of the classrooms, making all the pupils visible to the master and enforcing them to focus their attention on him alone; the same goes for the rest of the organization of school life, which could not but fascinate the founder of the Panopticon, Jeremy Bentham (p32). This fundamental fantasy, so closely linked to the very idea of education, was complemented by the institutional written and photographic records and reports gathering all kinds of information about each child, 'doubtless modelled on the files kept by the police and by prisons' (p42). In contemporary schools similar regimes of surveillance persist in a less obvious way, though not a 'hidden' one (as the notion of 'hidden curriculum', taken from the new sociology of education, might suggest).

How does all this machinery of government, exercised in schools of the modern age, affect the child's psychic reality? The transformation of the social into the psychic is neither reducible to the process of immediate reflection of the external, nor is it produced by a clean cut operation with no remnant; there is always a misfit caused by 'translation, displacement, repression and transgression' (p47).

In other words, 'these are stories not just about reason and intentionality,' as already pointed out in the introductory chapter, 'but especially about the messy dynamics of desire, fantasy and transgression' (p16). In Donald's analysis, as opposed to the 'post-Foucauldian orientation' of Ian Hunter and Nikolas Rose, the relation between power and body is mediated through consciousness and transformed through the formations of the unconscious. What prevents the achievement of the pedagogically prescribed goals, e.g. to educate a virtuous individual in a good society (and what, on the other hand, also prevents the possibility of total surveillance), is the intermediate space which forms an obstacle to transparency. It plays a crucial role in the relation of the self to itself, not as a simplified notion of the relation of the inside to the outside, but as the spatiality of the 'extimate' (p94), based on a paradoxical crossing of two distinctly separated surfaces, the external and the internal, which gradually slide into each other. This entails a far-reaching model of 're-spatialization' of the outside and the inside, the social and the psychic, the public and the private.

The theoretical interlude about the ways in which the social enters the individual psyche paves the way to a further conceptual issue, that of the question about how governmental technologies produce the individual as citizen (p135) and how the overlapping cultural apparatuses and technologies of education affect their selves. If the problem of becoming human proves to be such a difficult one in the context of the 'self' and its 'socialization', could the impossible task of education be better pursued through the idea of the formation of (virtuous) citizens?

In the inter-war period, education, aiming at such a goal, was the main target of the discourses on broadcasting of the time. Authors like Herbert Read and his *Education through Art*, the journal *Scrutiny* and its editor F.R. Leavis, the first director general of BBC John Reith, the founder of the British documentary cinema John Grierson, all had in common the idea of using cultural, symbolic authority as a means for 'policing' a democratic population. As the analysis of installing compulsory schooling has shown, education could be used as a counterpart to the threat of popular culture as well as against illiteracy or bad taste. However, in our century, this relationship became more ambivalent. It was meant to be an instrument of struggle against totalitarianism, the threats of fascism or bolshevism, but at the same time it offered mechanisms of control over the circulation of knowledge and public opinion. Returning once again to the polemical dimension of the book, such exposure of ambivalence and inner tensions, even contradictions, could be regarded as another point to be made in 'a consciously anti-ideological explanation', precluding the danger of functionalism in interpreting the school too simply as an ideological state apparatus.[1]

It is this ambiguity which is put at the centre of interest in the chapter on the re-regulation of broadcasting and education. The elaborate analysis of Thatcherism reflects upon the combination of neo-liberal 'rolling back' of the state with the neo-conservative espousal of cultural identity, authority and 'standards'. The alternative is sought for through the questions of what should be the limits of political power, and what should constitute a radical, democratic citizenship.[2] The answer could be said to lie in the absence of any straightforward answer: in an impossibility to define, plan or control the former as well as the latter. Namely, at the very heart of the logic of democracy, there is, as Claude Lefort put it, indeterminacy, and at the very heart of forming a democratic public and educating democratic subjects, there is a paradox because such an idea is not simply congruent with the concept of democracy itself. (Even the idea of teaching independence of mind is in a way paradoxical, since it can actually mean thinking 'as I tell you'.) Finally, this brings us back to the two initial steps in defining what sort of institution education is through the process of installing 'boundaries' and 'identities': 'Lefort's conclusion that 'the quest for identity cannot be separated from the experience of division' is clearly at odds with the Reithian vision of broadcasting as the integrating force in a mass society which could address, and thus institute, a divided population as the One of the nation-people' (p137-8).

Where, on the level of the individual, we have to deal with the displacement, transgression and misfit caused by the existence of a realm which is intermediate to body and power, there is, on the level of 'the art of government', a basic indeterminacy, an empty place, constitutive of its very functioning.

1. In relation to the theory of education, the exposure of ambiguities and inner contradiction (in the interplay of the cultural, the political and the economic) has an important polemical impact on more 'post-Althusserian' oriented analysis of schooling as well, specially in the world of M.W. Apple (*Ideology and Curriculum*, 1979, *Education and Power*, 1984, *Teachers and Texts*, 1988, *The Politics of Official Knowledge*, 1993; all by Routledge).

2. The problem with the claims for educating citizens is that they fail to see how 'governmental techniques produce the individual as citizen' (p135), how citizenship is constituted through discipline and pastoral technologies.

What is then the use of universal education? As discourses on higher education (J.H. Newman, F.R. Leavis) indicate, it seems to be impossible to avoid the eternal, even 'sclerotic' antinomy of liberal education vs. vocationalism with its particular narrow ends. Quite similarly, it seems to be out of the educationalists' reach to conceive the central issue of schooling, literacy and literary education as a path to consensual citizenship: though figuring as a means of social mobility, the latter still seems to be embedded in the logic of exclusion.³ The ambivalent power of literacy, therefore, has to be acknowledged, keeping in mind that even the choice between different languages and dialects is always a political act, as Gramsci pointed out.

What hinders the embodiment of democracy and human rights in education is not merely deviation from an ideal; inequalities, conflicts and incommensurabilities are rather indicative of an inner impossibility, 'an index of corruption' (p134), inherent in the process of education. This impossibility could be said to be twofold, related to the indeterminacy of democracy (the empty place of democratic government) as well as to the issue of how identifications operate within institutions – fantasmatic scenarios allowing the institutions to persist, a place in the paradoxical space of the psychic reality where the machinery of power can be anchored.

Therefore, after broadening the object of analysis from schooling to broadcasting, the product of the theory of subjectivity as developed in the 'brief theoretical interlude', i.e. the product of the process of re-spatialization, has to be put at the centre of interest. This could be described as an entity of what is left out, and is at the same time constitutive of the very inside: the abject. The concept of the abject, indicated also by the Lacanian *objet petit a*, is elaborated further in the chapter on 'the pedagogy of monsters'. Here, the act of expulsion is counterbalanced by the production in the real of fantasy.

Though never explicitly mentioned in the text, the idea of this 'beyond' (beyond language, beyond identities and agencies, construed in and through discourses) could be said to form an underlying presence and the *leitmotif* of the book. This is the dimension which disturbs 'identity', 'system' and 'order', forcing it into endless metonymical sliding of the symbolic, into an ever-open dynamics of delimitation and expulsion. And this is how ultimately, in such a re-spatialization of the cultural and the subjective, all the roads lead to Rome: diverse detective clues meet in the difficulty to cope with what could be called 'the other side of the Enlightenment' – with the dimension, in other words, from which the impossibility of Freud's 'impossible professions' derives.

In *Sentimental Education*, this 'other side' is most explicitly approached through the history of popular fears and fantasies, opening a new perspective on 'the popular' as well. Here again, the explanation of the tales about vampires, doubles, cyborgs, monsters as the 'dominant ideology' (as what has been repressed or oppressed in our civilization) brings about 'a certain reductionism' (p101) which has to be opposed and denounced. But it does not suffice either to say that the images of the monstrous are the images of the Other as a threat to identity, or to point out the mobility of 'identification'.

3. In the very subtitle of Hirsch's influential *Cultural Literacy* – 'What every American needs to know' – there is already an implication that 'those who do not know all this are in some sense *not* American' (p154).

What is at stake is the transgression of boundaries between the 'I' and the 'not-I', the human and the automaton, the live and the dead, the inside and the outside; it is the coming together of the radically different, of otherness, not 'being at home in a place', with the 'old and long familiar', but repressed (p106). This is the point of Freud's analysis of the uncanny which provides a common denominator of different approaches to the monstrous (Moretti, Wood, Todorov, Penley, Cixous).

The nature of ambiguity connects the uncanny to the notion of the sublime, as opposed to the beautiful, and, already in Kant, as what resists the tendency towards a closed, definitive system. Making a detour around the 'complex history' of the sublime (from Kant to Nietzsche), Donald traces his 'other history of the sublime', the one which proceeds from the Gothic novel with its principal themes of death and the supernatural as 'what cannot be represented', to melodrama as the 'vulgar sublime'. Here, the 'unreality, the excess and the irrationality' (as a counterpart to the familiar and the normal that erupts into the everyday world), 'are functional: they enable us to conceive the unpresentable' (p111).

This bringing together of the concept of the sublime and the concept of the popular is related to 'the modern sublime' of Kristeva, centered upon the representation of the unpresentable through a nondiscursive language with the notion of the abject (p113), and to Lyotard and his analysis of the postmodern as the refusal to domesticate the sublime. It is of particular importance for defining what kind of institution education is that, in Lyotard, the sublime has an aesthetic as well as a political dimension. The latter opens up with Lyotard's 'politics that would respect both the desire for justice and the desire for the unknown' (p114) which leads to a new conception of political pluralism and radical democracy, beyond and away from the projection of an ideal, either a particular form of community or a particular image of a supposedly universal good citizen (whether in the form of 'all round', 'whole' personality or in less totalitarian pleas for educating 'active and involved', 'psychologically balanced', 'critical' citizens).

What is finally at stake then, apart from the misfit in the formation of the psychic through the process of socialization and education, and apart from the indeterminacy of 'the art of government', is a fundamental impossibility, imminent to the goals of education themselves: not the the distance between the ideal and the possibility of its realization, but the inner crack of the idea itself, from the very outset.

It is in this post-Enlightenment perspective that the double relation of education and government to psychoanalysis becomes accessible to further theoretical elaboration. Let us therefore go back to the basic theoretical context as outlined in the introductory and the closing chapters of the book.

The impossible task of educating could be tracked back to yet another reference to Freud, to his idea of 'civilization and its discontents'. In this context, the process of knowledge accumulation and transmission reveals the impasses of the Enlightenment, exposing the impossibility of a clear division between the authority of reason and its other side (present also in Foucault, 'as inhabited by figures of madness, sexuality, death and the diabolical', p112). Negativity does not come from the outside and cannot be done away with – this could be said to be the ultimate clue for detection. It lies at the very core of psychic reality and of the progress of reason.

In a way, one can see that even the very Enlightenment idea which constitutes the foundation of education, Rousseau's notorious 'nature', is in incessant danger of turning into its opposite, into 'perversion'. It is because of this basic insight that all kinds of surveillance techniques, ensnared in the fantasy of transparency, had to be developed. Émile is not supposed to make a move on his own, a move not previously intended or anticipated by his tutor. The principle, in a peculiar way quite close to Bentham's panopticism, is developed to its utmost limits: the tutor must be in a state of perpetual vigilance, he must literallly see everything and know everything. Émile is never to be left alone, day or night: 'Look thus very carefully after the young man; he is able to get all the rest by himself, but this care has to be provided by you alone.'[4] However, in spite of all the efforts education does not seem to be able to avoid an ultimate failure, even a disaster.[5]

If the *Bildungsroman* could be read as an indication of the importance of education in western modernity, and Flaubert's *Sentimental Education*, by deconstructing the narrative of self-formation, as its irony, another recourse to literary tradition might perhaps be added at the very end to demonstrate the impossibility and the failure of education – the utterly ambiguous Henry James's *The Turn of the Screw*.

Here, the dimension of the fantastic and horrifying (described by Donald in 'the brief theoretical interlude'), as gradually deployed in the relationship between the governess and the children, derives from the ambiguity related to the uncertain boundaries between the perceptual delusion (at a certain point even the looming madness of the governess) and the transgression of the limit between the real and the unreal. However, the post-Enlightenment perspective adds another twist: because of the respatialization of the inside and the outside, the social and the psychic, nature and culture, education runs into a basic impossibility of positing a limit towards the evil, the perversion coming from the outside and the one stemming from the inside.[6] The fragile boundary is just the one of 'turning the screw', by which the natural becomes unnatural and supernatural, the virtuous becomes totally perverted, the well-intended and prescribed by the goals of education reveals an inner crack which cannot be resolved.

If we go back to the sources of the Enlightenment, this line of investigation could bring together Rousseau and Wollstonecraft (apart from reading Kant, who was the first to expose the impossible task of education and governing, with Sade and his pornographic pedagogy, as pointed out in the introductory chapter), and add another point to the discussion about the theoretical relevance of the theory of education. Both were 'adversaries of the Enlightenment', if we may say so; they did not fit into its mainstream and were

4. Jean-Jacques Rousseau, *Émile ou de l'éducation*, Oeuvres complètes, Bibliothèque de la Pléiade: Paris, Gallimard 1964, p633.

5. Cf. N.J.H. Dent, *The Rousseau Dictionary*, Basil Blackwell: Oxford 1992, p111.

6. In James's short story, the former is related to the supposed corruption of children by the servants, and the latter to the dubious voice of the child's nature itself, due to the paradoxical coincidence of nature with its extreme counterpart, perversion. I have developed the argument in more detail in my paper

particularly sensitive to its 'other side', and both were also the most engaged in rethinking the concept of education. Here again, in interpreting their ambivalence toward the perverse image of sexuality, of unclean and decadent sexuality, structured round an irreducible negativity in its core, the 'third position' (along the lines of Donald's analysis), has to be pursued. Beyond too simple an alternative between the prohibition or renunciation of desire, and its straightforward, even wild liberation, it could perhaps be best summarized with Lacan's *Ne pas céder sur son désir*, not to give way to one's desire.

And is this not, ultimately, the site where the interpretation of 'sentimental education' should proceed?

In exposing some of the main topics of contemporary theoretical debates and their close connection to the 'art of education,' Donald's book is an excellent example of 'defining' not only what kind of institution education is through 'transgressing the usual boundaries' of educational discourses. Speaking about education as one of the impossible professions, it develops a conceptual apparatus to define the very nature of this impossibility. It could be said, therefore, that *Sentimental Education* is of utmost importance for a fresh approach to the theory of education, clearing the ground for its new foundations. Along the way, it also provides an important contribution to the development of basic theoretical concepts as such.

'Where does the Misery Come from: On the Metaphor of Turning in Rousseau and Henry James', in *Mesotes*, vol.3, pp44-51, Vienna 1991.

Books Received January – April 1994

Richard M BARSAM, *Non-Fiction Film: A Critical History* Revised and Expanded London, Indiana University Press 1993 Hb. £57.50 Pb. £21.99

Vern L BULLOUGH and Bonnie BULLOUGH, *Cross Dressing, Sex and Gender* Philadelphia and London, University of Pennsylvania Press 1993 Hb. £49.50 Pb. £15.00

Blaise CENDRARS, *Modernities and Other Writings* Edited and introduced by Monique Chefdor; translated by Esther Allen in collaboration with Monique Chefdor French Modernist Library Lincoln and London, University of Nebraska Press 1992 Hb. £16.95

Jonathan CRARY and Sanford KWINTER eds, *Zone 6: Incorporations* London, MIT Press 1993 Hb. £58.50 Pb. £31.50

Wheeler Winston DIXON, *The Early Film Criticism of Francois Truffaut* with translations by Ruth Cassel Hoffman, Sonja Kropp, and Brigitte Formentin-Humbert Bloomington and London, Indiana University Press 1993 Hb. £25.00 Pb. £9.99

Terry EAGLETON, Derek JARMAN, *Wittgenstein: the Terry Eagleton Script, the Derek Jarman Film* London, British Film Institute 1993 Pb.

Diane P FREEDMAN, Olivia FREY, and Frances Murphy ZAUHAR eds, *The Intimate Critique: Autobiographical Literary Criticism* Durham and London, Duke University Press 1993 Hb. £42.75 Pb. £15.95

Ortwin DE GRAEF, *Serenity in Crisis: A Preface to Paul de Man 1939-1960* Lincoln and London, University of Nebraska Press 1993 Hb. £29.95

Claudion GUILLEN, *The Challenge of Camparative Literature* Translated by Cola Franzen Harvard Studies in Comparative Literature 42 Cambridge, Mass. and London, Harvard University Press 1993 Hb. £39.95 Pb. £15.95

Axel HONNETH, Thomas MCCARTHY, Claus OFFE and Albrecht WELLMER eds, *Cultural-Political Interventions in the Unfinished Project of the Enlightenment* London, Mit Press 1993 Hb. £31.50 Pb. £14.95

Jayne Anne KRENTZ ed, *Dangerous Men and Adventurous Women: Romance Writers on the Appeal of the Romance* London, University of Pennsylvania Press 1993 Hb. £23.70 Pb. £10.95

Vassilis LAMBROPOULOS, *The Rise of Eurocentrism: Anatomy of Interpretation* Princeton University Press 1993 Hb. £19.95

Lois MCNAY, *Foucault and Feminism: Power, Gender and the Self* Oxford, Polity Press 1993 Hb. £39.50 Pb. £10.95

George E MARCUS ed, *Rereading Cultural Anthropology* London, Duke University Press 1993 Hb. £42.75 Pb. £12.95

Chris MARKER, *La Jetee* cine-roman London, MIT Press 1993 Hb. £22.50

John MOWITT, *Text: the Genealogy of an Antidisciplinary Object Post Contemporary Interventions* Durham and London, Duke University Press 1992 Hb. £37.95 Pb. £13.50

Arthur NOLETTI Jr and David DESSER eds, *Reframing Japanese Cinema: Authorship, Genre, History* London, Indiana University Press 1993 Hb. £32.50 Pb. £15.99

Daniel PICK, *War Machine: the Rationalisation of Slaughter in the Modern Age* New Haven and London, Yale University Press 1993 Hb. £19.95

Richard RAND ed, *Logomachia: the Conflict of the Faculties* London, University of Nebraska Press 1993 Hb. £27.00 Pb. £11.95

Adrian RIFKIN, *Street Noises: Parisian Pleasure 1900-40* with a foreward by George Melly Manchester, Manchester University Press 1993 Hb. £35.00

Avital RONELL, *Crack Wars: Literature, Addiction, Mania* London, University of Nebraska Press 1993 Pb. £7.95

Michael SPRINKER ed, *Edward Said: a Critical Reader* Oxford, Blackwell 1993 Pb. £13.95

Radical Philosophy
A JOURNAL OF SOCIALIST & FEMINIST PHILOSOPHY

ISSUE 65   autumn 1993   £2.95

ENGLISH PHILOSOPHY IN THE FIFTIES

CULTURAL NATIONALISM & IRISH WRITING

FLESHY MEMORY: FREUD & FEMININITY

CRITICAL THEORY IN GERMANY TODAY

Truth & Eros • Liberalism & Justice
Islam & Science • Beyond Equality & Difference

INDIVIDUAL SUBSCRIPTIONS

3 issues: UK – £ 8.50   Overseas surface – £11/$20   Overseas airmail – £15/$30
6 issues: UK – £16.00   Overseas surface – £21/$36   Overseas airmail – £28/$56
(all prices include postage) Cheques payable to *Radical Philosophy Group*

We accept Visa, Acces/Mastercard & Eurocard. Please state your card no. and expiry date

From: Central Books (RP Subsciptions), 99 Walis Road, London E9 5LN

GOLDSMITHS' COLLEGE
University of London
Postgraduate Opportunities in the Department of Media and Communications

MA IN MEDIA AND COMMUNICATION STUDIES
MA BY RESEARCH; MPhil/PhD PROGRAMME

Our taught MA course is offered on either a full-time or part-time basis. Students will be based in the Department of Media and Communications, but will also be able to take optional courses offered by the Departments of Sociology, English and Anthropology. Students will take 2 core courses in *Communications and Cultural Theory*; 2 specialist courses in *Methodologies of Communications and Cultural Analysis* and will choose 4 optional courses (a total of 8, 10-week courses, in all). Students will also complete a supervised Dissertation on a subject of their own choice. Among the optional courses likely to be available are:

Optional Courses
Reconceptualising the Media Audience; The Media as a Public Sphere; Post-Colonial Criticism; Feminism, Psychoanalysis and Representation; Modernism and Post-modernism in the Arts; Literary History and Historicism; Literature and Popular Culture; Contemporary Cultural Production; Culture, Identity and Difference; Modernity and its Others; Political Communications; British Cinema.

MA MEDIA/COMMUNICATIONS BY RESEARCH

Students with an undergraduate qualification in Media, Communications or Cultural Studies can also be considered for an MA by Research, where the principal element is a supervised Extended Dissertation, supplemented by teaching in Methodologies of Research.

MPhil/PhD PROGRAMME

The department runs a lively doctoral programme for both full and part-time students. The department is recognised for the receipt of ESRC and British Academy awards. Students may take a range of courses to support their thesis research from the MA programme, together with tailor-made methodology courses, seminars, workshops and support groups.

Faculty Research Specialisms
Professor James Curran (The political economy and influence of mass media)
Professor Valerie Walkerdine (Psychology, post-structuralism, feminist theory)
Dr David Morley, Reader in Media Studies (Audience studies, cultural identities)
Dr Georgina Born (Technologies of cultural production)
Christina Geraghty (Film and Media theory)
Dr Sarah Kember (Photography, subjectivity, technology)
Gareth Stanton (Post-colonial criticism, Third Cinema, post-modernist ethnography)

Further Information and Admissions
Application forms and further information about the courses can be obtained from The Registry, Goldsmiths' College, New Cross, London SE14 6NW.
Telephone 081 692 7171.

A new journal in philosophy, literature and the social sciences:

ANGELAKI

volume one

No 1
The Uses of Theory
September 93
144 pages

No 2
Narratives of Forgery
December 93
160 pages

No 3
Reconsidering the Political
February 94
c.144 pages

volume two

No 1
Home and Family
May / June 94

No 2
Intellectuals and Global Culture
August / September 94

No 3
Authorising Culture
December 94

ANGELAKI
ISSN: 0969-725X

Volume 1, 1993/4, 3 issues (c.450pp)

Price (including postage and packing)
Volume: £12.00 / US$24.00

Single Issue: £4.50 / US$9.00

Cheques payable to Angelaki

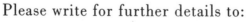

Please write for further details to:
**ANGELAKI, 44 Abbey Road
Oxford, OX2 0AE, UK**

A critical journal of the social sciences

Economy and Society

Contact editors: **Mike Gane**, *Loughborough University* and **Maxine Molyneux**, *Birkbeck College, University of London*

Economy and Society is a radical, interdisciplinary journal covering the social sciences, history and philosophy. With an emphasis on theoretical perspectives and on confronting the new issues facing the intellectual left today, the journal enjoys an outstanding reputation for rigorous critical scholarship.

Highlights for 1993 include: Markets, Morals and Powers of Innovation *Mark Elam;* Poland's New Political Culture: the Relevance of the Irrelevant *Sergiusz Kowalski;* Hyperreal America *Jean Baudrillard*

Special issue (Aug. 1993): Foucault and Politics: Liberalism, Neo-Liberalism and Governmentality, edited by *Andrew Barry, Thomas Osborne* and *Nikolas Rose*

ISSN: 0308-5147, four issues per volume
Subscription Rates for 1993
UK/EC: institution: £55.00 individual: £34.00
USA/Canada: institution: $95.00 individual: $64.00
ROW: institution: £60.00 individual: £38.00

For further information please contact:
David Bull, ROUTLEDGE JOURNALS,
11 New Fetter Lane, London EC4P 4EE, UK.
Tel: 071 583 9855 Fax: 071 583 4519

Back Issues

1 **Peter Wollen** on fashion and orientalism / **Denise Riley** on 'women' and feminism / **Dick Hebdige**'s sociology of the sublime / **Laura Marcus** on autobiographies / **John Tagg** should art historians know their place? / **Franco Bianchini** on the GLC's cultural policies / **Homi K. Bhabha**, **Stephen Feuchtwang** and **Barbara Harlow** on Fanon / Reviews – **Cousins** on Foucault, **McLennan** on Norris, **Schwarz** on Englishness and **O'Pray** on Powell and Pressburger.

2 **Mary Kelly**, **Elizabeth Cowie** and **Norman Bryson** on Kelly's Interim / **Greil Marcus** on subversive entertainment / **Georgina Born** on modern music culture / **Geoffrey Nowell-Smith** on popular culture / **Ien Ang** on 'progressive television' / **Alan Sinfield** on modernism and English Studies in the Cold War / **Tony Bennett** on Eagleton.

3 *TRAVELLING THEORY* – **Julia Kristeva** on the melancholic imaginary / **David Edgar** on carnival and drama / **Kobena Mercer** black hair – style politics / **Jacques Rancière** on journeys into new worlds / **Peter Hulme**'s Caribbean diary / **Bill Schwarz** on travelling stars / **Ginette Vincendeau** on chanteuses réalistes / **Steve Connor** on Springsteen / **Christopher Norris** on Gasché's Derrida.

4 *CULTURAL TECHNOLOGIES* – **Simon Frith** making sense of jazz in Britain / **Griselda Pollock** on Doré's London / **Colin Mercer** on entertainment / **Tony Bennett**'s exhibitionary complex / **Ian Hunter** setting limits to culture / **David Saunders** on copyright and literature / **Jody Berland** on television.

5 *IDENTITIES* – **Homi K. Bhabha** on the commitment to theory / **Philip Cohen** on Tarzan and the jungle bunnies / **Glenn Bowman** on Palestinian nationalist consciousness / **Kristin Ross** on Rimbaud and spatial history / **Kaja Silverman** on liberty, maternity, commodification / **Adrian Rifkin** on Carmenology / **Margaret Sotan**'s epistemology of the wandering woman / **Andrew Benjamin** on psychoanalysis / **Gill Davies** on heritage / **Les Back** on soundsystems.

6 *THE BLUES* – **Jacqueline Rose** on Margaret Thatcher and Ruth Ellis / **James Donald** how English is it? / **Benita Parry** on Kipling's imperialism / **John Silver** on Carpentier / **Mitra Tabrizian** and **Andy Golding**'s blues / **Barbara Creed** on *Blue Velvet* / **Joseph Bristow** on masculinity / **Graham Murdock** on Moretti's *Bildungsroman* / **Edmond Wright** on post-Humptydumptyism.

7 *MODERNISM/MASOCHISM* – **Victor Burgin**'s Tokyo / **Linda Williams** on feminine masochism and feminist criticism / **John Tagg** on criticism, photography and technological change / **Geoff Bennington** l'arroseur arrosé(e) / **Emilia Steuerman** on Habermas vs Lyotard / **Paul Crowther** on the Kantian sublime, the avant-garde and the postmodern / **Mark Cousins** on Lévi Strauss on Mauss / **Iain Chambers** being 'British' / **Adrian Forty** on lofts and gardens / **Lisa Tickner** on Griselda Pollock.

8 *TECHNO-ECOLOGIES* – **Peter Wollen** cinema: Americanism and the robot / **John Keane** on the liberty of the press / **S.P. Mohanty** on the philosophical basis of political criticism / **David Kazanjian** and **Anahid Kassabian** naming the Armenian genocide / **Paul Théberge** the 'sound' of music / **David Tomas** the technophilic body / **Félix Guattari** the three ecologies / **Margaret Whitford** on Sartre.

9 *ON ENJOYMENT* – **Slavoj Zizek** the undergrowth of enjoyment / **Peter Osborne** aesthetic autonomy and the crisis of theory / **Rachel Bowlby** the judgement of Paris (and the choice of Kristeva) / **Joseph Bristow** being gay: politics, identity, pleasure / **Gail Ching-Liang Low** white skins black masks / **Christine Holmlund** I Love Luce / **Line Grenier** from diversity to indifference / **Mark Cousins** is chastity a perversion? / **Simon Critchley** review of Christopher Norris.

10 *RADICAL DIFFERENCE* – **McKenzie Wark** on the Beijing demonstrations / **Paul Hirst** on relativism / **Cindy Patton** African AIDS / **Anna Marie Smith** Section 28 / **Tracey Moffatt** something more / **Susan Willis** Afro-American culture and commodity culture / **Hazel V. Carby** on C.L.R. James / **David Lloyd** on materialist aesthetics / **Peter Redman** Aids and cultural politics.

11 *SUBJECTS IN SPACE* – **Dick Hebdige** subjects in space / **Iain Chambers** on the Sony Walkman / **Meaghan Morris** on Sydney Tower / **Sam Appleby** on Crawley New Town / **Raphael Samuel** on brick / **Peter D. Osborne** on Milton Friedman's smile / **Victor Burgin** on Breton's Nadja / **Donatella Mazzoleni** on the city and the imaginary / **Ann Game** on Bondi Beach / **Nicholas Green** on monuments and memorials.

12 *NATION, MIGRATION AND HISTORY* – **David Morley** and **Kevin Robins** no place like Heimat / **Renata Salecl** national identity and socialist moral majority / **McKenzie Wark** Europe's masked ball / **Peter Wollen** tourist art / **Victor Burgin** paranoiac space / **Elizabeth Grosz** Judaism and exile / **Mitra Tabrizian** surveillance / **Gail Ching-Liang Low** narratives of empire / **Peter Middleton** vanishing affects.

13 *NO APOCALYPSE YET?* – **Angela McRobbie** new times in cultural studies / **Slavoj Zizek** the king is a thing / **Geoffrey Nowell-Smith** broadcasting: national cultures – international business / **Paul Du Gay** enterprise culture and the ideology of excellence / **Colin Mercer** neverending stories: the problem of reading in cultural studies / **Peter Nicholls** consumer poetics: a French episode / **Lyndsey Stonebridge** the subject of the father: from ethics to love / **Jenny Taylor** dreams of a common language: science, gender and culture / **Joseph Bristow** life stories: Carolyn Steedman's history writing.

14 *ON DEMOCRACY* – **Chantal Mouffe** pluralism and modern democracy: around Carl Schmitt / **Renata Salecl** democracy and violence / **Joan Copjec** the *Unvermögende* other: hysteria and democracy in America / **Mladen Dolar** the legacy of the Enlightenment: Foucault and Lacan / **Slavoj Zizek** act as the limit of distributive justice / **Zdravko Kobe** death of the political / **Bill Schwarz** exorcising the general: Gabriel García Márquez *Clandestine in Chile* / **Patrick Parrinder** Leeds, intellectuals and the avant-garde.

15 *JUST LOOKING* – **Kevin Robins** the postmodern city / **Charlotte Brunsdon** satellite dishes and taste / **McKenzie Wark** from Fordism to Sonyism / **Sarah Kember** the geometry of chaos / **Gill Frith** the female reader / **Christopher Norris** deconstruction versus postmodernism.

16 *COMPETING GLANCES* – **Kobena Mercer** skin head sex thing / **Jane M. Gaines** competing glances / **Couze Venn** subjectivity, ideology and difference / **Gregory Stephens** interracial dialogue in rap music / **Jean-Jacques Lecercle** ecstasy and discourse in the cinema / **Sandra Kemp** Derrida and dance / **Graham Dawson** the public and private lives of T.E. Lawrence / **Daglind Sonolet** the Christa Wolf reception in West Germany / **David Morley and Kevin Robins** techno-orientalism.

17 *A QUESTION OF 'HOME'* – **Ariel Dorfmann** present / **Doreen Massey** a place called home / **Tzvetan Todorov** bilingualism, dialogiam and schizophrenia / **Jamie Owen Daniel** on Adorno and the language of home / **Aine O'Brien** homeward bound / **Celia Applegate** the question of Heimat in the Weimar Republic / **Jeffrey M. Peck** rac(e)ing the nation / **Helen Fehervatu** homeland – November 1989 / **Jenny Bourne Taylor** re-locations from Bradford to Brighton / **Bill Schwarz** on Paul Scott / **Theodor W. Adorno** refuge lot the homeless / **Mary Ellen Hombs** on America's homeless / **Marianna Torgovnick** Slasher stories / **Irena Klepfisz** *Fradel schtok*.

18 *HYBRIDITY* – **Christopher Norris** old themes for new times / **John Frow** the concept of the popular / **Annie Coombes** inventing the 'postcolonial' / **Simon Frith** Adam Smith and music / **Andreas Bjørnerud** outing Barthes / **Rod Giblett** philosophy (and sociology) in the wetlands.

19 *PERVERSITY* – **Anne McClintock** the return of female fetishism and the fiction of the phallus / **Sue Golding** the excess: an added remark on sex, rubber, leather and ethics / **Beverley Brown** troubled vision: legal understandings of obscenity / **Grace Lau** perversion through the camera / **Stephen Johnstone & John Gange** an interview with Nayland Blake / **David Curry** decorating the body politic / **Alasdair Pettinger** why fetish? / **Anna Douglas** Annie Sprinkle: post post porn modernist / **Leslie Moran** buggery and the tradition of law / **Della Grace** xenomorphisis / **Parveen Adams** the three (dis)graces / **Louise Allen** looking good, feeling queer / **Sandra Kemp** painting as philosophy.

20 *WALTER BENJAMIN* – **Irving Wohlfarth** Benjamin's actuality today / **Sigrid Weigel** images in Benjamin's writings / **Victor Burgin** the city in pieces / **Zygmunt Bauman** Benjamin the intellectual / **Gillian Rose** out of the sources of modern judaism / **Axel Honneth** a communicative disclosure of the past / **Andrew Benjamin** shoah and remembrance / **Janet Wolff** feminism and cultural analysis / **Susan Buck-Morss** aesthetics and anaesthetics / **Martin Jay** Benjamin and the novel / **Julian Roberts** aesthetics of conflict.

Back issues cost £14.99 each
Make cheques payable to *Lawrence & Wishart* and send to:
Lawrence & Wishart, 144a Old South Lambeth Road, London SW8 1XX

NEW FORMATIONS

Now in its seventh year, *New Formations* has established a reputation nationally and internationally as one of Britain's most significant journals of cultural debate, history and theory. *New Formations* brings new and challenging perspectives to bear on the categories that frame cultural analysis and political action; as one reviewer writes, the journal has become 'a vital tool in honing an awareness of the politics of culture'.

WHY NOT SUBSCRIBE?
MAKE SURE OF YOUR COPY

The issues for 1994 are Nos. 22, 23 and 24.

Subscription rates, 1994 (3 issues)

Individual Subscriptions

UK	£30.00
Rest of World	£32.00

Institutional Subscriptions

UK	£50.00
Rest of World	£52.00

Please send one year's subscription starting with Issue Number _____

I enclose payment of _____

Please send me _____ copies of back issue no. _____

I enclose total payment of _____

Name: _____

Address:_____

_____

Please return this form with cheque or money order payable to Lawrence & Wishart and send to:
Lawrence & Wishart, 144a Old South Lambeth Road, London SW8 1XX